Canada's Governors General at Play

Culture and Rideau Hall from Monck to Grey, with an Afterword on their Successors, Connaught to Le Blanc

by
James Noonan
Carleton University

Dedication

For my parents,
Jim Noonan and Bertha Gannon

Canada's Governors General at Play

Culture and Rideau Hall from Monck to Grey, with an Afterword on their Successors, Connaught to Le Blanc

by
James Noonan
Carleton University

BOREALIS
BOOK PUBLISHERS

Ottawa, Canada
2002

Canada

*The Publishers acknowledge the financial assistance
of the Government of Canada through the Book Publishing
Industry Development Program (BPIDP), and of the
Ontario Arts Council, for our publishing activities*

National Library of Canada Cataloguing in Publication Data

Noonan, James
    Canada's governors general at play : culture and Rideau Hall
from Monk to Grey, with an afterword on their successors,
Connaught to LeBlanc

Includes bibliographical references and index.
ISBN 0-88887-190-2 (bound). —ISBN 0-88887-192-9 (pbk.)

    1. Governors general—Canada—Biography. 2. Canada—
Cultural policy. 3. Canada—History—1867-1911. I. Title.

FC26.GN65 2002   971.05'092'2   C2001-903308-7
F1005.N65 2002

Cover design by Bull's Eye Design, Ottawa
Typesetting by Chisholm Communications, Ottawa

Printed and bound in Canada on acid-free paper

Contents

List of Illustrations

Note: Illustrations from the National Archives of Canada are indicated by NAC.

Cover illustration: Lord and Lady Dufferin and guests at theatricals at Rideau Hall. (NAC C-059072).

Inside photograph of Rideau Hall, main entrance . From Department of the Interior Collection. (NAC PA-043784).

Introduction

This book originated in a letter from Ann Saddlemyer of the University of Toronto suggesting that I research the private theatricals of the Dufferin family at Rideau Hall since I was residing in Ottawa and was an active member of the Association for Canadian Theatre History, of whose journal *Theatre History in Canada* (now *Theatre Research in Canada*) she was then co-editor with Richard Plant. I agreed to do this and in due course produced a paper on the Dufferins which was delivered to my colleagues in the Association.

In my research I discovered that there had been much theatrical activity at Rideau Hall not only in the time of the Dufferins, but during the tenure of other Governors General as well. I also discovered that the holders of that office were interested in many other facets of culture, and thought it would be interesting to research their varied cultural activities. I was also aware that the Social Sciences and Humanities Research Council of Canada administered the Jules and Gabrielle Léger Award "to promote research and writing on the historical and contemporary contribution of the Crown and its representatives in Canada." It seemed to me that the cultural activities of Canada's Governors General would fit this description, so I applied for the award and was granted it in 1986. As I continued my research, interrupted at times by teaching, organizing conferences, and other writing projects, I realized that the remarkable men and women and their families who resided at Rideau Hall had many cultural interests beyond theatre—art, sculpture, literature, music, crafts, education, sport, science, agriculture, technology, and religion. So I use the word culture broadly in this book, and have tried to bring to light these various interests of Canada's viceregal families and how they may have influenced Canadians in these several fields.

In some cases, like the Dufferins' private theatricals or the Mintos' athletic prowess, these activities have been given prominence in their respective chapters. Where none such activity has predominated, as in the case of Monck or Lisgar or Stanley, I have made a more general survey of their cultural interests. One area I have not explored is their political activities, since these have been treated in most books and articles on the Governors General of Canada. To put in context their lives in Canada and elsewhere, however, I have pointed out the important issues of Canadian politics during their tenure here, as well as some political issues with which they were involved before and sometimes after they resided in Canada.

I have also attempted to give some idea of the personalities of these nine Governors General, their backgrounds and the positions they held in Great Britain and Canada as the case may be. Where their spouses or children were particularly active in cultural activities in Canada, I have examined their involvement as well, and how they supported and supplemented the work of the Governor General. This is true especially of Lady Dufferin and Lady Aberdeen, who pursued and fostered their own cultural interests when their husbands had other interests or did not have the time or good health to get very involved in activities other then their political responsibilities.

This book is not restricted to the public face of culture like the plays at Rideau Hall or the exhibitions of the Royal Canadian Academy of Arts or the activities of the Royal Society of Canada. I have also noted the private cultural activity of the Governors General and their families both in Ottawa and in their travels across Canada and elsewhere. Thus I have sought their reactions to plays and concerts and agricultural fairs as they performed their viceregal duties in towns and cities of the new Dominion, as well as in cities such as New York, Boston, Washington, San Francisco, Santa Barbara, and even beyond North America, in England and Ireland, in Spain and Italy, in India and Russia before and after their tenure in Canada.

The book is mainly about those who served as Governors General from Confederation in 1867 to the early twentieth century, i.e., the nine Governors General from Monck to Grey, whose term ended in 1911. This group corresponds with the men and women covered in the first volume of R.H. Hubbard's *Rideau Hall*, which has been an invaluable resource and inspiration for my own work. While those Governors General who followed Grey did not for the most part sponsor events as visible as the Dufferin theatricals at Rideau Hall, or the Aberdeen historical balls in Ottawa, Montreal and Toronto, or Grey's re-enactment of the battle of the Plains of Abraham in Quebec City, some, such as Bessborough and Massey and Vanier, made significant contributions to Canadian culture. Indeed their personal and public cultural activities might be the subject of another book just as Hubbard wrote another volume on Rideau Hall and its occupants from 1911-1977.

My sources include general works on Rideau Hall, as well as biographies of several Governors General. In the cases of Monck, Dufferin, Lorne, Aberdeen and Minto I have been fortunate that letters, diaries and journals have been published. Where none such original sources have been available, as in the case of Lisgar, Lansdowne, Stanley and Grey, I have relied more heavily on newspaper accounts and articles that have appeared in various magazines and journals. Putting all these resources together, a composite of the cultural life of the early residents of Rideau Hall since Confederation has emerged that is both fascinating and unknown to the majority of Canadians. It is hoped that this book will fill a void in the cultural history of Canada, and that those who read it will see a side of our Governors General and their families that is for the most part unsuspected, and in so doing gain pleasure as well as knowledge from their stories.

I wish to thank many people and institutions who have been helpful with the work that created this book. My gratitude goes, first of all, to the Social Sciences and Humanities Research Council of Canada, which put its trust in me before the book was begun by awarding me the Jules and Gabrielle Léger Fellowship. Carleton University has also been supportive in many ways through the Faculty of Graduate Studies and Research that awarded me money and funded several capable students to go through newspapers, journals and magazines at the National Archives of Canada and elsewhere searching for information on Governors General, through the Department of English, which recommended many of these students to me, and through the office of the Dean of Arts, which also helped fund the project. Students who did research for me included Kerry Badgley, Patricia Cook, Chris Eaton, Kevin Gildea, Barbara Hulme, Suzanne Klerks, Katie Marshall, Shelagh Ord, Marion Phillips, Elizabeth Rothwell (Queen's University, Canada), and David Wylynko.

I am also grateful to the staff of the National Library of Canada, the National Archives of Canada, the Canadian Royal Heritage Trust, the libraries of Carleton University and the University of Toronto, the Archives of the Province of Ontario, the British Museum, the National Register of Archives (London, England), the National Portrait Gallery of England, the Bodleian Library and the Rhodes House Library, Oxford, the Plunkett Foundation for Cooperative Studies, Oxford, the Archives of the Department of Paleography and Diplomatic of Durham University, England, the National Library of Scotland, the National Library of Ireland, Trinity College Library, Dublin, the Public Record Office of Northern Ireland, and the Royal Commonwealth Society Library in London, England.

Many academics and other individuals have been generous with their time, information, and suggestions when I consulted them, including Ann Saddlemyer of the University of Toronto; Richard Plant, Natalie Rewa, and Arthur Zimmerman of Queen's University, Canada; David Gardner, actor, director, teacher and theatre historian; Heather McCallum, founder of the theatre section of the Metropolitan Toronto Reference Library; Patrick O'Neill of Mount Saint Vincent University; Denis Salter of McGill University; Anne Spitere of the Canadian High Commission in London; R.H. Hubbard, author of the seminal book *Rideau Hall: An*

Illusrated History of Government House from 1867 to the Present (1977); Lindy Dufferin, widow of the last Earl of Dufferin; June, Marchioness of Aberdeen, who gave me permission to work in the Muniment Room at Haddo House, Scotland; Sir Oliver Miller, Keeper of the Queen's Pictures; Lord Howick of the Grey Estate in Howick, England, grandson of the former Governor General of Canada; Mrs. Iris Young, former librarian of the Earl of Derby's Estate and the Stanley Estate and Stud Company; and Pat Marsden of sports radio 590 AM "The Fan" in Toronto.

A special note of thanks is due to two people—Corinne Allan and Maurice Sullivan—who helped me develop some computer skills so I could put the manuscript of this book on computer files and disks, and thus make the work of the helpful and vigilant publishers at Borealis Press—Glenn Clever and Frank Tierney—less onerous.

Finally, I wish to thank my wife Norma, whom I met and married during my work on this book, and who was always supportive and encouraging, even on the many occasions when I came home late for supper from the National Library and the National Archives in Ottawa.

Lord Monck.
(NAC C-003621)

Chapter 1

Before the Theatre at Rideau Hall

There is little evidence that Canada's first two Governors General, Lord Charles Stanley Monck (1867-1868) and John Young, Lord Lisgar (1869-1872) fostered culture at Rideau Hall or elsewhere in Canada. It would not be until the time of the Dufferins in 1873 that Canada had a vigorous supporter of culture in the Governor General's residence. However, it is worthwhile exploring to what extent culture was a concern of the two men who preceded Dufferin, and of their families, and why they did not do more to foster Canadian culture.

Lord Monck

Charles Stanley Monck (1819-1894) had been Governor General from 1861 until Confederation, and during most of that time he resided at Spencer Wood, the vice-regal home outside Quebec City. Because he spent six years as Governor General before Confederation, and only one year after, evidence of his cultural interests will be given before as well as after that crucial date in Canadian history. And because culture in a public figure is intimately linked with his social life and hospitality, these elements in the life of Monck will be examined as an expression of his willingness to foster culture in Canada.

The principal sources of information on his cultural activities are his own letters, his sister-in-law, Feo Monck's journal for 1864-1865, *My Canadian Leaves*, and various newspapers of the time. Lady Elizabeth Monck (1824?-1892), his wife, kept a diary-letter which she sent to her sisters in England, but that has unfortunately been lost except for some fragments.

1

Lady Monck.
(NAC PA-027932)

Part of the reason for minimal social and cultural life during their time in Canada, and especially in Ottawa, was that the Moncks were not wealthy, and the salary of a Governor General was not great. One writer said of Monck's life in Ottawa:

> Very little entertaining was done by him. He had no carriage and pair save when John Tozer, a well-known "citizen of credit and renown" scoured the city for horses and drove a spanking four-in-hand down to the Hall for His Excellency. The latter's usual way of reaching the city was by boat (Randall 151).

Near the end of Monck's tenure, Parliament had even voted to reduce his salary, but its wishes had been overridden by the Imperial Parliament. The issue prompted much debate in Canadian newspapers, especially since a reduction would affect Monck's successors rather than himself. The *Montreal Gazette*, taking its cue from *Le Journal de Québec*, suggested there was more reason to reduce Monck's salary than that of his rumoured successor, Lord Lisgar:

> *Le Journal de Québec*, commenting on the rumoured appointment and the rejection of the recent bill to reduce the Governor General's salary, asks whether the Dominion Parliament can find anything in the nominee's social and political position to induce it to accept the decision of the Imperial Government so far as it is contained in the disallowing despatch. The brief sketch we have given of Sir John Young's services, induces us to believe the Canadian Parliament will be satisfied with the manner in which the Imperial Government has, or is, about to, supplement its despatch. In any event, Sir John's claims to title and distinction far outweigh Lord Monck's. (Sept. 22, 1968, p. 2)

This sharp criticism of Monck was countered a year earlier when the *Ottawa Citizen* wrote an editorial condemning an attack by the *Gazette* on Monck's hospitality:

> Lord Monck has his public duties, but it is clearly no part
> of his duty to give hungry members of Parliament a taste of
> the contents of his larder and cellar. He may, as best suits
> him, provide board and lodging for public representatives
> or observe strict social exclusiveness. We do not believe the
> general public cares one jot whether the Governor General
> invites few or many persons to sit at his table. (Oct. 11,
> 1867, p. 2)

But the public did care about Monck's hospitality and generosity, and these various newspapers showed the public's
ambivalence towards Monck's wishes for privacy. Indeed on
his arrival in Ottawa on June 28, 1867 for his swearing in as
Governor General of the new Canada Monck declined a public reception by the people of the capital. Though he did
accept a reception from them in October of that year, the
snub seems to have caused relations between Monck and the
people of Ottawa, indeed of all Canada, to remain cool for
the year that remained of his term in Canada. The feeling was
shared by the Members of Parliament, as noted again by the
Montreal Gazette when Monck finally took up residence at
Rideau Hall:

> However painful it may be to make the observation, it is no
> less true that the bond which would unite the Governor
> General and the Representatives of the people in Canada,
> has not been strengthened the last few years. The weaning-
> off process has, we believe, already proceeded so far, that
> during the whole of last session very few members of either
> House ever sat at Lord Monck's table, or even performed
> the ordinary courtesy of making their calls, before leaving
> town or on arrival at the seat of Government. (*Quebec
> Mercury*, Oct. 9, 1867, p. 2)

This coolness, which made it virtually impossible for
Monck to contribute much to culture in Canada, manifest-
ed itself in other ways. After his swearing in on July 1, 1867
Monck remained in Ottawa only one week before returning

to Quebec City and his beloved Spencer Wood. His family did not accompany him to the swearing in, and, when Rideau Hall was finally ready for occupation in October of that year, joined him a month later. For the first anniversary of Confederation Monck did not even come to Ottawa, but remained in Quebec, and "visited the forts at Point Lévi ... and then drove to the camp of the 60th Royal Rifles ... listening to the band of the Regiment" (*Quebec Mercury*, July 2, 1868, p. 2). Indeed, at the one-hour levee he held that year, he was criticized because "that will be a decidedly cheap reception, and no doubt originates in the laudable idea of doing away with wine-bibbing even on New Year's Day" (*Quebec Mercury*, Jan. 3, 1868, p. 2).

Monck had other priorities, and they were diplomatic and military rather than social and cultural. Both he and the British Government were concerned about peace with the United States during and immediately after the American Civil War. He was also concerned about the defence of Canada's borders against the Fenians after the Civil War. He took these things very seriously, and was praised for his success in dealing with them. He even went as far as publishing a letter of disapproval of a volunteer officer (*The Leader*, Dec. 9, 1867, p. 2).

In fact, most of Monck's cultural interests were connected with his interest in the military. One of the few plays he is listed as patronizing in Ottawa was performed by the amateurs of the P.C.O. Rifle Brigade (*Ottawa Times*, June 27, 1866, p. 2). Several newspapers in Ottawa, Toronto and Montreal noted his giving prizes and a speech, a rare thing for Monck outside diplomatic and political duties, to the Rifle Association in October and November of 1867. If he had a real interest in music, it was in that played by military bands. Often the Quebec newspapers note that a military band played in the garden of the Governor General's residence of Spencer Wood, and in his final summer in Canada we read that a Band of the 53rd Regiment will play on the Esplanade in Quebec on Tuesdays at 7 p.m., and on Thursdays at 5 p.m.

"in the Governor's Garden ... during the remainder of the summer, weather permitting" (*Quebec Mercury*, Aug. 4, 1868, p. 2). Other musical groups Monck seemed little interested in, though when Marshall & Doyle's Mikado troupe came to Quebec a matinee was attended by Lady Monck and her daughters, as well as by Monck's brother Richard, then his military secretary, and Richard's wife Feo (*Quebec Mercury*, Sept. 18, 1867, p. 2).

Monck seems to have given little public support to science and education in his years in Canada. One organization he did patronize and receive was the Natural History Society, on two occasions in Ottawa, in 1866 and 1868. On the second occasion he received an address from the Society (*Quebec Mercury*, May 21, 1868, p. 2).

Monck was more interested in agriculture and sports than in science and education. In a letter to his friend Edward Ellice, after comparing the Toronto Cattle Show favourably with the Royal Shows at home in Ireland, he wrote: "... I say this with some authority, as I have all my life been a practical farmer myself, and been very much engaged in cattle shows at home" (Batt 56). Speaking more generally of Monck's character, Elizabeth Batt, his great-granddaughter, wrote:

> For all his mature judgement and steadiness of character, Monck was very much of a boy at heart, and a great deal of the pleasure Henry (his elder son) derived from outdoor pursuits arose from the fact that his father enjoyed them every bit as much as he did. One of the horses was Henry's special property, and they went on riding expeditions together. Both father and son were keen fishermen, and in Canada, this sport could be enjoyed on a scale they had never known in Ireland. (Batt 73)

They satisfied their love of both fishing and hunting mostly on the Saguenay River, as would several Governors General after them. The Quebec papers duly noted their absences from the city to enjoy pleasure trips on the Saguenay, as did Montreal's *La Minerve* when the Monck family and guests

The Monck Family at the south front of Rideau Hall, 1868. Photo by Samuel McLaughlin. (NAC C-005966)

left Quebec City on board the steamer *Napoleon III* for a fishing and hunting trip (Aug. 20, 1867, p. 3). No doubt this was one of the attractions that led the Moncks to spend more time in Quebec than in Ottawa even after Confederation. Other sports they could also enjoy more readily in Quebec than in Ottawa, such as cricket (*Quebec Mercury*, May 30, 1866, p. 2) and the annual games of the 30th Regiment on the Esplanade, when "The carriage of the Governor General, containing Her Excellency Vicountess Monck, the Hon. Mrs. Monck (Feo), Col. Irvine, A.D.C., and Capt. Pemberton, A.D.C., drove on to the grounds about two o'clock and remained to the close. The band of the 30th played a full programme, to the gratification of the immense crowd assembled" (*Quebec Mercury*, Sept. 21, 1867, p. 2). It is noteworthy, however, that the Governor General is not listed among those in the coach, even though he was at Spencer Wood at the time. This was often the case when members of the viceregal family took part in various forms of entertainment. Monck also consented to become patron of the Victoria La Crosse (sic) Club in Ottawa, but it was with some irony that the local newspaper reported: "The Victoria La Crosse Club will open their great match to-day at two o'clock p.m. His Excellency has consented to become the patron of this club, which, of course, will have the effect of making it one of the best in the country" (*Ottawa Citizen*, May 24, 1866, p. 2).

One of the few entertainments Monck described was in a letter dated October 2, 1863 to his son Henry, who was en route back to England. He tells the boy about his family—Lady Monck and their three other children—going to see the P.T. Barnum circus: "General Tom Thumb is here now; they are all going to see him today. Stanley (their youngest) calls him 'le petit Tom Pouce'" (*Monck Letters* 22). So delighted were they with the performance of the dwarfs that they invited members of the troupe to Spencer Wood, as the Governor General tells his son a week later: "Last Saturday, Mama had Tom Thumb, his wife, his sister, and Commodore Nutt out to lunch at Spencer Wood. They drove out in their carriage and four, and after lunch Stanley got into the carriage and drove about in it" (*Monck Letters* 23). The newspaper reviews of the performances and the reception of the audiences were ecstatic, as reflected in this review in the *Quebec Mercury*:

> The levees of those miracles of humanity—General Tom Thumb and wife, Minnie Warren, and the famous Commodore Nutt—commenced yesterday at the Lecture Hall, Ann street. As might have been anticipated from the widespread reputation of this incomparable miniature quartette, the Quebec public were not backward in extending towards them a cordial and hearty reception. The fashion and elite of the city thronged the morning and afternoon receptions of the little folk, and hundreds of anxious visitors, unable to obtain admittance to the evening exhibition, were obliged to turn away in disappointment. (Oct. 2, 1863, p. 3)

When Monck himself did attend or patronize a play or a concert it was often out of a sense of duty and often included some military performers. Thus the *Quebec Mercury* reported:

> It is very pleasing to see the esprit de corps of the 25th K.O.B.'s, manifested by all, from its Colonel downwards, joining in a dramatic performance, given on Thursday, for the benefit of the family of a deceased subaltern in that Regiment.—The officers of the garrison and their friends mustered in strong force in the body of the Music Hall. His Excellency the Governor General was present, and the galleries and pit were crowded with soldiers and others. (Jan. 5, 1865, p. 2)

He was also patron of a farewell concert by a Mr. Pearce, Mus. B., Oxon., and Organist to the English Cathedral, who was leaving Quebec after holding that post for several years. In a review of the concert, directed by Mr. Pearce, all the performers were praised including the Band of the 25th Borderers, which "played with its usual sweetness and taste" (*Quebec Mercury*, April 25, 1865, p. 2), though there is no evidence that Monck attended. Nor is there evidence he attended the double bill he patronized at Her Majesty's Theatre in Ottawa consisting of Buckstone's popular play *Green Bushes* and the farce *The Artful Dodge*, even though it was announced that "the P.C.O. Band will play their best music" (*Ottawa Times*, July 24, 1866, p. 2). His brother Col. Richard Monck attended the farewell concert of the K.O.B. in aid of a regimental charity that included two plays, the burlesque extravaganza *Aladdin, or The Wonderful Scamp* by Henry J. Byron, and the comedy *Little Toddlekins* by Charles Matthews. Monck had his own reasons for not attending these plays, though they were hardly those suggested by Feo in her journal:

> Everyone laughed at me because I said I begged of the G.G. not to go to the theatricals, as *on dit* that Booth is in Canada, and knowing that the G.G. is a Northern sympathizer, Booth might try and shoot him. (Monck 158)

Lincoln had been shot one week before these plays were scheduled. A more plausible reason for not attending might be that at the end of the extravaganza one of the characters recited a farewell composed for the occasion, typical of the inflated verse that would be used under later Governors General to mark similar occasions at Rideau Hall. It concluded:

> Ten rapid months have scarcely flown, since we,
> True birds of passage, came across the sea,
> And found with you a resting place,
> And smiles of welcome lighting up each face.
> Fondly we hoped to make a longer stay,
> But now that dream's dispelled—we must away—
> Alas! we're here just long enough to make
> Us feel, how sad it is so soon to break
> Your friendly bonds, and lose the happy spell
> You've round us wove so quickly and so well.
> Yet must it be—for adverse powers compel!
> Long shall the mem'ry of your kindness dwell
> Among us, our regrets 'twere vain to tell!
> FAREWELL! the Borderers bid you all FAREWELL!

Perhaps Monck explained his reluctance to get involved in entertainments best in a letter to his son Henry in January, 1863, early in his career in Canada: " ... last night there was an amateur theatrical performance by the non-commissioned officers and men of the 60th which I hear was very good and very well attended, but unfortunately we were lazy and did not go" (*Monck Letters* 7). Most of the events described here took place before Confederation, but from the evidence it is clear that Monck attended or sponsored even fewer after July 1, 1867.

One member of Monck's entourage who did revel in all forms of entertainment available to them in Canada was Feo, his sister-in-law, married to his brother Richard, military secretary for part of Monck's tenure in Canada and then after Monck had left. Her full name was Frances Elizabeth Owen Cole Monck. *My Canadian Leaves* is the title of a journal she wrote for her father, Owen Blayney Cole, from May 16, 1864 to May 30, 1865, during her first residence in Canada. The journal reflects the enthusiasm, vivacity, powers of observation, and manifold interests in life and its expression in culture, interests that were suppressed or ignored by the Governor General. In her journal we get an idea of the many social and cultural events that went on around her even as political events developed that would bring about the Canadian Confederation two years after she left. She was interested in balls, in dances, in theatre, in concerts, in travel around Quebec City, in Anglican churches and Catholic nuns, and in people of both high and low estate, and she records them all with verve in the pages of her journal.

She had a certain musical talent herself and displayed it on occasion, though not as often as we might expect. It may have seemed inappropriate to her status for her to perform in public often, unlike Lady Dufferin, who regularly acted on the stage for large audiences at Rideau Hall.

One occasion on which Feo did not hesitate to display her talent was at a fund-raising concert on Saturday, May 9, 1868 for St. Bartholemew's Anglican Church in Ottawa, of which the cornerstone had been laid that morning by the Governor

General. Feo's husband was on a second tour of duty in Canada, and she was more than pleased to join other singers and performers at Her Majesty's Theatre to help the fledging church across from Rideau Hall which would become known as the Governor General's church. This concert was attended by Lord Monck as well as "the most fashionable audience that ever assembled on a similar occasion in this city" (*Ottawa Times*, May 11, 1868, p. 2). While neither Feo nor anyone else is singled out for their musical ability, she is recognized for her generosity in taking part in the performance: "... The Hon. Mrs. Monck is also justly entitled to the highest praise for having consented to appear as a singer on the occasion" (*Ottawa Times*, May 11, p. 2). Perhaps if Feo had taken part in more concerts the Governor General would have encouraged the cultural life of Canada more enthusiastically.

Indeed a preference for the arts was part of the life of Feo's family. Her younger brother, Blayney Cole, undertook a career on the stage, a choice which was duly reported by a Quebec newspaper: "An English newspaper, *The Era*, has announced that Mr. Blayney Cole has chosen a career in the theatre. Mr. Cole is the brother of Frances ... and nephew of Viscount Monck, Governor General of Canada" [my translation] (*La Minerve*, Nov. 7, 1866, p. 2). He was Monck's nephew by virtue of the fact that his and Feo's mother was the elder sister of Monck's wife. Monck himself was puzzled by Blayney's decision and wrote to his son Henry accordingly: "What an odd thing it is of Blayney Cole to choose to go on the stage!" (*Monck Letters* 284). His reaction showed his own disinterest in the arts, and his failure to appreciate the artistic bent both Blayney and Feo inherited from their father.

In defence of Monck's lack of involvement in cultural affairs in Ottawa, it must be remembered that he did not move into Rideau Hall until October, 1867, four months after Confederation, when additions had been completed on the 1835 structure, and he left Ottawa for Quebec City in June 1868 after Parliament rose, to await the family's departure for England on November 14, 1868. Thus they lived in

Ottawa only eight months after Confederation, hardly time to establish any cultural traditions. An editorial on his departure from Canada even saw virtue in the limited social life of the Moncks: "...he has set the example of modest and prudent social life which it would not be by any means unhealthy for people in more obscure positions to imitate" (*Ottawa Times*, Nov. 18, 1868, p. 2).

Still, he had his critics even as he prepared to leave Canada and after he had returned home to his estate in Ireland. Speculating on who Monck's successor would be Ottawa's *Le Canada* reflected: "Lord Monck seems greatly to enjoy his life in his palace at Spencer Wood, when he's not travelling up the Saguenay ... the next Governor General ... has a very simple task to perform in succeeding in our tiny capital: do just the opposite to what Lord Monck did" [my translation] (Aug. 27, 1868, p. 2). On the day Monck sailed home from Canada, *Le Journal de Québec* wrote a lengthy editorial summing up his career, which ended: "Lord Monck proved that he had more tact for political life than for social life, and while he was without reproach in the one, he did not understand the demands of hospitality and of official life. That is why he leaves behind no regrets at his departure as well as no enemies" [my translation] (Nov. 14, 1868, p. 2).

Two weeks later, as Lord Lisgar was about to arrive in Quebec, the same paper looked forward to a new regime of social life and hospitality: "... we hear much good of the future viceroy. We also hear much praise of Lady Young. We are promised wonderful receptions at Rideau Hall ... a complete contrast with the arrogant solitude in which Lord Monck lived" (Nov. 28, 1868, p. 2).

These were harsh words indeed for the departing Governor General. While much was expected of his successor, it would seem that he would not have to try very hard to surpass the social and cultural life offered to Canadians by the Moncks.

Perhaps Monck was not so much arrogant as simply tired. Having accomplished his main task of seeing Canada into Confederation, he had no interest in stimulating social

Lord Lisgar.
Photo by W.J. Topley (NAC PA-027026)

or cultural life in Ottawa or elsewhere in Canada. As Morton commented somewhat sadly: "His year (in Canada after Confederation) was only the completing of a task and the filling in of time" (*Monck Letters* xxiv). He had limited his function to a narrow definition of the role of Governor General which barely included cultural patronage.

Lord Lisgar

Monck's example of modest social life was not followed by his immediate successor, Sir John Young, Baron Lisgar (1807-1876), who accepted the position of Governor General after others had rejected it because Prime Minister Macdonald had proposed a reduction in the incumbent's salary. Perhaps because this proposal was finally not accepted by the Queen, Lisgar and his wife Adelaide felt obliged to use his $50,000 salary as Governor General to entertain at Rideau Hall regularly, if not lavishly. And their generosity was reciprocated by Canadians in Ottawa and elsewhere, who were honoured to see their feelings toward the Queen's representative reciprocated as Monck had not reciprocated them.

John Young's past suggested he did not need to save the salary he earned as Governor General from 1868-1972. He was the eldest son of Sir William Young, first baronet, whose home was Baillieborough Castle, county Cavan in Ireland. His father was a director of the East India Company, which is the reason the future Governor General was born in Bombay in 1807. He inherited the baronetcy on his father's death in 1847. Educated at Eton and Oxford, he later studied at Lincoln's Inn and was called to the bar in 1834. He served as a Tory member of parliament for county Cavan from 1831 to 1855, and was appointed a lord of the treasury in 1841 and a secretary of the treasury in 1844. Under Lord Aberdeen he was chief secretary for Ireland from 1852-1855, when he was appointed Lord High Commissioner of the Ionian Islands, a position he held until forced to resign for political reasons in 1859. In 1861 he was appointed Governor General and

Commander-in-Chief of New South Wales, where he remained until 1868, the year he was appointed Governor General of Canada and Governor of Prince Edward Island, which did not join the Dominion of Canada until 1873, the year after Young left the country.

Young's most serious political challenge in Canada was the first rebellion of Louis Riel in 1869-1870. Partly because of his handling of this delicate situation, he was created Baron Lisgar in October 1870, a month after Riel fled to the United States. His new title was Baron Lisgar of Lisgar and Baillieborough. In 1835 he had married Adelaide Anabelle Dalton. They had no children.

While Lisgar was not officially sworn in as Governor General of Canada until January 1869, he and his wife arrived in Ottawa to begin his new duties in November of the previous year. On their arrival they were greeted by 7000 citizens in a reception that was described as "très brillante" (*Courrier du Québec*, Nov. 30, 1868, p. 2), and one "which caused almost a complete cessation of business in Ottawa" (my translation) (*Courrier du Québec*, Dec. 2, 1868, p. 2).

Anxious to make the new Governor General and all the federal politicians feel welcome in Ottawa, a Citizens Ball was held for them on May 5, 1869 at the Skating Rink, the only venue in the capital capable of accommodating the numbers who attended. It was described as "the most brilliant social gathering which has been held in Canada since the visit of His Royal Highness the Prince of Wales in 1860" (*Citizen*, May 6, 1869, p. 2). The ball was the first in a series of entertainments given in that session of Parliament, the second being a grand promenade concert followed by a conversazione (*Times*, May 6, 1869, p. 3). They also patronized and attended other balls in Ottawa, such as the Bachelors Ball, and a number of Calico Balls, often held to raise money for various causes including the Irish Protestant Benevolent Society (*Times*, Apr. 18, 1872, p. 2).

The vice-regal couple responded by giving a series of balls themselves on special occasions, like the first visit of Prince

Arthur when he served in Canada for several months in 1869-1870 with the 60th Rifle Battalion. On this occasion there were 2000 present in the Senate chamber on February 25, 1870 to meet the prince and join in the festivities. One fey description of the event used Shakespeare's "Seven Ages" speech to illustrate the variety of those in attendance:

> Shakespeare's 'Seven Ages,' or perhaps it were more correct to say 'five of them were present,' though for the nonce their own peculiar characteristics ... were forgotten and but one uniform desire seemed to possess them. The 'Lover' forgot his sighing since his mistress was present to smile on him. The 'Warrior' who had but just before gained the bubble reputation at the cannon's mouth, now yielded unresistingly to the more powerful charms of beauty. The Justice—'Capon Lined'—forgot his wise saws and modern instances, and became juvenile again. (*Globe*, Feb. 26, 1870, p. 1)

Such were the flights of rhetoric which a vice-regal ball could inspire in the 1870s. The Lisgars were also more ready than their predecessor to give dinners regularly and to mark special events such as the Queen's birthday (*Citizen*, May 26, 1871, p. 2).

Although the Lisgars were active in giving dinners, receptions and at homes, these were not always the lively and exciting events that we might expect from a vice-regal couple. One person who has testified to this is Edmund Allen Meredith (1817-1898), who was Under-Secretary of State during the time of the Moncks, the Lisgars, and the Dufferins. He kept a journal from 1844 to 1898, in which he described dinners at Rideau Hall with the Lisgars as gloomy and filled with awkward silences (NAC). Florence Randal is even more graphic in her description of the solemnity of the Lisgars:

> It is said that on a day when guests were invited till the hour of eight p.m., the gas went out at the fateful stroke, and the forlorn guests, huddled in the dark on the steps,

waited impatiently for their carriage to "block the way". In a letter written by a Nova Scotian in 1872, this pen picture of the times is given: "I shan't libel Lord Lisgar, and therefore I won't say that the parties are very numerous or very pleasant. 'God Save the Queen' plays you out at ten o'clock…" (Randal 151)

The Lisgars were fairly ecumenical for their time. Their own allegiance was to the Church of England, and they attended regularly services at the Anglican Church while in Canada. Like the Moncks, they were generous to St. Bartholemew's Church, which was still raising money for its building fund during their tenure. Accordingly, Lisgar donated $100.00 on Christmas Day in 1870 to the church. As one newspaper noted, "This is not the first instance of our Governor's generosity" (*Chronicle & Quebec Gazette*, Jan. 4, 1870, p. 2). He was also active in the affairs of the Anglican Diocese of Ottawa, and often attended meetings of its Mission Board and its Auxiliary Bible Society, of which he was the patron. Indeed, he was not hesitant to give advice to the Mission Society, as when "His Excellency spoke at the close of the meeting, urging that subscriptions should be general, and not thrown on a few wealthy individuals. He said he was opposed to church endowments, which had done much harm in the past to the progress of the Church" (*Globe*, Jan. 20, 1869, p. 1). On one occasion, while Lady Lisgar attended the Bachelors Ball at the Rink Music Hall in Ottawa, the Governor General was presiding at a mission meeting (*Chronicle*, Feb. 1, 1871, p. 2). But he also received and gave addresses to both the Wesleyan Conference (*Globe*, June 19, 1869, p. 1) and to the Presbyterian Church (*Globe*, June 30, 1869, p. 1). He and his wife visited Catholic schools and convents, and one of his last public acts before leaving Canada was to attend the opening in Montreal of a new Catholic Commercial College (*Chronicle*, June 20, 1872, p. 2).

His relations with Quebec, particularly in Quebec City, were more tenuous. A large Citizens Ball was given for the

Lisgars at the Music Hall in Quebec City on July 21, 1869. However, the Mayor of Quebec was not invited since the Quebec City council had voted against a reception for the Governor General a month earlier (*Le Canada*, June 19, 1869, p. 2). And even before the ball, Lisgar had to face an unfortunate incident with the St. Jean-Baptiste Society. At a levee in the Quebec capital on July 12 of that year, an altercation took place over the presentation of addresses by various national societies. The St. Jean Baptiste Society claimed precedence, but other societies objected. When these other societies offered to draw lots, the St. Jean Baptiste group refused. As a result the Governor General declined to receive any of them. He did, however, receive the consuls, judges, Roman Catholic clergy, the Anglican Synod, and the Board of Trade (*Globe*, July 13, 1869, p. 1). *The Globe*, which followed this story closely, reported that as a result of the disturbance, the invitation to the President of the St. Jean-Baptiste Society to a banquet for the Governor General three days later was withdrawn. Drawing on a report from an English newspaper in Quebec, it gave more background to the social snub to the Society:

> The *Chronicle* says the conduct of the St. Jean-Baptiste Society was preconcerted, and that it was known to several high in power, whose duty it was to have prevented His Excellency from being subject to so unseemly an altercation at the door of his reception room. It says a party of five (papal) Zouaves, from St. Sauveur ... roughs in uniform ... were placed in the passage to insult citizens and rudely repulse the Protestant Bishop and the members of the Synod. (*Globe*, July 15, 1869, p. 1)

It would not be lost on the editors of the *Globe* that the date of the levee was July 12, when Toronto was having its own celebrations to mark the victory of the Orangemen at the Battle of the Boyne.

Two years later, Lord Lisgar was not present at a St. Jean-Baptiste celebration in Ottawa which passed without incident.

He was represented by the Prime Minister, Sir John A. Macdonald, who expressed the Governor General's apologies to the Society. The report of his sentiments and of the message the Prime Minister would deliver to him was tinged with irony, whether intentional or unintentional, in view of the incident in Quebec City two years previously and, indeed, of subsequent Canadian history:

> Sir John A. Macdonald regretted the absence of His Excellency the Governor General, but he would take the earliest opportunity to convey to His Excellency a knowledge of their loyal sentiments. He would have much pleasure in recounting to His Excellency the splendid procession which so many had witnessed in Ottawa that day. His Excellency was enjoying a pleasant relaxation after the labours of the year; he was enjoying the beauties of nature amid the loyal inhabitants of Lower Canada, whose magnificent scenery was abundant. He was glad their useful Society was so prosperous; its object was to do good, and he was satisfied it afforded much comfort to the needy, and it also encouraged and fostered that spirit of patriotism and loyalty which has ever characterized the career of Frenchmen in Canada. (*Times*, June 27, 1871, p. 3)

At the time of the Ottawa celebration, the Governor General was with Mr. Molson on a fishing trip in the Gaspé.

Lady Lisgar was not with him on the fishing trip. She had left for a visit to England, one of several trips she took to England or the United States while he remained in Canada. The reason seems to have been no dissatisfaction with her role as first lady in Canada, but may have been partly due to her poor health. Although she was very active in social activities in Canada, there were times when she could not accompany her husband to official functions for health reasons, and one occasion when the Governor General arrived two days late for a visit to Saint John, New Brunswick because of his wife's illness (*Globe*, Aug. 28, 1869, p. 1). It was not unusual for her to leave on a trip abroad and for him to go on a hunting or

*Group in the Conservatory at Rideau Hall, with Lord Lisgar
seated at left, and Prince Arthur seated at right, 1870.*
Photo by W.J. Topley (NAC PA-026355)

fishing trip immediately afterwards, as when he went off to the Gaspé in Mr. Molson's steamship.

In fact, there was a careful division of interests and social responsibilities between the Lisgars. She was responsible for much of the entertaining that was expected of the vice-regal couple. Very often the newspapers announced or reported that Lady Lisgar was holding a reception or an at home for members of parliament or other parts of the social elite in Ottawa. There was a clear distinction between the two events. An "at home" was less formal than a "reception" and included fewer guests. An at home might include games and light-hearted revelry, like the one at Rideau Hall on October 18, 1869 when Prince Arthur was visiting Ottawa. At this event, which was called a "merry social", we are told that the Prince joined in the games "with much hilarity" (*Chronicle*, Oct. 20, 1869, p. 2). On the other hand, Lady Lisgar gave a reception on December 19, 1871 for the Grand Duke Alexis of Russia, son of the tsar, on his state visit to Ottawa, which was "well attended" by "all the elite" (*Daily Witness*, Dec. 20, 1871, p. 4). In 1869, the Lisgars' first full year in Canada, she held a series of receptions after improvements had been made to Rideau Hall: "A large room has been made by the removal of partitions. The Conservatory was beautifully illuminated last night with Chinese lanterns, and with the plants and shrubs in full bloom, had a beautiful effect" (*Globe*, April 17, 1869, p. 1). The receptions continued regularly until the end of June when Parliament was prorogued and the Lisgars embarked on a three-month tour of Canada that began in Montreal, went on to Quebec City and the summer levee there, continued into the Maritimes, and ended in South-western Ontario.

The Lisgars were so well coordinated that on some days each entertained in their own fashion. Thus, on April 15, 1869 he had some members of parliament to dinner, while she held an "at home" for some fifty ladies and men from 9 p.m. to 11 p.m. And on January 1, 1870 the Governor General held his second levee on Parliament Hill, while his wife gave a reception at Rideau Hall the same day. Her invitations made it quite clear as to when the guests should arrive and when they should leave. She also made it clear how they should dress. Accordingly, for her first reception on December 17, 1868 it was announced that "Persons appearing at Lady Young's reception to-morrow p.m., will not require to do so in full dress, but in ordinary walking costume" (*Globe*, Dec. 17, 1868, p. 1). She was also generous in patronizing bazaars to raise money for worthy causes such as the building of the Free Presbyterian Church on Bank St. in Ottawa; over the two days of the bazaar, at which "Gowan's band was not the least attraction" (*Times*, March 19, 1870, p. 3), $1,000 was raised.

The Lisgars certainly took their social duties seriously, and entertained the Canadian people regularly and appropriately, thus avoiding the practice of their predecessor Lord Monck, who had been so severely criticized for his failure to entertain whom and when he should.

One visitor they had entertained with relish was Prince Arthur, the third son of Queen Victoria, who, as Duke of Connaught, would become the tenth Governor General of Canada in 1911. He was only nineteen when he came to Canada to serve in Montreal in the first battalion of the Rifle Brigade, a duty in which he would see his first active service during a Fenian raid on Canada in 1870. The enthusiasm and youth of the young prince induced the sixty-three-old Governor General to engage in some of his earliest sporting activities in Canada. Lisgar met the Prince in Halifax on August 22, 1869 and, after accompanying him on a visit to Niagara Falls and other parts of southern Ontario, met him again in Ottawa on October 11. During the Prince's stay at Rideau Hall he visited several attractions around Ottawa and the Ottawa valley, including the Chaudière Falls, a bulk head dam, a suspension bridge, a crib and raft on the Ottawa River, Messrs. Perley & Petters' mill, Messrs. Bronson & Weston's mill, and Levi, Young and Co. (*Chronicle*, Oct. 13, 1869, p. 2). Before their arrival in Ottawa they had gone hunting on Long Point Reserve where, one paper stated, "The Governor General (was) about the most lively of the party, and enjoy(ed) the amusement with the greatest relish" (*Globe*, Oct. 1, 1869, p. 1). After a ball and an "at home" for the Prince at Rideau Hall, and a promenade concert at the Skating Rink, the Prince and the Governor General left on a hunting trip for a week at the camp of a Mr. Reynolds on the Nation River. Lisgar apparently entered into the spirit of this hunt as much as the earlier one at Long Point, for, during the first two days, he "devoted himself to shooting woodcock, at which he proved himself an adept, (and on October 22) His Excellency turned his attention to the deer. As he is evidently a finished sportsman, we have no doubt that he will give a good account of any that come his way" (*Citizen*, Oct. 23, 1869, p. 2). This estimate of the Governor General's skill as a hunter was confirmed by another paper which reported that he "gave evidence of being a keen sportsman and accurate shot, having in thick cover brought down a number of woodcock in capital style" (*Times*, Oct. 16, 1869, p. 2). After the hunting expedition the Prince left to join his battalion in Montreal.

While Lord Lisgar was not a particularly avid sportsman in Canada and did not encourage sports the way some of his successors did, he enjoyed them as a form of leisure either as a spectator or an active participant from time to time, as shown by his outings with Prince Arthur. He was quite adept at sports like hunting and fishing that he would have engaged in on his Irish estates. It is not surprising, then, that the one cup he donated in his name was given to the Ottawa Rifle Association. The cup was described in detail:

> The design of this prize cup is very chaste and elegant, both in its proportions and finish. It stands about six inches in height, the whole burnished, except a pretty wreath of maple leaves, forming a band around it, near the top, which is dead finished. On one side are his Excellency's monogram and orders. The foot is very simple, and in good keeping with the containing portion. The gold lining

is of the richest colour ... altogether it is as pretty and unpretentious a little cup as one could wish for, and then it is sterling silver. (*Times*, July 5, 1869, p. 3).

The article went on to say, "We understand that his Excellency will give a cup annually to each Provincial Rifle Association, viz.: to the Dominion, Ontario, Quebec, Nova Scotia, and New Brunswick, and to the Metropolitan." Shortly before his departure from Canada, he extended the scope of his prizes to Canada's newest province by offering one "to the best marksman in the 'Lisgar' (Manitoba) Rifle Company" (*Citizen*, June 5, 1872, p. 1).

Virtually all the newspapers, English and French, followed the Governor General's plans for a fishing trip of several weeks in the Gaspé in 1871, the trip which overlapped with the festival of St. Jean Baptiste. The date of his departure from Ottawa (June 8), as well as his destination, were carefully noted. One paper wrote of how government departments were rushed before his departure: "This has caused some hurry in the Government Department to get ready documents requiring the Governor's signature" (*Daily*, June 8, 1871, p. 2). The *Globe* noted how off Quebec City he breakfasted on the outgoing mail steamer *Scandinavian* at the invitation of steamship and railway magnate Sir Hugh Allan before continuing on Mr. Molson's steam yacht (*Globe*, June 12, 1871, p. 1). On another day it was noted that he had gone fishing at Rimouski (*Courrier d'Outaouais*, July 12, 1871, p. 2). It appears that Lisgar's motives for fishing were as much social as sporting.

For other sporting events the Governor General was happy to be a patron or a mere observer. Thus he agreed to become the patron of the Toronto Yacht Club shortly after his arrival in Canada (*Globe*, Dec. 12, 1868, p. 1); and the day after his arrival in Quebec City in 1871 he agreed to be the patron of the Quebec Regatta (*Chronicle*, Sept. 12, 1871, p. 2). On his first extended visit to Montreal he visited the Victoria Skating Rink where he was warmly greeted and intrigued by what he saw. After meeting the President and Directors of the Club, he was

> at once conducted by them to the gallery over the entrance, the band of the 78th playing the national anthem. A large body of skaters of various ages were already disporting themselves on the ice, and the sight, on which the setting sun shed its rays, was very beautiful, and no doubt fully enjoyed by His Excellency, who watched it for a considerable time ... Though the numbers of skaters and visitors was not so large as perhaps might have been anticipated, the scene was very animated. The gas was partially lit, and as the shades of evening came down was lighted all over, including the beautiful coloured lamps. The rink was decorated with flags, likewise with festoons of evergreens, and His Excellency cannot fail to have carried away with him the recollection of one of the most beautiful and striking pictures that the city affords to its winter visitors. (*Daily*, Feb. 6, 1869, p. 2)

A sport more dear to his Excellency's heart was horse-racing, and in this way he was involved with the Queen's Plate race on at least one occasion. At its inception in 1860 the race had no permanent home, and moved from one Ontario city to another until it was was settled in Toronto in 1883, where it remains to this day. In 1872 it was Lisgar's decision that the prestigious race for "50 guineas", initiated by Queen Victoria, be run at the Ottawa Turf Club. And so at the end of May of that year he and his wife, along with several members of Parliament, witnessed the running of "the oldest uninterrupted stakes race on the continent" (Marsh 1812), "which was won by Mr. Simpson's horse, 'Fearnaught,' of Guelph" (*Chronicle*, June 1, 1872, p. 2).

When it came to the arts the Lisgars showed a genuine but not an avid interest, so they could not be called leaders in the arts for the Canadian people. Their involvement, such as it was, was with music rather than theatre or art. And many of the concerts they attended or patronized were for organizations or causes, as would be expected of them in their position. On occasion one or both of them were patrons of a particular concert; of the two Lady Lisgar had the more serious interest in music. Thus one of the first concerts patronized by the Governor General in Ottawa was the annual Grand Concert of the St. George's Society in aid of their Christmas fund. The music was performed by both amateurs and by a military band: "The committee have secured the services of the best amateur talent and placed the directorship in the hands of Mr. Fripp, organist of Christ Church. The splendid band of the P.C.O. Rifles will play some of their best selections" (*Times*, Dec. 5, 1868, p. 2). The same Mr. Fripp organized and conducted a Grand Promenade Concert at the Skating Rink during the visit of Prince Arthur in aid of St. Bartholemew's Church. Lady Lisgar was patroness of the event. The concert itself was followed by a dinner in honour of the distinguished visitor. And the local musicians were bolstered by the Prince's own battalion: "The band of the 60th Rifles will contribute their valuable aid. The chorus will comprise about seventy of the leading amateurs of the city" (*Times*, Oct. 14, 1869, p. 3). She also patronized, though she could not attend, a Grand Concert at the Skating Rink Music Hall in aid of St. Alban's Church, another Anglican church in Ottawa (*Citizen*, April 27, 1870, p. 3). Underlining the ecumenical nature of Lady Lisgar was her patronage of a Grand Concert at the same Hall for the new school of the Ladies of the Congregation Notre Dame of Ottawa. The newspaper report went almost too far out of its way to point out both her and the audience's broadmindedness in supporting such a cause:

> It was indeed a most pleasing spectacle to witness a large assemblage of our most respectable citizens burying all thoughts of class and creed, and meeting together to give their countenance and assistance to the best cause that can engage the attention of the public. We hope we may have the delight of witnessing many events similar to that in the Hall last evening, and we trust we may ever be able to say that in the capital of the Dominion nothing can prevent its

liberal hearted and liberal minded people from encouraging and supporting sound education no matter what be the nature of the Institution in which it has its abode. (*Times*, May 31, 1871, p. 3)

One concert patronized by Lady Lisgar which did stir some controversy was a Grand Italian Operatic Concert by Signora Maria Gellie, an Ottawa woman "who had been favourably received at Milan last year, and more recently had been creating quite a sensation in New Jersey" (*Times*, May 12, 1870, p. 3). When the concert, which included other distinguished artists, had been advertised she was attacked as a fraud by the Toronto *Mail* newspaper. The *Ottawa Times*, which had already given her an enthusiastic advance billing, was incensed by the charges and wrote a vigorous article in her defence:

> A woman is coming here to sing. True. That woman is the Signora Maria Gellie, and that woman is not a humbug. The Signora could not be more than a woman, but she is nevertheless a lady and no swindle, as the *Mail* absurdly and unjustly alleges. She is an Ottawa woman. She is an accomplished woman. She has obtained the highest honours at Milan, where operatic music is not unknown. She has been appreciated where Jenny Lind, being only a woman, was appreciated, and there are very many here, who will gladly pay a dollar to hear one 'screech' of that voice which by times elicits laughter or tears. It is shameful in a *Mail* to abuse a female, because that female is a woman. (*Times*, May 17, 1870, p. 2)

This eloquent rebuttal of the *Mail* article apparently persuaded the concert-going public in Ottawa that Maria Gellie was genuine, for the very positive review of her concert the next day noted that "the audience ... filled the Hall ... (with) over 600 people present" (*Times*, May 18, 1870, p. 2), though the capacity of Her Majesty's Theatre was actually 1000. No such controversy attended a concert patronized by Lady Lisgar on

April 18, 1871 at the Skating Rink Music Hall. Two performers were given top billing: Madame Elena Waters, an operatic singer, and F. Jehin Prume, a violinist of renown in Europe and North America. Like Maria Gellie, Mme. Waters had Ottawa connections, having taught music there some years previously. She was warmly welcomed back by the French paper *Le Courrier d'Outaouais*, which encouraged all music lovers to attend. "A ce soir donc, et en foule, au Skating Rink" (*Courrier d'Outaouais*, April 18, 1871, p. 2) were its directions. But while both performers were given glowing praise in a review the following day, and the hall was filled with an audience that included the elite of society, "which didn't hurt things at all" [my translation] (*Courrier d'Outaouais*, April 19, 1871, p. 2), the paper noted that the number of French-Canadians in the audience was small. It expressed embarrassment over this poor turnout, and said that this often happened when the ticket prices were slightly elevated for a particular concert. The ticket prices, as advertised in the paper, were 75 cents for reserved seats, 50 cents for unreserved seats, and 25 cents for seats in the gallery (*Courrier d'Outaouais*, April 17, 1871, p. 3). (The top price for the concert by Maria Gellie was $1.00.) No mention was made of Lady Lisgar being among the elite at this concert even though her name was included in the advertisement as a patron.

It is thus difficult to say whether the Lisgars actually attended the performances they patronized or were expected to attend, since the reviews rarely said they were there. Perhaps the review would have said so if they did attend, as it sometimes did, so we might assume they were not present unless they were positively identified. Thus, among the few plays their names were connected with, there is no record they actually did attend any of them. Still, the plays, both military performances, are worth noting. The first, under the patronage of the Governor General, was performed at Her Majesty's Theatre in Ottawa by the 60th Royal Rifles, Prince Arthur's battalion, on March 3, 1870. The local newspapers gave the play their enthusiastic backing and did all in their power to encourage the locals to attend: " ... every care will be taken to insure an amusing entertainment, and we hope our military friends will have plenty of well-merited applause for their exertions" (*Times*, March 1, 1870, p. 3). On the day of the performance, the same paper wrote: "This, one of the most celebrated among the many distinguished regiments of the British line, contains at present many clever men even in its ranks, whose educational and histrionic acquirements are of no mean order ... By all means, then, let the gallant and admirably well-behaved 60th have a good house" (*Times*, March 3, 1870, p. 2). The plays were a drama *The Midnight Watch* by J. Morton, and a farce *To Paris and Back for £5*, as well as a "Grand Comic Scene" entitled "Shylock", presumably from Shakespeare's *Merchant of Venice*. Every performance of the evening was highly praised, including the songs and band music that supplemented the drama, but special praise was lavished on the soldier who performed Shylock: "(Corporal) Putman's scene from 'Shylock' was inimitable— he was encored, and kept the audience in roars. The farce was well done—it went off like a champagne cork—. The fine band, though last mentioned, was not the least attraction of the evening" (*Times*, March 4, 1870, p. 3).

Another performance by the "Military Amateurs" on behalf of charity took place on April 2, 1870 at the Rink Music Hall in Ottawa. Again, the local paper did its best to ensure a full house on the day of the performance: " ... from all appearances a crowded house is likely to await the corps ... Lady Young, we understand, will be present, and both the audience and performance promise to be brilliant. Those who are going—and who is not?—should secure their seats early this morning" (*Citizen*, April 2, 1870, p. 2). In the enthusiastic review the following day no mention is made of Lady Young's presence.

There is little evidence that the Youngs had any particular interest in art, or that they had much opportunity to indulge it in Canada if they did. Two visits to art institutions have been recorded. Both Lord and Lady Young visited l'Institution Nationale des Beaux-Arts Appliqués à l'Industrie, a school of design established by l'abbé M. Chabert in the building which housed the school of the Sisters of the Congregation Notre Dame in Ottawa. On this occasion it is reported that "Their Excellencies were real connoisseurs in examining the works (of M. Chabert's pupils), and carefully pointed out to those who accompanied them the most distinguished works" (*Canada*, July 3, 1869, p. 2). Those who accompanied them included Sir Georges Étienne Cartier and the Mayor of Ottawa. After M. Chabert made an undisguised request for state support for his institution, the Governor General, though he had not been aware that he was expected to give a speech, diplomatically replied that the institution was indeed worthy of such support, and used the example of schools of design in England and Ireland, often encouraged by the late Prince Albert, which contributed to the progress of industry in these countries. His interest in the practical results of education is clearly evident in his impromptu speech, and was no doubt the main reason he visited the Institution: "He thought that the best models should be placed before the mechanic, that he might be able to investigate the principles of correct taste. Art does not better genius, but shows it the right path in which to proceed" (*Times*, July 3, 1869, p. 3). Less practical was Lady Lisgar's visit, accompanied by Lady Belleau, wife of the Lieutenant Governor of Quebec, to the workshop of the Quebec City painter Eugène Hamel, nephew of the famous portrait painter, Théophile Hamel (1817-1870) (*Courrier d'Outaouais*, October 8, 1870, p. 2). She seems to have been drawn by the pride and desire of her hostess to display the talents of "notre artiste canadien-francais".

Lisgar's concern for education, both formal and informal, and its importance for the growth and development of Canada, was shown in other ways. In 1871 he "sent his name to Dr. Meredith ... to be enrolled (with a) life membership of the Literary and Scientific Society (of Ottawa), as one of the twenty who subscribe $50.00 to relieve the institution from embarrassment. The act was purely voluntary on his part, no one having solicited the donation" (*Citizen*, May 5, 1871, p. 3). In a similar spirit he had served as patron of the annual festival of its predecessor the Ottawa Mechanics' Institute and Atheneum (Gaizauskas 66).

In fact, Lisgar's most consistent cultural concern in Canada was for strong and vibrant educational institutions, particularly institutions of higher education. In this spirit he visited Laval University for a convocation ceremony, and replied in both English and French to the rector's address of welcome (*Chronicle*, July 10, 1869, p. 2). During Prince Arthur's visit to southern Ontario in 1869 they visited several educational institutions including the Hellmuth Ladies College in London, the Wesleyan Female College, the Central School and the Dundurn Deaf and Dumb school in Hamilton, and various schools in Toronto including the University of Toronto, the Normal School, Upper Canada College, and Osgoode Hall. At the University of Toronto he vouched for the centrality of universities in the life of Canada:

> In truth it is impossible to over-estimate the value of well regulated national Universities. They are the rich storehouses of wisdom, from which the seeds of knowledge may be sown broadcast throughout the land—the centres of sound principle and high moral bearing; the scenes of many a friendly contest for the early laurels of literature; the fruitful sources of many a trusted and life-long friendship; the homes of traditions and cherished memories. (*Globe*, Oct. 5, 1869, p. 4)

In the course of his speech he reflected the practice of the time when he referred to the "well-educated and high-principled men" who would go forth from its portals, and "that greatest of all benefits—a sound and Christian education" these men would receive at the university, though Trinity College was the only denominational college in the University of Toronto at the time since the university had become secularized in 1850. Women were admitted to the university only fifteen years later in 1884.

On his tour of the Maritimes in 1869 he again emphasized the importance of education at a levee in St. John, New Brunswick, where "He praised the energy of the people, pointed to the resources of the country, and urged the adoption of a good system of education by which the people would be prepared for the destiny before them" (*Chronicle*, Sept. 9, 1869, p. 2).

His most extensive visit to any educational institution was to McGill University earlier that year. The Governor General was by Royal Charter one of the visitors of the university, and he visited it carefully, including the Museum of Natural History and the Geological Museum. He was escorted through various departments of the university, and, accompanied by Principal Dawson, examined the collections in the Natural History Rooms for forty-five minutes, and was particularly interested in "the series of Canadian mammals and birds, also the specimens of Australian birds, with the latter of which he was familiar owing to his recent residence in New South Wales" (*Daily*, Feb. 4, 1869, p. 2). At a Convocation on February 3, he received an address, and again gave some of his thoughts on the importance of education, though again he stated that he had not come prepared to give a speech:

> I feel, as all intelligent men must feel, the deepest interest in the progress of education in this country, as in the country I have left. Education in Great Britain and the Dominion of Canada is not a luxury, but an absolute necessity, not only for individual advantage, but for the safety of the country. Where suffrage is so diffused, as to be nearly universal, education must be made as general and extensive, for there is no evil can threaten a country's freedom so great as that arising from ignorance, intrenched behind the bulwarks of prejudice and delusion with which it surrounds itself. It is a necessity for government and every lover of humanity to foster education by every means possible ... (Applause.). (*Daily*, Feb. 4, 1869, p. 2)

His serious interest in education is further seen in the fact that on this same week-long residence in Montreal, he also visited the Villa Maria convent, and the schools of the Christian Brothers.

There were some lighter moments during his visit to Montreal. He attended a concert of the Amateur Musical Union at McGill, and was scheduled to be driven around the mountain of Montreal. The attempt, however, was unsuccessful:

> His Excellency, with the Hon. John Rose, Col. McNeil and Mr. Hogan, started in a sleigh drawn by four spirited horses, but nature was too strong for even such a team. The drive was sound by Mile End, but when in the neighbourhood of the Côte des Neiges, the snow had drifted to such a degree, blocking up the road, that it was found necessary to return without fetching the far-famed compass round the Mountain. (*Chronicle*, Feb. 6, 1869, p. 2)

It was also in Montreal that Lisgar performed his last public function before leaving Canada at the end of his term, the opening of a new Roman Catholic Commercial College on Plateau St.: "Lord Lisgar was present to witness the ceremonies, and he replied to several addresses which were presented to him" (*Chronicle*, June 20, 1872, p. 2). The newspaper reports do not say whether he had come prepared to make his reply. Three days later he sailed back to England on Sir Hugh Allan's steamship the *Scandinavian*.

Lisgar's resignation had come rather suddenly for Canadians. At the beginning of April 1872 the papers simply announced that he had requested to resign and that his resignation had been accepted, though he had one more year to serve as Governor General. Furthermore, his replacement, the Earl of Dufferin, was announced at the same time. Unlike the departure of Monck, Lisgar's was announced with regret and genuine fondness. One newspaper summed up the sentiments of most Canadians when it wrote:

In all His Excellency performed the duties of his office faithfully and well, and in a way which was in all respects satisfactory, to not only his sworn advisers, but to the members of the Opposition. Lord Lisgar will ever be held in kindly remembrance here, and he may rely upon it that the people of Canada will watch his future career with interest, sincerely wishing that he may yet be spared many years to the Queen and country whose faithful and efficient servant he has ever been. (*Times*, June 14, 1872, p. 2)

As he and Lady Lisgar left Ottawa on the steamer *Queen Victoria*, "A large number of distinguished persons were present at the Queen's Wharf to bid the party farewell. The Ottawa Field Battery fired a royal salute, and, as the steamer cast loose from the shore, three hearty British cheers were given by the assembled multitude, which he acknowledged by raising his hat" (*Chronicle*, June 17, 1872, p. 2).

A farewell banquet was hosted by the citizens of Montreal at the St. Lawrence Hall after Lisgar had opened the new Commercial College there. It was chaired by Sir Hugh Allan in the absence of the Mayor of Montreal, and attended by the Lieutenant Governors of Nova Scotia and New Brunswick, the Premier of Quebec, members of both the House of Commons and the Senate, and the Consul General of the United States. Affairs of state kept the Prime Minister, Sir John A. Macdonald, in Ottawa, while illness prevented the Lieutenant Governor of Quebec, Sir Narcisse Belleau, and the Mayor of Montreal, Charles J. Coursol, from attending. Many tributes were paid to the departing viceroy recognizing the success of his work in Canada and the fairness with which he had carried out his task. In the course of the many speeches and toasts, Lord Lisgar stated confidently: "I will not further trespass on your indulgence than to reiterate my thanks and say that in leaving Canada I leave no serious difficulties for my successor; there are no clouds in the Canadian political sky, no harassing questions to engross his attention on his arrival" (*Canadian*, vol. 6, July 6, 1872, p. 3).

Whatever he thought of the absence of the Lieutenant
Governor of Quebec and the Mayor of Montreal, he probably didn't notice until he received the report of the banquet
in the *Courrier d'Outaouais* that the feast of St. Jean Baptiste
was four days hence; on the same page of the paper was an
advertisement for a "Soirée Musicale et Dramatique" at the
home of l'Institut Canadien Français in Ottawa (*Courrier
d'Outaouais*, June 22, 1872, p. 2). One of the performances
on the program was a "pantomime comique" entitled "Les
Tribulations d'un Anglais". If Lisgar saw no clouds in the
Canadian political sky, it was because they were too close for
him to see. And if he failed in one thing during his tenure in
Canada, it was to make French Canadians feel truly at home
in the Dominion.

Nevertheless he is still respected for his abilities as a constitutional Governor General, and in the *Dictionary of
National Biography* was praised for "leaving behind him in
Canada a reputation for ability and sound judgment" (Carlyle 1297). Indeed Sir John A. Macdonald "considered him
the ablest governor general he had known" (Miller 1217). He
returned to his estates in Ireland where he died four years later
on October 6, 1876. Lady Lisgar later married Sir Francis
Charles Fortescue Turville of Bosworth Hall, Leicestershire,
who had once been the Governor General her husband's secretary. She died in 1895.

*   *   *

Both Monck and Lisgar had performed the political tasks
assigned to them in Canada with diligence and responsibility.
Lisgar even went beyond this in responding to the social
expectations of the inhabitants of the new Dominion. But if
Canadians looked to their first two Governors General for
leadership in culture and the arts, they were disappointed.
Fortunately this situation would soon change with the arrival
of Lord and Lady Dufferin in June 1872.

Works Cited

Batt, Elizabeth. *Monck: Governor General, 1861-1868*. Toronto: McClelland & Stewart, 1976.

Le Canada (Ottawa).

Canadian Illustrated News (Montreal).

Carlyle, Edward Irving. "Sir John Young," *Dictionary of National Biography*, vol. xxi. Eds. Sir Leslie Stephen and Sir Sidney Lee. Oxford: Oxford University Press, 1949-50: 1296-7.

Chronicle & Quebec Gazette (Quebec).

Courrier d'Outaouais (Hull).

Courrier du Québec (Quebec).

The Daily Witness (Montreal).

Gaizauskas, Barbara. *Feed the Flame: A Natural History of the Ottawa Literary and Scientific Society*. M.A. Thesis. Carleton University, Ottawa, 1990.

The Globe (Toronto).

Le Journal de Québec (Quebec).

The Leader (Toronto).

Miller, Carman. "Lisgar, Sir John Young, Baron," *The Canadian Encyclopedia*, 2nd ed. Ed. James H. Marsh. Edmonton: Hurtig, 1988: 1217.

La Minerve (Montreal).

Monck, F.E.O. *My Canadian Leaves*. Dorchester: Dorchester County Express Office, 1873. Facsimile edition published by University of Toronto Press for Canadian Library Service, Toronto, 1963.

Montreal Gazette.

Morton, W.L., ed. *Monck Letters and Journals*. Toronto: McClelland & Stewart, 1970. Carleton Library no. 52.

NAC (National Archives of Canada, E.A. Meredith, Journals 1844-1899, June 10, 1869. MG29, E15, vol. 7. Reel M-188.)

Ottawa Times.

Quebec Mercury.

Randal, Florence Hamilton. "Rideau Hall – Past and Present," *The Canadian Magazine* 12, 2 (1898-1899).

Lord Dufferin.
Photo by Guy Piron, Paris (NAC C-051650)

Chapter 2

Drama in the Days of Dufferin, 1872-1878

It was indeed a remarkable couple who presided over the political, social and cultural life of Ottawa from June 1872 until October 1878. Their background made the Dufferins particularly qualified to encourage and participate in the theatrical life of the new Dominion. They were the first couple to serve a full term at Rideau Hall; Lord Monck, the first Governor General, served only one year in that position after Confederation, and Lord Lisgar three years. Dufferin was eminently qualified to be Governor General. Indeed, D.M.L. Farr, writing in 1958, said: "Of the eighteen men who have filled the office of Governor-General of Canada since Confederation, the most accomplished was probably Frederick Hamilton Temple Blackwood, Earl of Dufferin" (Farr 153). His background included not only a classical education at Eton and Oxford, which gave him an enduring interest in drama and in culture generally, but some distinguished ancestors whose lives and occupations made it natural for him to maintain an interest in the theatre. Frederick Blackwood was, on his mother's side, the great-grandson of the Anglo-Irish playwright Richard Brinsley Sheridan, and he was extremely proud of that.

In fact, he seemed as fascinated by the drama in the life of Sheridan as by the plays themselves. A speech given by him at Bath on September 5, 1898, twenty years after his departure from Canada, was summarized by one of his biographers thus:

> It was there that Sheridan passed from boyhood into manhood, formed his early friendship with Grenville and Halhed, and tried his wings as an author; it was from the varied and brilliant society in Bath that he drew the characters of his two immortal comedies; above all things it was there

Lady Dufferin.
Photo by W.J. Topley (NAC PA-026533)

that he met that divinely beautiful and angelic creature who became his wife under such romantic circumstances. It was to that neighbourhood that destiny recalled him to tend and comfort her upon her tragic death-bed. ... A hundred years had passed since that event, but he was sure they had not forgotten that, though the great grandson of Sheridan he also claimed as his progenitrix that sweet songstress who ravished the ears of their forefathers with notes, which she still seems to prolong in the guise of St. Cecilia on the canvas of Sir Joshua Reynolds. (Black 357-8)

But Sheridan and Elizabeth Linley were not his only distinguished ancestors nor the only ones whose lives contained high drama. An earlier ancestor, Thomas Sheridan,

Papist and Jacobite, was accused of complicity with the Popish plots but whatever may have been the truth of this charge he gained his acquittal by proving that he had eleven times taken the oath of Conformity. His son, the next Thomas, Swift's friend and versifying correspondent, lost his benefice in the Church because, being one of the Irish Viceroy's chaplains, he selected for his sermon on Queen Anne's birthday the text, "Sufficient for the day is the evil thereof." (Lyall 8)

His son, also named Thomas Sheridan, was the friend of Samuel Johnson and the father of R.B. Sheridan. Sheridan's son Thomas seems more noteworthy for the three lovely daughters he engendered than for any public achievements; these highly acclaimed ladies were the Duchess of Somerset, Lady Caroline Norton, and Helen Selina Sheridan, Countess of Gifford, the mother of Lord Dufferin.

Helen Selina married Price Blackwood, fourth Baron Clandeboye, and bore the future Governor General of Canada, their only child, in Florence on June 21, 1826, when she was nineteen years of age. They were living in Italy to avoid his family's disapproval of their marriage. She became the most important influence in her son's life, especially after his father died when he was fifteen. She also introduced him to many of the leading literary figures in England of the time. In a memoir which introduced her *Songs, Poems and Verses* (including a play by her entitled *Finesse*) Dufferin said: "... through their intimacy with my mother, I became acquainted with all the remarkable literary men of the day, including Dickens, Thackeray, Stirling-Maxwell of Keir, Carlyle, the late Mr. Venables, Charles Butler, Macaulay, Kingsley, Proctor, and others" (Helen 77).

A biography of Dufferin written by his nephew Harold Nicolson is entitled *Helen's Tower* after the name of a monument he built to his mother on their estate in Clandeboye, Northern Ireland. The memoir contains some glowing tributes to her, which are described thus by another of his biographers: "In his filial solicitude to do justice to the memory of his beloved mother, Lord Dufferin seems to have fairly exhausted the language of affection" (Black 4). Here are two examples of the language to which Black was referring:

> ... the chief and dominant characteristic of her nature was her power of loving. Generally speaking, persons who love intensely are seen to concentrate their love upon a single object; while, in my mother's case, love seemed an inexhaustible force. Her love for her horse, for her dog, for her birds, was a passion, and the affection she lavished on her own mother, on me, on her brothers, sisters, relations, and friends was as persistent, all-embracing, perennial, and indestructible as the light of the sun. However little, as I am obliged to confess to my shame, I may have profited by these holy and blessed influences, no one, I am sure, has ever passed from boyhood to manhood under more favourable and ennobling conditions. (Helen 76)

Writing of her death in 1867 he went even further:

> Thus there went out of the world one of the sweetest, most beautiful, most accomplished, wittiest, most loving, and lovable human beings that ever walked the earth. There was no quality wanting to her perfection; and I say this, not prompted by the partiality of a son, but as one well

acquainted with the world, and with both men and women. There have been many ladies who have been beautiful, charming, witty, and good, but I doubt whether there have been any who have combined with so high a spirit, and with so natural a gaiety and bright an imagination as my mother's, such strong unerring good sense, tact, and womanly discretion. (Helen 102)

These statements might make one speculate about the nature of the relationship between mother and son. More grist for the speculative mill is provided by the fact that she agreed to a second marriage—to the Earl of Gifford, who was closer to her son than to her in age—only after she was assured by doctors that the illness from which he was dying was incurable. The wedding took place on October 13, 1862. Lord Gifford died two months later.

Lord Dufferin's marriage to Hariot Rowan Hamilton, a distant cousin, took place ten days after his mother's second marriage, on October 23, 1862 at his bride's home of Killyleagh Castle, County Down, some twelve miles from Clandeboye. She was nineteen and he thirty-six. The marriage by all accounts was a happy one, and produced seven children, four boys and three girls, two of whom were born in Canada. Harold Nicolson made an intriguing comment on their marriage when he said: "I was conscious ... of some quality in their relationship which was deep and strange ...," but then added: "Nor do I wish again to witness such agony of human despair as assailed her when he died" (Nicolson 143-4). Dufferin's admiration for his wife was attested to in an incident he recounted to his eldest son: "The King of Greece told his sister—who repeated it to me—that there was no lady in Europe could enter a room like Lady Dufferin" (Nicolson 145).

Before coming to Canada Dufferin held various diplomatic positions including Lord-in-Waiting to Queen Victoria, British representative in the negotiations at Constantinople over the massacre of Christians in Syria, undersecretary for India and then for War, and Chancellor of the Duchy of

Lancaster. On his departure from Canada he was named ambassador to Russia and then Turkey, Viceroy of India, and ambassador to Italy and later to France. In 1896 he retired to his estates in Ulster, but his last years were troubled by the fall of an investment company he had sponsored and by the death of his eldest son and heir in 1900 in the Boer War. After Lord Dufferin's death in 1902 his wife outlived him by thirty-four years.

Throughout his life Dufferin showed an enduring interest in drama and the theatre. We read of his going to the theatre in London, Dublin, Rome, Paris and Edinburgh. He was an avid reader of plays, which gave him support at crucial moments in his life. During the difficult negotiations in Syria in 1860, where he acted as a kind of nineteenth-century Philip Habib, he wrote a letter to the Duchess of Argyll in which he stated:

> My sole consolation here is reading Shakespeare: every morning while my hair (my black hair) is being brushed, I read a couple of scenes in some pleasant comedy, filling the room with a vision of sunshine, roses, and quaint old-world merriment. It does take one so out of the present. (Lyall 117)

After speaking of a play and an exhibition Dufferin attended in Paris in 1889, his official biographer added, " … art and the drama (were) everywhere and always irresistibly attractive to him" (Lyall 482). In a letter he wrote from Rome in 1890 Dufferin stated: "I intend going through all my Classics, both Greek and Latin, as fast as I can. How delightful it is to have such resources and to be able to take pleasure in them" (Lyall 404). In his journal for December 30, 1895, while he was still ambassador to France he gave "a long list of the Greek classics that he has read wholly or partly during the year—the Greek tragedians, eleven plays of Aristophanes, portions of Thucydides, Plato, Plutarch, Lucan, and others" (Lyall 541). Besides, we are told, "His knowledge of Egyptology was above that of the ordinary amateur—and his study of the Persian language ... became a solace and an exercise of his later years" (Nicolson 246). One of his acquaintances, H.M. Butler, then Master of Trinity College, Cambridge recalled that in 1892, "at the grand Tercentenary Festival of Trinity College, Dublin, I saw him eagerly watching from a box in the theatre close to the stage the excellent acting of *The Rivals*, the masterpiece, as some might hold, of his renowned ancestor" (Black 389). Shortly before his death, Lady Dufferin recorded in her journal that he was desperately ill when he gave the Rectorial address at the Edinburgh Convocation on November 14, 1901, after which he attended a concert and then the theatre (Nicolson 278). Three days later he returned to Clandeboye, where he died on February 12, 1902.

While Dufferin wrote no plays himself, there was a high dramatic quality to many of the speeches he delivered. They reflect both his classical studies and the florid style of the Victorian period. Two examples will illustrate this, one just prior to his departure for Canada, the other just before his departure from it. In a speech at a banquet given in his honour in Belfast on June 11, 1872 he said:

> In fact, ladies and gentlemen, it may be doubted whether the inhabitants of the Dominion (of Canada) themselves are as yet fully awake to the magnificent destiny in store for them—or have altogether realized the promise of their young and virile nationality. Like a virgin goddess in a primaeval world, Canada still walks in unconscious beauty among her golden woods and by the margin of her trackless streams, catching but broken glances of her radiant majesty, as mirrored on their surface, and scarcely recks as yet of the glories awaiting her in the Olympus of nations. (Leggo 31)

These words were greeted by loud and long cheering. His farewell speech to both Houses of the Canadian Parliament, delivered in the Senate Chamber on April 16, 1878 was no less magniloquent. It read in part:

I found you a loyal people, and I leave you the truest-hearted subjects in Her Majesty's Dominions. I found you proud of your descent and anxious to maintain your connection with the Mother Country; I leave you more convinced than ever of the solicitude of Great Britain to reciprocate your affection of her dependence on your fidelity in every emergency. I found you—men of various nationalities—of English, French, Irish, Scotch, and German descent, working out the problems of Constitutional Government with admirable success; I leave you with even a deeper conviction in your minds that the due application of the principles of Parliamentary Government is capable of resolving every political difficulty, and of controlling the gravest ministerial crises, to the satisfaction of the people at large, and of their leaders and representatives of every shade of opinion.

... I shall be able to assure her (Majesty) that not a leaf has fallen from her maple chaplet, that the lustre of no jewel in her transatlantic diadem has been dimmed. (Earl of Dufferin 257)

In the same speech he paid tribute to Lady Dufferin and the popularity and influence she shared with him while they were in Canada. His words, along with many of her own in *My Canadian Journal* and those of other writers on the administration of Lord Dufferin, attested to a less aloof and cold woman than the one Marian Fowler described in *The Embroidered Tent* (Fowler 218). Whatever aloofness she did show may have been due to her shyness as much as anything else. If she had difficulty in adapting to the Canadian wilderness and lifestyle in her travels around the country, she was very much at home and made many others in Ottawa at home for the private theatricals that were presented at Rideau Hall, in many of which she took a leading role. Her nephew Harold Nicolson told us how satisfying and liberating was this activity for her. He wrote:

I can recall ... even from the time of my boyhood, certain surprising moments when she would discard her stateliness and appear wholly different. Such moments were always connected with some form of travesty, whether charades, dumb-crambo, practical jokes even, or merely dressing up. It was as if the more human sides of her nature could only escape from their covering of shyness by adopting an impersonal alibi. On such occasions she would lose all rigidity, abandon her deportment and become frivolous and enchanting to the very movements of her eyes and hands. Even so does a stammerer forget to stutter when he sings. (Nicolson 160)

Nicolson then went on to describe an episode in which she prepared him as a young boy for a stage presentation:

At my dress rehearsal I repeated the poem sulkily and with the utmost economy of gesture. My aunt, with ardent eyes, watched my performance. She then rose and said, "Try to do it something like this." Whereat she ceased to be my aunt and became two separate people (one of them clearly nymph and the other clearly swain) whose antics I watched with fascinated embarrassment. "There," she said gaily, giving me a rare pat of affectionate regard: "when you get on the platform, all you have to do is to copy exactly what I did." (Nicolson 161-2)

The affection which Lady Dufferin came to win from Canadians was shown at her departure from Ottawa and also from Quebec, whence she left for England on August 31, 1878, some two months before her husband. Of their last day in Ottawa, June 7, William Leggo wrote:

The parting was a painful one. Their Excellencies had so wound themselves around the hearts of the people of Ottawa that the scene did not bear the impress of officials moving to another sphere of action, it was more like that of dear and warm personal friends parting forever. Her Excellency was deeply agitated, and tears were seen in the eyes of many, who could not have betrayed more emotion had they been saying "farewell" to those connected with them by the closest ties of affectionate relationship. (Leggo 743)

A local journal in Quebec wrote of her last farewell:

> As we stood upon the steamer and looked upwards towards the city we saw crowds of people clustered here and there upon the rocks above us. Durham Terrace was black with them. High up at the Citadel flags floated, and good-by signals were being made from her late home, which the Countess responded to with many a tear and friendly wave of her handkerchief.
>
> The departure of Lady Dufferin is a source of unfeigned regret to the people of Canada ... Many were the sorrowful prayers that went up yesterday, both publicly and privately, that God would watch over and bless her, give her of the fruit of her hands, not only in the warm love and gratitude of the people of Canada, but wherever, in the Providence of God, she might be led. (Leggo 757-8)

* * *

In Canada the Dufferins showed the social side of their natures in their public and private entertainments, so much so that the Duke of Argyll wrote Lord Dufferin to protest: "I hear terrible things about your expenditure. People say that you will be entirely ruinated. Do not be too Irish or too Sheridanish; it is an awful combination" (Nicolson 155). But combine them they did and in no way more successfully than in the private theatricals presented at Rideau Hall. These theatricals fell into two distinct parts, the plays for general audiences that were presented regularly in the late winter and spring, and the children's plays which were performed on New Year's day and sometimes repeated in January. The best source for all of these is Lady Dufferin's *My Canadian Journal*, a book comprised of letters written regularly to her mother, and published first in 1891; a new edition, annotated by Gladys Chandler Walker, was published in 1969. We are also fortunate to have a complete record of the adult plays in the form of a souvenir program entitled "Plays at Government House 1872 to 1878" (NAC 1). This record shows the Dufferins lost no time in launching the theatricals for which they became celebrated.

The first item on the program was for December 23, 1872, two months after their arrival in Canada. It was called a "Concert Costume" and consisted mainly of solos and duos from the operas of Mozart, Donizetti, Rossini, and Boieldieu sung by members of the Ottawa community who would figure prominently in the theatricals. The last selection of the evening was the only Canadian work on the program; it was entitled "Canadian Boat Songs" sung "By all the Amateurs." The theatricals proper began the following March 1873 and continued each year until the April before the Dufferins' departure from the capital. The plays were usually presented in Lent when the Governor General did not give fancy balls. A season consisted of from two to four plays, with sometimes two plays presented on the same program, each program being repeated with usually a week or two between performances of the same play. The plays were mostly chosen from the popular mid-Victorian genres of domestic comedy and farce, by such authors as Tom Taylor, Tom Robertson, W.S. Gilbert, J.M. Maddox, R. Theyre Smith, J.R. Planché, and Palgrave Simpson. An evening's entertainment would usually consist of a comedy followed by a farce. Sometimes the play or plays would precede an elaborate dinner for all the guests. That is what happened after the first play, *To Oblige Benson* by Tom Taylor. Lady Dufferin described it in her journal:

> We had a great party to-night, and opened our new room ... they found 300 chairs arranged in rows, in front of a very pretty little stage ... The entertainment began with music, and was followed by "To Oblige Benson," which went off admirably. People were particularly delighted with Fred's performance—he did the part of Trotter Southdown; and Mrs. Southdown was excellent, too. (Dufferin 57)

Six days later a farce, *The First Night* by J.M. Maddox, was presented and Lady Dufferin was no less pleased with the results:

> People were quite surprised and delighted with *The First Night*. The old actor was splendidly done by M. Kimber, and the singing introduced before and during the piece was excellent. (Dufferin 58)

In every subsequent year, except for 1875 when Lady Dufferin had her last child, Frederick, on February 26 (two days after the performance of the first two plays of that year), she took part in every program, and sometimes in two plays on the same program. This intimate involvement with the plays, along with her enduring interest in the theatre, is what makes her journal such a valuable source of information and insight into the theatricals at Rideau Hall and the human situations surrounding them.

The following year the entertainment consisted of selections from Rossini's opera *Semiramide* and the play *One Hour*. A week before the performance Lady Dufferin gave the first of several accounts of play rehearsals in her journal: "We were very busy at home preparing everything for a full-dress rehearsal of a selection from the opera *Semiramide*, and the little play *One Hour*, in which I myself take part. The rehearsal was successful, the servants making up the audience" (Dufferin 107). She also took part in the next program of two plays a week after *One Hour* closed, this time in the title role of *The Dowager*. Her comment after this performance was:

> In the evening our play came off, and was a great success. People seemed to listen with eyes and ears, and to be delighted ...
> When I had shaken hands with the "six hundred," and we were alone again, we had our supper, of which we were all very glad, for acting makes one so hungry. (Dufferin 109)

Performance of the operetta **The Maire of St. Brieux** *at Rideau Hall, March 1875.*
(NAC C-062664)

1875 was the year of *The Maire of St. Brieux*, an operetta in one act written for the Dufferins' Private Theatricals by Frederick A. Dixon with music by Frederick W. Mills. The action takes place in the Breton village of St. Brieux about 1800, and involves a plot to depose the consul Napoleon and replace him by the rightful heir to the French throne. The plot is foiled by the Maire but because he has unwittingly implicated himself by letting one of the spies with whom he is in love use his mail to send messages to Paris, the guilty parties are not punished. In less than inspired verse the Maire addresses the audience in his final speech:

> What an escape I have had to be sure!
> Once I get clear, I'll not try any more,
> If I had married a woman like that,
> She would have led me the life of a cat,
> Moral: a widow is best left alone,
> She'll have her own way and you will have none.
> So should a widow seem charming to you,
> Think of the fate of the Maire of St. Brieux.

This is followed by the Chorus chanting:

> Garlands we bring and roses we strew.
> Hail to his Honour the Maire of St. Brieux.
> The Maire of St. Brieux, the Maire of St. Brieux.
> Hail to his Honour the Maire of St. Brieux. (Dixon 33)

Then the curtain falls.

The cast included seven soloists and a chorus of fifteen. Lady Dufferin was pleased with the production and added some interesting personal and social commentary on the one performance she saw:

> My baby boy ... is now five weeks old, so I was able to be present at the second representation of the "Maire of St. Brieux," of which the first performance had been extremely successful ... The music is very pretty and the whole play excellent. It is very interesting to bring out a new thing on

one's own stage, and even the author and composer must have been satisfied with the actors and singers who played in it. The prima donna, Mrs. Anglin, both sang and looked charmingly, and the Maire himself, Mr. Kimber, was quite perfect. (Dufferin 166)

The operetta also had a successful performance at the new Opera House in Ottawa on Saturday, March 25 the following year (*Ottawa Free Press*, March 27, 1876, p. 1), which was attended by the Dufferins. On that program it was preceded by Brough's farce *No. 1 Round the Corner*, in which Dixon played a leading role.

The two plays produced together on two separate evenings in 1876 were *School* by Tom Robertson and *A Happy Pair* by R. Theyre Smith. It must have been a hectic time for Lady Dufferin since she acted in both plays. We get some idea of this from her comments on the rehearsals as early as January 29, even though the first performance was not given until March 29. We also get an idea of the woman's energy and social nature when she writes on that Saturday in January: "The thaw was so decided this morning that we gave up all idea of outdoor amusements. At two we rehearsed 'School,' which is to be our next play. As soon as the people had collected afterwards we danced, and I made the elderly people join" (Dufferin 175). On February 8 there seems to have been a difficult early rehearsal for she says: "The Marquis and Marquise de Bassano arrived this afternoon, just as we were finishing a laborious rehearsal of part of 'School'" (Dufferin 176). Things were going better three days later for she writes: "... in the afternoon we rehearsed the first two acts of 'School'—very successfully. Mr. Kimber and Miss Fellowes remained for dinner, and in the evening the other twenty-eight singers arrived, and we rehearsed the singing quadrilles, lancers, and waltz" (Dufferin 176).

The quadrilles were in preparation for the most extravagant entertainment of the Dufferins at Rideau Hall, a Grand Fancy Ball on February 23 for which 1500 invitations were issued and, one commentator tells us, nearly all of them accepted (Stewart 432). Another tells us: "The skill of Paris, London, New York and Boston were invoked for the occasion, and the result was an entertainment which far surpassed anything of the kind ever yet seen in British North America" (Leggo 426-7). Lady Dufferin's description of the performance itself is dated March 1, although the program gives the first date of performance as March 29. Possibly on March 1 a dress rehearsal was given for special guests since she tells us on that day:

> The Comte de Turenne arrived for the play. The actors dined early, in D.'s room. Then I went to dress for Mrs. Honeyton, in the "Happy Pair". Then the "School" arrived, and began to dress in one room, and the men had another (sic), and the guests came crowding in, and got off their things in the school-room, and there was painting and curling and excitement going on everywhere.

It was another busy day at Rideau Hall. Then she speaks of her brother Fred, who was an aide-de-camp of Dufferin as well as an actor:

> Fred and I began the performance with "A Happy Pair," and had a very warm audience, which was pleasant. "School" is a difficult piece for amateurs; but I must say it was an unequivocal success. Every part was well done. It was quite new here, so the audience liked it immensely. (Dufferin 179)

The following year was a busy one for the theatre activities of Lady Dufferin, who performed in all three plays that were presented in February and March. Her comments also show some of the problems with gaslights on the stage at Rideau Hall. On February 15 she writes:

> We had an evening rehearsal of some plays we are getting up, and all the actors came to dine first. Of course there were several things to be improved: the gas did not go out

Masquerade Ball given by Lord Dufferin, February 23, 1876.
(NAC C-006865)

when it should, etc.: but by working hard we got it all right. (Dufferin 236)

On February 16 they had a successful dress rehearsal of *Our Wife* and of *The Loan of a Lover*, and then on February 17 they were rehearsing their March production, *A Scrap of Paper* by Palgrave Simpson, even though the other two plays had not yet opened for their public (Dufferin 236). When they did open, the problem with the gas was the reverse of the one reported at the rehearsal—it didn't go on this time. Lady Dufferin lamented:

> Great misfortunes happened today ... at seven we had no gas at all! ... all the passages and dressing-rooms in a miserable light; for by eight o'clock only a glimmer of gas had appeared. The stage was lighted up with candles, which dripped over us, and had to be replaced between each scene. It was so depressing.
>
> People declared they were delighted; and certainly they did not mind the want of gas half as much as I did. At the end I felt much more tired than usual, owing to the worry. (Dufferin 236)

One is inclined to be sceptical about the delight of the Rideau Hall audiences especially when they knew they would be entertained by their hosts with dining or dancing after performances. This feeling is reinforced by the effusive praise of a contemporary like George Stewart, whose book on the Dufferins came out the year their tenure in Canada ended. At times he is even careless with his facts. Speaking of these plays, he wrote:

> In March several theatrical entertainments were given [actually two of the three were given in February] where Her Excellency, who adds histrionic talents of a high order to her many other accomplishments, sustained the leading roles with fine effect. Her Gertrude in the bright little farce *The Loan of a Lover* [the program listed her playing the role of Ernestine] and Suzanne de Rousseville in Palgrave

*Lady Dufferin playing a leading role in W.S. Gilbert's **Sweethearts** at Rideau Hall (April, 1878) "with all the skill and delicacy and spirit which characterize her efforts in this way"*

(NAC PA-148607)

Simpson's comic drama *A Scrap of Paper*, were inimitable in their way, and Her Excellency achieved a genuine artistic triumph by her performance of these clever parts. (Stewart 516)

In spite of his effusiveness, Stewart does reinforce the general admiration of the acting ability of Lady Dufferin.

The last two plays at Rideau Hall under the auspices of the Dufferins were presented on April 2 and 5, 1878. They were *New Men and Old Acres* by Tom Taylor, whose *To Oblige Benson* was the first play they had sponsored, and W.S. Gilbert's *Sweethearts*. In both Lady Dufferin played a leading role, "with all the skill and delicacy and spirit which characterize her efforts in this way" (Stewart 597). However, she failed to impress Senator John B. Glasier, "who went away from our theatricals 'because he did not come all the way down here to see a lot of love-making'" (Dufferin 290). Glasier, sixty-nine years old at the time, was a lumber merchant from New Brunswick who served in the Parliament there and was made a Senator in 1868 (Dufferin 290). His departure is ironic in view of the fact that Lady Dufferin herself had walked out of a play in New York some four years earlier when it took an unsavoury turn.

Perhaps the most memorable speech of these last two evenings was an epilogue which Lord Dufferin composed and his wife delivered after each performance. "The worst of it was," she wrote, "that it made the audience so melancholy that the evening ended tearfully" (Dufferin 287). Stewart confirmed this when he said: "during the recital of (it) she was visibly affected, and many in the audience could scarcely refrain from shedding tears" (Stewart 597). The epilogue reviewed in a sprightly way all the adult theatricals which had been presented by the Dufferins, and was a clever summary of the titles of many of the plays:

But soon emboldened by our Public's smile,
Our Muse attempts a more ambitious style,
"The Dowager" parades her stately grace,—

"Our Wife" declares two husbands out of place,—
To "School" we send you, and—a sight too rare—
Show you for once, a really "Happy Pair,"
Then having warned your daughters not "to Lend"
Their only "lover" to a Lady friend,—
We next the fatal "Scrap of Paper" burn,
And follow with "one Hour,"—"Jacques"—in turn,
"Semiramis,"—a Debutante's "First Night,"—
Winging at each essay a loftier flight,
Until at last a bumper house we drew
With the melodious "Maire of St. Brieux!"

After paying tribute to the audience and the actor, she bid adieu to her faithful Canadian friends:

And now one last farewell,—a few months more
(To the audience) And we depart your loved Canadian shore,
Never again to hear your plaudits rise,
Nor watch the ready laughter in your eyes
Gleam out responsive to our author's wit,
However poorly we interpret it,
Nor see with artist pride your tears o'erflow,
In homage to our simulated woe …
For know—whatever way our fortunes turn—
Upon the altars of our hearts shall burn
Those votive fires no fuel need renew,
Our prayers for blessings on your land and you. (NAC 2)

* * *

The children's plays at Rideau Hall took various forms and developed later than the adult plays as an annual event. There is no record of any children's plays the first New Year the Dufferins were in Canada. The following New Year, 1874, there is a record of "a little play" being produced but no title or author is mentioned. Stewart says:

A parlour dramatic entertainment was given at Government House on New Year's Day, when the children of Lady

Dufferin and Lady Fletcher sustained the principal parts.
The eldest actor was but ten years of age, while the
youngest actress, Lady Victoria Blackwood, was only eight
months old. Lady Dufferin acted as general manager and
prompter, and the play was quite cleverly performed.
(Stewart 280)

Lady Dufferin went into some detail in her description of the
plot and in her enthusiasm for these important moments in
the lives of the child actors:

I have been busy the last few weeks teaching the children
to act a little play, to be performed before an audience this
New Year's Day ...

Every member of our two families (ours and Colonel
Fletcher's) between the ages of twelve years and eight
months appears either in the play or in the tableaux which
come after it, and I only wish you were here to see how well
they do it, and how pretty they look!

In the piece they represent imps who, clad in the gayest
attire, are invisible to mortal eye the moment they put on
certain bright-coloured caps, and visible again directly they
take them off. The fun of the play consists in the way in
which they are supposed to appear and disappear, plaguing
the life out of a gigantic mortal, who either cannot see his
tormentors at all, or whose frantic attempts to catch them
when he does, only lead him into the traps they have prepared for him.

My little troop entered fully into the spirit of the plot,
and were so delighted with Fred's acting in the part of
"Grumps", the troubled mortal, that they were really holding their sides with laughter, and there certainly was more
nature than art in their representation of the mischievous
imps. (Dufferin 99-100)

The play was performed at Rideau Hall on two other occasions—on Saturday, January 10 after a party and dance, and
on Tuesday, January 27 when the children performed "to
about fifty of their contemporaries" (Dufferin 101-2).

On the same program in 1874 was a number of tableaux vivants, which were a feature of the Dufferins' years at Rideau Hall. These were silent representations of fictional or historic events in which all the children could take part. Lady Dufferin described them with a mother's perception and indulgence:

> The tableaux were equally successful, and though an eye was occasionally opened during the "Sleeping Beauty in the Wood" scene, and then conscientiously shut up again with unnecessary firmness—though one infant preferred to sleep with his legs in the air, and another made an uncalled-for announcement in the middle of a tableau vivant—the whole performance was most charming and successful, and actors, parents and audience were all equally delighted. (Dufferin 99)

On January 29 the ballroom was used for a concert and more tableaux in aid of "our little church." We are given more details about the subjects of these presentations when Lady Dufferin writes:

> Three very pretty tabeau (sic) closed the entertainment:— The Death of Cleopatra; the Expulsion of Hagar; and a group of flower-girls, Nelly being one of them. Cleopatra was very handsome, and beautifully dressed. I think they will have cleared fifty pounds. (Dufferin 102)

Once again that year on March 28 Lady Dufferin mentions tableaux being presented in the dining-room along with a band and some singing, but makes no comment on them (Dufferin 107). We hear of them again the following New Year when she describes the care that went into their presentation:

> The tableaux were very pretty. I had to be behind the scenes, and so only managed to see one myself, which I will describe to you.
>
> The foreground of the stage was painted in dark colours to represent a cavern, and the back opened, displaying a

brilliant grotto in gold and silver and red. Hermie stood on a raised rock of gold at the top; beneath her sat three little ones, with baby in the centre, who was enchanted with her position. Terence lay at their feet in his red moon-costume, and grouped beneath were Archie, Nelly, Maud, Edward, etc. They were lighted up with various coloured fires. Baby amused us so by giving three cheers in the middle of the performance. The other tableaux were scenes in a tournament: the Encounter, the Result, and the Coronation of the Victor. (Dufferin 164-5)

The only other contemporary comment on them is by Leggo, who says, "The tableaux will not speedily be forgotten," and then goes on to list the adults and children who took part in them (Leggo 379).

The interest of Lord Dufferin in presenting these tableaux at Rideau Hall is intriguing in the light of a letter sent him by his mother on the subject when he was at Oxford some thirty years earlier. She wrote:

> Your Tableaux Vivants sound to me much like bad pantomimes; nothing is so pretty or pleasing as a breathing representation of some great chef d'oeuvre which we all know and recognize, for the memory and imagination are both affected by it. But silly people putting themselves in affected attitudes to represent imaginary persons, has always appeared to me a waste of time, energy, and candlelight. (Lyall 48)

Perhaps he was not swayed so much by his mother as some of his effusive writings would suggest.

One other children's performance at Rideau Hall in 1875 was a pageant given by the Dufferin children on their parents' return from a visit to England. The text is two pages long and consists of a detailed description of the entry of the participants and then the speeches by three of the principals entitled "Canada's Welcome", "Autumn's Welcome", and "Winter's Welcome". The finale is described thus:

Thereupon did the Pages present their severalle offerings, and so, to the musick of an exceeding noble marche, did the Pageante return whence it came, and being again sette about the Pedestal, it was there illumined most pleasingly by divers marvellous bright lights; whereat the Hangings did descende to the musick of
GOD SAVE THE QUEEN.
And so the Pageante was ended. (NAC 2)

No author of the pageant is given. Perhaps it was the children themselves or their tutor, F.A. Dixon; the children had clearly inherited the Sheridan enthusiasm for theatre.

The most elaborate of the children's plays were those of the same Frederick Augustus Dixon (1843-1919), which were presented on New Year's Day each year from 1875 to 1878. Dixon, who was born in London the same year as Lady Dufferin, came to Canada in the early 1870s, and for a short time was a writer for the Toronto *Mail*. Later he was appointed tutor to the Dufferin children and established a close and enduring relationship with the family. The children affectionately called him "Dicky-bird" in letters they wrote to him. Leggo praised him in these glowing words:

> How can the brilliant F.A. Dixon be sufficiently thanked for the original plays which formed so marked a feature in the recreations of Rideau Hall? In rendering the beautiful librettos and operettos (sic) composed by this accomplished gentlemen (sic) hundreds of the readers of these lines will recall with pleasure the excellent performances of Mr. E. Kimber, the Usher of the Black Rod, (etc.). (Leggo 380)

Dixon was also one of twenty-five distinguished persons in the procession of the famous Grand Fancy Ball of 1875, "which entered the ball room and passed through to the foot of the throne" (Leggo 426).

The first of his plays performed at Rideau Hall—if the unidentified play of 1874 is not by him—was *Pussy-Cat Mew-Mew*. It is the only one of the children's plays not published, but Lady Dufferin gives a good description of it in her journal:

> The play took place upon a small stage erected in the ante-room to the ball-room. Mr. Dixon wrote the piece and painted the scenes. "Pussy-cat, Mew-mew" was the name of the play, and it went off very well. Fred was excellent in the part he undertook, and was well made-up, with red stockings, red knickerbockers, a brown blouse, and red wig. Fred Ward was the Master-magician, in a dressing-gown covered with mysterious signs. Nelly looked very pretty in white tarlatan and gold, a crown on her head, and a wand in her hand. Archie was a prince in green and silver; Terence, the "Man in the Moon," in red. Hermie, a pink fairy; and all the others in the same style of costume in different colours. Terence's first appearance was through the full moon, and he did his part very well. All have much improved in acting since last year. (Dufferin 164)

The next three New Year's plays are all published: *Little Nobody*, *Maiden Mona the Mermaid*, and *Fifine the Fisher-Maid*. *Little Nobody*, like *Maiden Mona*, is subtitled "a fairy play for fairy people," and is the story of a character named Nobody, who becomes a somebody by saving a beautiful Princess from an Ogre and an Ogress. The cast included all but the youngest of the Dufferin children, who was not yet a year old. Written in rhyming couplets, the play abounds in puns and riddles, as in the following exchange:

> NOBODY: His *way's* to make himself at home at once.
> OGRESS: Her *waist's* at any rate no *waste* of time.
> NOBODY: These foreigners don't think that any crime
> (Dixon, *Little* 22).

The staging was elaborate, as we see in this description of both it and the audience:

> My children had invited all the workpeople and their children to come to teas and to see their play, "Little Nobody",

written by Mr. Dixon. He has taken great pains with the scenery, which is quite beyond that of a mere amateur state. There is a street and a castle, with a background of sea and sky, followed by a magnificent transformation scene, in which a silver-dressed fairy stands behind a star of many colours, the rays of which gradually part and open, leaving her supported on each side by minor fairies of the female sex, while two male fairies sit in cars underneath. This is the last scene of the play, and while this gorgeous sight is in the background the active performers in the piece are grouped in the front. We had an appreciative audience, filling the room. (Dufferin 173)

However, at a later performance on January 17, there were problems that showed the dangers of gaslight in theatres of the time. Lady Dufferin described the ensuing confusion:

"Little Nobody" began, and went most successfully till near the end. In the middle of the last beautiful fairy transformation scene there was a fire, which might have been very bad. The man attending to the limelight held a candle under an indiarubber pipe containing gas. The pipe melted, and the gas burnt furiously. There were people rushing about, water flowing, and a great scrimmage going on, during which the imperturbable queen of the fairies continued her speech. Darkness ensued; then we lifted the curtain and threw a roselight over the scene. But of course the grand effect was spoilt and the author and the carpenter burnt their hands a little. (Dufferin 174)

Very little is said of *Maiden Mona the Mermaid* either by Lady Dufferin or by other contemporaries. She refers briefly to it as "a little play" on January 1, and even misnames it "Fifine, the Fisher Maid" in speaking of the last performance, "which went off extremely well. They like the appreciativeness of a grown-up audience" (Dufferin 233). She does give an indication of the care she put into the staging when she writes: "There was a scene in the play in which all go down to the bottom of the sea. I managed this by having green tarlatan, upon which fishes were pasted, drawn up slowly in front of the children to a certain height above their heads, showing the depth of the water" (Dufferin 233). The plot concerns a mermaid who helps two princes, Noodle and Doodle, regain the kingdom from which they have been expelled by a bad uncle. In the program the play was called *Noodle and Doodle*, but the text published later that year gave it its proper title. The program has an interesting note about the youngest Dufferin child, Frederick—not yet two years old—who plays a Fairy, "who only appears if he feels so inclined" (NAC 3).

The verse is again in rhyming couplets, and is more natural and witty than the verse in *Little Nobody*, although Dixon still indulges his weakness for puns. In trying to identify his brother, Doodle asks:

> Did you like sugar on your bread and butter?
> Used you to play at marbles in the gutter?
> (Dixon, *Maiden* 36).

This is better than many lines in the previous play. In fact, an analysis of the three published children's plays would show a growing sophistication of the verse. Perhaps Dixon was adapting his style to the gradual maturity of his young actors. The last of the three, *Fifine, the Fisher-Maid; or, The Magic Shrimps*, has the cleverest verse of all. It is the story of Fifine, who makes her fortune by selling shrimps that have the magical power of sweetening sour temperaments. It also includes some satire on marriage, politics, and evolution. In greeting Queen Bessina as she arrives on the Enchanted Isle, Fernando, Fifine's helper, says:

> We've fourteen dukes, nine bishops and a Turk,
> All sent here by their loving wives and daughters
> To have their tempers cured by shrimps and waters.
> (Dixon, *Fifine* 29)

The play was another popular success, and ended with fourteen lines recited by Terence in this their last Christmas play:

The years have slipped away so very fast,
This fairy tale is, sad to say, our last.
Before another merry Christmas Day
The "company" will all have gone away;
An ocean will divide our little band
From all but memory of your kindly land;
And when we meet again in after years,
Some may be Generals and some Premiers;
Some Nobodies—for some you know must be.
There'll be no ogres, though, I clearly see.
One thing is certain; we shall all have grown,
And some, perhaps, have "fairies" of our own;
But still we'll not forget, though old and tall,
"The Children's Christmas Play" at Rideau Hall.
(Dufferin 281)

This farewell speech is reminiscent of the more elaborate one by Lady Dufferin at the final adult play in April that same year.

The attention which Lady Dufferin gave to this and other plays is confirmed by a letter she wrote to Dixon on October 25, 1877, while the play was being prepared. It reads in full:

Dear Mr. Dixon,

I return the play with many thanks. I like it very much indeed & think it will be very pretty.

Capt. Hamilton & I have on reading it, thought of the changes in the casting of the characters, which we think would be an improvement.

It is (I submit it with diffidence to the author's consideration) that Terence should do Sir Pops—Basil, Mercury—& Capt. Hamilton, Prince Emerald—the advantages are—1st that Terence would do the scene with Pops so much better than Basil, & it is one of the best scenes in the piece—Basil likes Mercury, & will do it very well—and if Fred is Prince Emerald, the old, & young actors will be more mixed together, which I am sure will give spirit to both their performances.

The Princess Zou-Zou is a little hurt at having so little to say! but I tell her I am sure more is coming for her—

Could she not be a *very* passionate child. I think Hermie would come out in any *very* marked part—as she is shy & requires an effort, to overcome her timidity, which she does not require for a quieter part. [Lady Dufferin could be speaking of herself here as well as of her daughter.]

I feel certain the piece will go better with these alterations, if you don't object—& Fred will read out the long poems so as to do them full justice.

Please let me have the *faintest* idea of the costumes.

I remain

Yr. truly

H. Dufferin. (NAC 2)

However, in the script we read that Captain Hamilton played Mercury, Terence, Prince Emerald, and Basil, Popinjay Pops (Dixon, "Cast of Characters," *Fifine*). So it appears that Dixon as director knew what he wanted and could resist even motherly and vice-regal pressure. Stewart confirmed the popularity of this and all the children's plays Dixon wrote for the Dufferins when he said, misnaming the play:

"Fifine, the Milk-Maid," [sic] was the delightful little fairy extravaganza, which ushered in the "season" at Rideau Hall, on New Year's Day, 1878, and like all of these entertainments, it proved a gratifying success. (Stewart 561)

A final note shows the appreciation of all the children for these delightful plays of Dixon. It is contained in a letter of December 21, 1893 to Dixon from the Dufferins' son Terence, who was then twenty-seven. Terence was working in the British Embassy in Paris where his father was ambassador. He wrote to acknowledge a wedding gift sent to him by Dixon after his recent marriage to an American, Flora Davis of New York, and made reference to the plays:

We are getting up some very mild theatricals for Christmas, for one of the Secretarys (sic) of this Embassy is very good at writing burlesque songs, though I do not think he comes up to you, and our whole attempt is much less ambitious than those Christmas theatricals which used to amuse us so much in Canada. (NAC 3)

The last performance on which Dixon worked for the Dufferins was a Punch and Judy show which he gave at a bazaar held at Rideau Hall on May 1, 2, and 3, 1878 to raise funds to help pay off the debt on the local church, St. Bartholemew's, which the Dufferins attended. Leggo quotes a short account of the show:

> The most amusing feature of the bazaar was Punch and Judy—Mr. Dixon, the young gentleman who did the manipulation, was kept very busy, for there was an incessant demand for tickets, and we know of some elderly gentlemen who visited the show more than once. 'Punch and Judy' are immortal, they will live as long as 'Jack the Giant Killer.' Mr. Brodie, the playman, was almost as amusing as the show itself. Dressed up in the proper costume of the character, with a huge drum suspended from his neck, he kept up a constant stream of visitors to the show room, and his intensely humorous face attracted the amused attention of the hundreds of people, old and young, who thronged Rideau Hall. (Leggo 731)

Lady Dufferin tells us, "An orange ticket, 25 cents, admits the juveniles, and many of the old people too, to the mysteries of 'Punch and Judy'" (Dufferin 291). Her concern for the show and for the practical business of the bazaar may be seen in a letter she wrote Dixon on April 4, a month before the bazaar. She said:

> I hope you won't think me very changeable, but for several reasons or rather difficulties—I think perhaps it will be wiser to confine our "shows" to that of "Punch & Judy" & not attempt other attractions. We shall all have our hands full, & it will be a pity for you to be shut up in a box all the time—when I am sure you can be making money for us in a way more amusing to yourself—. (NAC 2)

She went on to give a detailed list of the items already collected for the bazaar, and concluded by asking him to "Excuse the writing of one overwhelmed by bazaar business" (NAC 2). Leggo paid a glowing tribute to her efforts in this regard in words that would match Lord Dufferin's praise of his mother:

> Lady Dufferin, by this bazaar, added one more brilliant to the diadem of usefulness which she has, with so much goodness and so unselfishly, been framing since her arrival in Canada. It is, perhaps, a small star, but it will never cease to shine, and, when she is far off in Britain, we shall see its long line of light tipping the waves of the Atlantic, bidding us to remember—what we never can forget—the gentleness, the kindness of the warm-hearted Countess of Dufferin. (Leggo 732)

Dixon left Rideau Hall when the Dufferins' term ended, and took a job in the civil service in Ottawa, first in the Department of Public Works and then in the Department of Railways and Canals. When he died in 1919 he was Chief Clerk of the Correspondence branch of that department. Besides working on the book *Picturesque Canada* and assisting Baedeker with his *Handbook of Canada*, Dixon published five other plays, including *A Masque Entitled Canada's Welcome* for the arrival of the Dufferins' successors, the Marquis of Lorne and his wife Princess Louise, the daughter of Queen Victoria. The masque was given before them at the Opera House in Ottawa on February 24, 1879, and more will be said of it later. The Lornes had no children, and life at Rideau Hall in their time was very different from the days of the Dufferins. This may well be the reason that no more children's plays came from the pen of F.A. Dixon.

* * *

When we turn to the plays attended or patronized by the Dufferins outside Rideau Hall, we get a broader view of plays that were popular in Canada, England, and the United States at the

time. The names of Tom Taylor, Tom Robertson, Dion Boucicault, Sheridan, Goldsmith, Ellen Price Wood, Anatole France,
Octave Feuillet and Mark Twain are among the playwrights
they saw, and are more easily identified than the authors of
some of the plays produced at Government House. The best
source of information on these plays is again Lady Dufferin's
My Canadian Journal, which sometimes merely mentions that
they saw a play, sometimes gives a title or, more rarely, an
author, and sometimes gives some of her own criticism of the
play or the performers, or some personal and pointed comments on the audiences. The journal thus becomes a record of
an intelligent playgoer's guide to theatre in the 1870s.

The places in Canada where the Dufferins attended plays
were Ottawa, Toronto, Montreal, Halifax and, shortly before
their departure, the Island of Orleans. The number of plays
they saw in Ottawa may seem small in view of the fact that
they lived there most of the time. But their theatrical activity
in the winter and spring of each year in the capital was centred on Rideau Hall, and they often spent the summer residing at the Citadel in Quebec City. The late summer and fall
were the times of their extensive travels to various parts of
Canada and the United States.

What they did see in Ottawa was not the standard fare
they attended elsewhere. Lady Dufferin's first entry recounts
their attendance at a series of tableaux in December 1873
similar to the ones they themselves put on. She gives further
insights into the demands of this genre with just a slight tone
of condescension:

> We attended an amateur performance in aid of a charity. It
> was very good indeed. The first part consisted of "wax-
> works" done by the beauties of Ottawa. They certainly
> have a talent for tableaux, for I never saw anything more
> perfectly still than they were—although they were "on
> view" for nearly half-an-hour at a time. Each one was
> wound up in turn, and went through its performance
> admirably. (Dufferin 97)

On December 27 they attended a performance at St. Joseph's College of the only play in French she mentions, although she says nothing of its content or author. Her description is more evocative of a happy day in the Christmas season:

> The house was beautifully illuminated outside, and we had songs and addresses, and a little French play acted by the students. It was a good night for sleighing, and the drive home was pleasant. (Dufferin 98)

The following May the Dufferins attended a performance at Gowan's Opera House by Mrs. Scott-Siddons of excerpts from several of Shakespeare's plays (*Ottawa Times*, May 4, 1974, p. 3). In November 1876 Lady Dufferin accompanied her children and some friends to see the midget Tom Thumb of the Barnum Circus, who in real life was Charles Edward Stratton (1838-1883). She writes of the children's enjoyment:

> We filled two boxes, and the delight of the children made it very amusing ... The dwarfs did some little plays, one having a man in the part of a "mischievous monkey" in it, who once made a dash at our box, and was received with shrieks. (Dufferin 232)

As they approached the end of their time in Ottawa, the Dufferins seemed more involved in local theatre than in the past. They attended two plays on successive evenings, *Jane Eyre* and *East Lynne*. Lady Dufferin made little comment on the plays, although she said of the first: "In the evening we went to see Charlotte Thompson in 'Jane Eyre'. She is not a handsome woman, but so good an actress that she makes you quite forget her face" (Dufferin 291). The last record of their involvement with theatre in Ottawa is their patronage at the Grand Opera House the week of April 30-May 5, 1878 of what seem like very different plays by Van Laer and Farren's Temperance Dramatic Organization, and by Eliza Weathersby's Froliques. The first group presented *Devotion, or Woman's Love* and *Drunkard's Home* (*Ottawa Free Press*, April

30, 1878, p. 3; May 1, 1878, p. 3); the second gave the city *Hobbies*, described in the advertisement in the *Ottawa Free Press* as "their Refined Entertainment, a highly original, serio-comic Burlesque Extravaganza" (May 1, 1878, p. 3). The Dufferins' taste in theatre was certainly not limited to any one genre. Lady Dufferin made no mention of their attending these performances, which coincided with the bazaar being held at Rideau Hall; she seems to have been more interested in raising money for their "little church" than in the Temperance Dramatic Organization or Eliza Weathersby's Froliques.

The Dufferins attended several plays on their visits to Toronto. The first they saw there—perhaps the first they attended in Canada—was Dion Boucicault's *London Assurance* at the Royal Lyceum Theatre on October 26, 1872. Lady Dufferin commented: "The theatre is small, but very pretty, and 'London Assurance' was well given—especially the part of Lady Gay Spanker, by Mrs. Morrison" (Dufferin 35). In August 1874 they apparently arrived late at a theatre and were greeted with cheers in the midst of the performance. "The actors," Lady Dufferin reported, "who were in the midst of a tragic part, could not imagine what the noise was about" (Dufferin 147). The Dufferins gave their patronage to, but were unable to attend a gala performance at the opening of Mrs. Daniel Morrison's new theatre, the Grand Opera, on September 21, 1874. The play was *The School for Scandal* by Lord Dufferin's great-grandfather, with Mrs. Morrison playing the role of Lady Teazle (Dufferin 147). In January 1877 they attended Boucicault's *Arrah na Pogue* (Dufferin 235), and in September 1878, after Lady Dufferin had left Canada, her husband paid a final visit to Toronto where he attended the popular *Mercy Merrick, or the New Magdalen* by Wilkie Collins at the Grand Opera House. Dufferin published no personal memoir of his life in Canada and made no mention of this or other plays in his speeches, but Leggo recorded his attendance at this performance in which Miss Ada Cavendish played the role of the heroine (Leggo 825).

Although the Dufferins made several visits to Montreal, Lady Dufferin never mentioned by name any play they saw there. Indeed, it was only in the last year of their days in Canada that she mentioned going to the theatre in Montreal at all. One performance they attended was a military demonstration which greatly impressed her. She wrote: "The house was crammed, and presented a most brilliant spectacle. The piece was, in its way, unique, for it was made the excuse for a grand military display" (Dufferin 284). She then described it in detail and added an interesting note on their escorts at the close of the evening: "We did not leave the theatre till midnight, and then were dragged by the snow-shoers of Montreal to the hotel" (Dufferin 284). The next day she recorded another tribute to them at an unnamed musical at the Sacred Heart Convent:

> At the far end was a stage with rustic arbours on it and quantities of flowers. On it was performed an original musical operetta, in which all the flowers took part, and which ended in the "Rose" carrying a magnificent basket of flowers to His Excellency, each of her attendants holding a ribbon attached to it. (Dufferin 285)

In her last mention of a play in Montreal in May she spoke simply of going "to the theatre" (Dufferin 293).

Their theatre-going in Halifax is more detailed and happened on their only trip there in August 1873 when they were on a state visit to the Maritime provinces, including the latest member of Confederation, Prince Edward Island. Shortly after their arrival Lord Dufferin had to return to Ottawa to prorogue Parliament as a result of the Pacific Scandal that led to the overthrow of the Macdonald government. Stewart gives some of the details of the productions they attended:

> The Countess and her brother, Lieut. Hamilton, remained at Halifax, and participated in the further entertainments which were included in the programme. The Garrison theatricals were most successful. The different parts were

assumed by amateurs entirely, and the cast embraced a
number of Halifax ladies and gentlemen, and some of the
officers belonging to the 60th Rifles. This performance was
held in the Spring Garden Theatre. (Stewart 263-4)

Again it is Lady Dufferin who provides us with more details
of the performances, as on August 11: "After dinner we proceeded to the theatre, where we saw "Still Waters Run Deep"
[by Tom Taylor] and "Under the Rose" [by Anatole France]
acted by amateurs. There were some excellent actors, and I
enjoyed it" (Dufferin 81-2). On August 16 she wrote: "I gave
a dinner to the amateur actors on board the *Druid*, and afterwards went to see them do "Caste" [by Tom Robertson],
which was very amusing" (Dufferin 83). This information
helps to confirm that the same plays were being done in the
Garrison theatres as in the main theatres in Canada and the
United States and, with the arrival of the Dufferins, on the
stage of Rideau Hall itself.

In October 1874 the Dufferins visited the eastern United
States, and went to theatres in New York, Boston and Baltimore. In a letter to the Duchess of Argyll on his return to
Ottawa Lord Dufferin spoke of the excitement of the visit in
blunt words that would never be used in his public utterances:
"After the solitude, desolation, and incompleteness of Ottawa
the sights and sounds of city life were very exhilarating" (Lyall
233). In New York the Dufferins were wined and dined and
taken to the theatre or opera almost every night of their two
week stay there. They saw the opera based on Hugo's novel
Ruy Blas twice, and Donizetti's *Lucia di Lammermour* once. In
commenting on *Ruy Blas*, Lady Dufferin's fussiness came out:
"The performers were not of the Patti order. The box we had
was very open, and had none of the privacy of an English one"
(Dufferin 154). She was more impressed with *Lucia*, partly
because the title role was sung by Albani, the stage name of the
Canadian soprano Emma Lajeunesse. Although she was
somewhat casual about being late for the opera, Lady Dufferin's pleasure with it showed a budding sense of Canadian

nationalism when she said: "… we only missed the first act of *Lucia*, and enjoyed the rest very much. Albani, who sang for the second time here, was very well received, and we are proud of her as a Canadian" (Dufferin 158).

In New York they also attended the opera bouffe *Madame Angot*, and an Octave Feuillet play in translation, *The Romance of a Poor Young Man*. One play they walked out of, and Lady Dufferin didn't even record its title. However, she did give us a brief description of it: "We had not been there three minutes before we found it was such a piece which we could possibly not (sic) stay to see. Imagine the history of the temptation and fall of man in burlesque upon the stage!" (Dufferin 155). The most interesting play they saw was based on Mark Twain's novel *The Gilded Age*, and this play is one of the rare works on which both Lord and Lady Dufferin commented. They were impressed by its American flavour and summarized the plot. Lord Dufferin's comments, in the letter quoted above to the Duchess of Argyll, make us regret that he did not more often give his impressions of the plays he saw:

> As you may suppose, we did not neglect the theatres, but we only witnessed one genuine American play. It was very amusing, and the principal character well acted, typifying the native speculator who ruins himself and his friends several times over by his magnificent operations. The first act concluded with the blowing up of a river steamer in which everybody had sunk their fortunes. Next we had a seduction, and the young lady transformed from the needy daughter of a settler into a gaily dressed female log-roller in Washington. She eventually reappears in a ball-dress, shoots her lover in her father's drawing-room, and is then acquitted by a sympathizing jury. The parts of the play which told upon the audience with unfailing success were jocose allusions to the corruption of the Senators and members of the Congress. (Lyall 234)

But it was Lady Dufferin who was the more perceptive critic as she commented on the acting: "The principal actor was excellent—Raymond by name—and the woman was good in the tragic parts, but looked much too wicked in her innocent days at the beginning of the play" (Dufferin 154).

It is Lord Dufferin who tells us of another unidentified American play he saw on a stop in Baltimore after a brief visit to Washington and the President of the United States, Ulysses Grant. Some misunderstanding caused him to miss a society dinner in Baltimore, and so he writes: "I had to content myself with the play, which was interesting, as we were given a drama laid during the time of the recent American War, with Stonewall Jackson and Federal and Confederate officers for the chief performers" (Dufferin 235). In Boston the Dufferins attended one of the monthly meetings of the Saturday Club as guests of the poet Longfellow, and had the pleasure of dining with Lowell, Emerson, the two Danas, and Oliver Wendell Holmes. The Dufferins attended two plays there at different theatres, and Lady Dufferin made some of her few comments on theatres themselves, and on the selection of plays. Comparing the New York and Boston theatres they attended, she wrote:

> In the evening we went to the Boston Theatre—a fine one, with spacious entrance-hall. The theatre itself, very large and beautifully decorated, finer than any we saw in New York. The piece was *Belle Lamar*, a story of the War, interesting and well put upon the stage. Here they have a farce both before and after, while in New York there was only one piece given in each theatre. (Dufferin 160)

The next night they went to the Museum Theatre, and of it she said: "It is not so fine as the Boston, but it is uncommon in one way. You pass through a museum to it—statues, pictures, stuffed animals, etc. The play was *Arkwright's Wife*, by Tom Taylor—very good indeed. The heroine was pretty and graceful" (Dufferin 161). At this, the last play on their trip, she was on familiar territory, since Taylor's plays were among those presented at the first and last of her own theatricals at Rideau Hall.

One reference to their theatre-going is found in a touching letter from Lord Dufferin to one of his sons who sent him a letter when they were visiting New York. It reveals the tender side of the Governor General's nature as well as his proclivity for the theatre. He writes to "My dear little boy" from Breevoort House commenting on a horse the boy has just named Prince, and describing the streets of this "very big town." Then he concludes:

> We have been to one or two plays, and have seen a number of very interesting people, but Papa is so busy, and so many persons insist upon seeing him all the morning he has only time to write his little boy this hurried line. He is nonetheless his dear little boy's dutiful Papa.
> (signed) Dufferin. (NAC 2)

It is easy to see how the theatre habits of the parents were passed on to the Dufferin children.

The last city in the United States where Lady Dufferin reported going to the theatre was San Francisco, in August and September 1876. Since the Canadian Pacific Railway was not yet completed, they travelled by rail through the United States on a journey to British Columbia, San Francisco being their connecting port with Vancouver Island on both legs of the trip. In August, on the first part of the journey, they saw two plays in San Francisco on successive nights, *Geneva Cross* and *Brass*. Little is said of the plays themselves, but we get some idea of the physical demands of travel on Lady Dufferin and of her dedication to the theatre when she says with reference to *Geneva Cross*: "We enjoyed the play, though I, at any rate, began to feel the effects of having risen at six and travelled day and night for many days" (Dufferin 196). When writing of *Brass* she says: "General McDowell, the hero of Bull's Run, dined with us, and we took him to a special performance of *Brass* in our honour. We had a good box, and enjoyed that very ridiculous play" (Dufferin 197).

On their return trip they went to a Chinese play. For the Dufferins it was one of the most exhilarating theatre experiences of their lives. On September 26 Lady Dufferin wrote:

> D. and I agree that we would have come the whole journey for the sake of seeing the Chinese Theatre.
> We went with the necessary appendage of a policeman. The pit was full of Chinamen, as was the gallery, with the exception of a small place in front of the musicians. A Chinese play is not an affair of hours, or of days, but of months. You can have about six hours a night of it as long as it lasts. We went for half an hour, and stayed two, and then left most reluctantly.
> The music is of the bagpipe order. D. was charmed with the minor key and the barbaric tunes. When we arrived the stage was occupied by a company of aristocratic Chinamen, and it was evident an important council was being held. The councillors were magnificently dressed in gold and embroidered satin and various-shaped head-dresses. The acting we might consider stagey, but it seems to suit the dress and the people. They did it with such an air! (Dufferin 226)

She concluded by describing an after-theatre visit: "Having torn ourselves away from the theatre, our guide took us to see the "Joss House" or Chinese church … " (Dufferin 226). The visit to the Joss House must not have lasted long, for Stewart tells us that "A visit to the Chinese Theatre and a Chinese restaurant occupied the greater part of (that) night" (Stewart 496). Like many people today, it seems the Dufferins enjoyed going for Chinese food after a night at the theatre.

The last play Lady Dufferin saw in Canada was, appropriately, *She Stoops to Conquer*. It was performed on the Island of Orleans on August 6, 1878 while she was staying in Quebec City prior to her departure from Canada some three weeks later. The somewhat crude conditions in which the play was presented were more typical of the homegrown theatre of Canada at the time than many more elaborate productions the Dufferins had attended on their travels or had presented at Rideau Hall. She described those conditions:

> ... we were engaged to attend an amateur theatrical per-
> formance on the Island of Orleans. We landed at eight
> o'clock and drove to what had been a carpenter's shop, but
> was now converted into a "Theatre Royal." The "green-
> room" was a tent.
>
> In front of the stage there were banks of flowers, two lit-
> tle arbours in the corners, and seven figures dressed in pow-
> der and Dolly Varden costumes ...
>
> The play was "She Stoops to Conquer," and it went off
> very well. The Tony Lumpkin was admirable, and the
> prima donna handsome. She is a Mrs. Watson, and had
> arranged the whole thing. (Dufferin 304)

It might also be said of Lady Dufferin's theatre work in Canada, especially at Rideau Hall, that she "had arranged the
whole thing." In a sense, too, she had stooped to conquer the
hearts of Canadians by embracing many things that were
originally strange to her in this huge land. The tear-laden
farewells on August 31 as she sailed from the harbour of
Quebec would show how well she had conquered. And in a
quite literal sense, as we have seen in her involvement in the
productions at Rideau Hall, she had stooped both before and
behind the scenes to begin a threatre tradition in the country's most prestigious residence.

We have much to be grateful for to the Dufferins for
their enthusiasm and encouragement of theatre in Ottawa
and elsewhere in Canada during their six years here. While
many of their successors would follow their example and
would encourage other cultural activities the Dufferins were
not involved in, none would surpass the Dufferins' personal
involvement in theatre and the stimulus they gave to a the-
atre-hungry public in this new nation.

Works Cited

Black, Charles E. Drummond. *The Marquess of Dufferin and Ava: Diplomatist, Viceroy, Statesman.* London: Hutchinson, 1903.

Dixon, Frederick A. *Fifine the Fisher-Maid.* Ottawa: A.S. Woodburn, 1877.

———. *Little Nobody.* Toronto: Adam, Stevenson, 1875.

———. *Maiden Mona the Mermaid.* Toronto: Belford, 1877.

———. *The Maire of St. Brieux: an operetta in one act.* Ottawa: J. Bureau, 1875.

Dufferin, Lady. *My Canadian Journal.* Edited and annotated by Gladys Chandler Walker. Toronto: Longmans, 1969.

Earl of Dufferin. *Speeches and Addresses.* Edited by Henry Milton. London: John Murray, 1882.

Farr, D.M.L. "Lord Dufferin: a Viceroy in Ottawa." Culture 19 (1958): 153-64.

Fowler, Marian. *The Embroidered Tent.* Toronto: Anansi, 1982.

Helen, Lady Dufferin (Countess of Gifford). *Songs, Poems and Verses.* Edited, with a Memoir and some Account of the Sheridan Family, by her Son The Marquess of Dufferin and Ava. 3rd ed. London: John Murray, 1894.

Leggo, William. *The History of the Administration of the Earl of Dufferin.* Montreal: Lovell, 1878.

Lyall, Sir Alfred. *The Life of the Marquess of Dufferin and Ava.* London: Thomas Nelson, 1905.

Nicolson, Harold. *Helen's Tower.* London: Constable, 1937.

Ottawa Free Press.

Ottawa Times.

NAC 1 (National Archives of Canada, MG28, I139, vol. 8, Government House, 1872-1879).

NAC 2 (National Archives of Canada, MG27, IJII, Dufferin Family Correspondence, 1873-1878).

NAC 3 (National Archives of Canada, MG27, IJII, Dufferin Family Correspondence, 1880-1917).

Stewart, George, Jr. *Canada under the Administration of the Earl of Dufferin.* Toronto: Rose-Belford, 1878.

vc MARQUIS of LORNE. GOV GEN. Nov 25 1878 — Oct 23. 1883 >.

Lord Lorne with his coat of arms.
(Metropolitan Toronto Reference Library)

Chapter 3

Theatricals, Art and the Royal Society
Under the Lornes, 1878-1883

If he were to carry on the traditions and vice-regal splendour established by the Dufferins, the next Governor General would have to be someone very special. To their love of Canada and enthusiasm for its future the Dufferins added an interest in spectacle, theatre, and social life, and became a presence at Rideau Hall that attracted international attention. It would be difficult to find a better couple to add to the emerging respectability of the fledgling capital and its imperial domain on the banks of the Ottawa River.

Benjamin Disraeli, the British Prime Minister at the time, was not only an astute politician; he was also a man with a vision for the British Empire and a plan for implementing that vision in the colonies. He also had the ear and sympathy of Queen Victoria. With such advantages he came up with the brilliant proposal that the next Governor General of Canada should be the Queen's son-in-law, John Douglas Sutherland Campbell, Lord Lorne, heir to the Dukedom of Argyll in Scotland, who had married the Queen's sixth child and second youngest daughter Louise in 1871. Disraeli felt the choice would flatter Canadians and would be "an instrument to proclaim the greatness and unity of the Empire", as Canadian historian Stewart MacNutt said (MacNutt 8).

Lorne and Louise were young, attractive, and talented. Their arrival at Rideau Hall in 1878 was heralded like the coming of Jack and Jacqueline Kennedy to the White House in 1960. Welcome arches greeted them in the various cities they visited, including two in Ottawa—one on Wellington Street with the words "Hail Daughter of the Queen," and the other at Rideau Hall. Lorne was just thirty-three and his princess thirty-one. They had been married seven years but—

unlike the Dufferins and the Kennedys—had no children and were to have none. Thus, life at Rideau Hall would be much different than it was under the Dufferins, including the new couple's involvement in theatricals there.

Lorne's appointment was not universally acclaimed. Misgivings were expressed as to both his and Louise's suitability for life in the pioneer Dominion. Although Lorne had been a member of parliament for Argyllshire and had worked as secretary for his politically acute father, who was Secretary of State for India, some people questioned his experience and intelligence for the position of Governor General. Sir Henry Ponsonby, private secretary to Queen Victoria, cited the opinion of Lady Dufferin, who told him, "Lorne was very vague in his conception of the duties of his office but the real difficulty was, how Louise would treat people in Canada—if as royalty, there will be trouble, but if in the same way Lady Dufferin did, they will be flattered" (Gwyn 184). Whatever truth there may be in this vain comment of Lady Dufferin, it is clear that Louise had misgivings herself about her forthcoming six-year residency in Canada, not the least of which was the weather. Lorne tried to relieve her anxiety on this count when he assured her that "she would be much more comfortable than she had ever been in Kensington Palace" (Epton 157). Such was not to be the case.

There were also misgivings in Canada about how the vice-regal couple, especially the princess, would take to their new home. Typically, some of these arose from what we now label the Canadian inferiority complex with regard to our social and cultural maturity. They were expressed particularly in the Toronto *Globe*:

> We have few attractions for the great and rich in this country. Those who find enjoyment in the show and glitter of life are not apt to think well of Canada. It so happens, however, that both the Marquis of Lorne and his consort are possessed of qualities which render them independent of many sources of amusement. The Marquis is of literary tastes, with a disposition to engage in public business ...

> The Princess has artistic tastes which can be indulged
> almost as well at Ottawa as at London and, like all the
> daughters of the Queen, she is clever and industrious.
> (Epton 157)

There was no doubt that the new Governor General and his
wife had backgrounds that would enable them to contribute
to the development of art and culture in Canada. Although
he was an indifferent scholar and wrote of his unhappy life at
Cambridge in a pamphlet entitled *The Handicaps of a University
Education*, he was interested in literature. He had
attended readings by and made the acquaintance of Tennyson,
the poet laureate. He had published some verse and
some stories before coming to Canada, including *The Book of
Psalms, Literally Rendered into Verse*, and *Guida and Lita, a
Tale of the Riviera* (1875), an adventure story of love and war.
His younger sister, Frances Balfour, reflecting on his literary
ability wrote: "He had an astonishing facility in writing
rhyming prose, which sometimes rose to the level of poetry.
His ballads partook of the nature and length of ancient sagas,
and he and I would shout them together in, to me, an
uncomprehending unison" (Balfour 81).

Lorne wrote non-fiction as well. While in Canada he
published a pamphlet entitled *The Canadian Northwest*
(Ottawa, 1881), the text of a speech he delivered after his
tour of Manitoba and the Northwest. He later wrote several
books about his experiences in Canada, which were published
after his tenure as Governor General, namely, *Canadian Pictures
Drawn with Pen and Pencil* (London, 1894), *Memories
of Canada and Scotland* (Montreal, 1884), *Yesterday and
Today in Canada* (London, 1910), and *Passages from the Past*
(two volumes, London, 1907). He wrote a book on politics,
Imperial Federation (London, 1888), and published a life of
Queen Victoria one year after her death (London, 1902;
1909). To a volume called *Three Notable Stories* (London,
1890), which contained "The Melancholy Hussar" by
Thomas Hardy, Lorne contributed "Love and Peril: A Story

of Life in the Far Northwest," a sentimental tale about the love of a white man for an Indian girl, and the Métis uprising of 1885. He also published two volumes of *Intimate Society Letters of the Eighteenth Century* (London, 1910).

Though not a poet of marked ability, Lorne wrote many poems on Canadian subjects, some of which may be found in an appendix to J.E. Collins's book on Lorne's tenure in Canada; the four lyrics are entitled "River Rhymes," "Legend of the Canadian Robin," "The Prairie Roses," and "Cree Fairies." Collins also gives an assessment of Lorne's talent as a poet; the critique is a combination of appreciation and understated derision:

> Those (poems) founded upon Indian legends give his lordship an opportunity of displaying his talent for verse-writing at its best, since description of externals, and story telling, rather than reflection and subtle analysis, are the prominent possessions of his muse. His work is always cultured; he sometimes writes with much imagination and strength, but frequently, in the midst of a passage exhibiting these qualities, the impulse leaves him, and he concludes with lines that are mere polished lassitude. With such grace and culture as his lordship possesses, it would be unnatural for him to write, even heedlessly, an uncouth line; but a lack of "the capacity for taking trouble," and a haste that will not permit itself to ply the file long enough upon what it is fashioning, are the abiding faults in the author's method of workmanship. (Collins 366-7)

After his trip to the Northwest Lorne wrote a long poem entitled "Westward Ho" which, if it does not show his poetic talent at its finest, does bear witness to his high recommendation of immigration to his adopted home. Here is an excerpt from the poem:

> The West for you boys, where God has made room
> For field and for city, for the plough and for loom.
> The West for you girls, for our Canada dreams
> Love's home better luck than a gold-seeker's dream.

Away and your children shall bless you, for they
Shall rule o'er a land fairer far than Cathay. (Epton 161)

He composed a poem with more genuine emotion to mark
the naming of the province of Alberta after his wife, whose
full name was Louise Caroline Alberta:

In token of the love which thou hast shown
For this wide land of freedom, I have named
A province vast, and for its beauty famed,
By thy dear name to be hereafter known.
Alberta shall it be! Her fountains thrown
From alps upon three oceans, to all men
Shall vaunt her loveliness e'en now; and when,
Each little hamlet to a city grown,
And numberless as blades of prairie grass
Or the thick leaves in distant forest bower,
Great peoples hear the giant currents pass,
Still shall the waters, bringing wealth and power,
Speak the loved name—the land of silver springs—
Worthy the daughter of our English kings. (Duff 199)

One story, though disputed, has it that the jewel of the Rock-
ies, Lake Louise, was also called after the princess.

Lorne also did some sketching and painting in Canada,
but Louise was the one who had superior talent in this direction. She was an accomplished sculptress and artist before
coming to Ottawa. Among her works, as noted in her *Life
Story*, are a bronze memorial in St. Paul's Cathedral to colonial soldiers who died in the Boer War; a bronze of Nelson;
an oil portrait of Paderewski; and a portrait of her father-in-
law, the Duke of Argyll, that hung in Lorne's study at Kensington Palace. For the wedding of her younger brother
Leopold in 1882 she painted a Dutch landscape in oils while
Lorne painted a view of Quebec. And for a special edition of
the British magazine *Good Words* that same year she contributed six sketches of Quebec which Lorne prefaced with a
poem on the beauty of the city. In Canada and during her

visit to the United States Louise was constantly sketching. In fact, she had a moveable hut built so that she could sketch out of doors unbothered by wind and cold. And after the Lornes left Canada, Louise sculpted a statue of her mother which was unveiled by the Queen in 1893 on the grounds of Kensington Palace, with the inscription:

> VICTORIA R. 1837
> In front of the palace where she was born, and where she lived till her accession, her loyal subjects of Kensington place this statue, the work of her daughter, to commemorate fifty years of her reign. (Duff 341)

The tributes to Louise's talent show that she was not praised merely for who she was, but for real artistic ability. Commenting on her devotion to her art and the effect of her painting, one Edwardian artist wrote:

> Princess Louise's water-colours are very charming. She is an industrious sketcher and is quite devoted to it, and I think is never happier than when at work. She can keep on at it for long hours, never seeming to get tired until she has finished ... She is remarkably quick with her pencil—very often she will draw a thing (with her left hand) sooner than explain in words her meaning. One can see from her little thumb-nail sketches that she is a sculptor because there is modelling in her lines, expression in her outlines showing that she is very familiar with the forms of things, not only with the surfaces. She is no mean caricaturist. Her style of work is very varied and she is not afraid of anything. She has an instinct for composition and her work is very harmonious. Never anything jarring in composition or execution. (Duff 312-3)

The same volume contains an appendix entitled "The Art of Princess Louise" by critic Hilary Hunt-Lewis, which outlines her training and career as an artist. He notes that in 1898 she was unanimously elected an Honorary Fellow of the Royal Society of Painters and Etchers, and concludes with the tribute:

A long life and an active one lay behind Her Royal Highness Princess Louise and through all its trials and difficulties, its glories and its joys, she used her exceptional gift for the best aims and fostered in all with whom she came into contact, her own high ideals of art. (Duff 344)

Her knowledge of art was manifested on a visit she paid to an exhibition of the Academy of the Normal School in Toronto. She knew what she liked and showed her preference in the way in which she toured the exhibition in a limited amount of time. Here is how one writer described her visit:

Her Royal Highness made a rapid but apparently thorough review of the most striking pictures. Her style of "doing" the exhibition differed materially from that of nearly all the other visitors. Instead of moving leisurely about looking at a painting here and there, and referring in a deliberate way to the catalogue, she moved quickly, looking at each picture which attracted her attention earnestly as if desirous of learning as much as possible of its character at a glance. Her manner was that of one deeply interested in what she saw who yet knew she could not see all she would wish unless she devoted her attention earnestly to the paintings. (*Globe*, June 4, 1983, p. 6)

Her example might well be followed by gallery visitors who are similarly pressed for time in visiting an exhibition.

Canadians might have benefited much more from this active patronage of art by such an accomplished first lady in their midst for five years. But the potential of the talented and revered first lady in Canada was never realized because Princess Louise spent less than half her time in Canada during her husband's tenure as Governor General. Although this is not the place to examine all the reasons for her absences, the issue is important in so far as it helps explain why the Lornes did not contribute more to the cultural and even the political life of Canada. As the author of a recent biography of the Lornes stated, "Lorne's administration did not live up

Janet Hall, diarist.
(NAC PA-132171)

to expectations in promoting a closer link between Canada and the British crown. The Queen's own daughter seemed to let the side down" (Stamp 205).

A brief survey will show how little time Louise did spend in Canada. The Lornes arrived in Halifax on November 23, 1878 after a rough voyage across the Atlantic on the *S.S. Sarmatian*. They proceeded to their new home in Ottawa, where they arrived on December 2—not the best month to settle in the backwoods capital, especially for one who was fearful of a Canadian winter. Louise's fears for that first winter must have been realized for she spent much of the next winter in England "ordered by her physicians," notes diarist and Rideau Hall watcher Janet Hall (Hall 112). Louise left Ottawa on October 17, 1879 and returned to the capital on February 6, 1880 having been met by Lorne in Halifax "after a stormy voyage" (Hall 119). The voyage was a presage of more trouble for Louise in Canada. Just a week later, on February 14, she was on her way with Lorne to a drawing-room in the Senate Chamber to mark the opening of a new parliament. Suddenly the horses bolted with their sleigh and dragged it four hundred yards. Louise was injured in the accident, as Lorne describes in his diary: "Louise has been much hurt, and it is a wonder her skull was not fractured. The muscles of the neck, shoulder and back are much strained, and the lobe of one ear was cut in two" (Duff 181). Accounts disagree on the seriousness of the accident, some commentators such as Gwyn suggesting Louise used it as an excuse for a much longer absence from Canada from July 31, 1880 until she was met by Lorne in Quebec in early June almost two years later (*Lorne Diary*, June 4, 1882).

During Louise's prolonged absence, Lorne left Canada to join her for two months from November 1880 to January 1881. On her return to Canada Louise did not come to Ottawa since parliament did not then sit in the summer months. As they did almost every summer, the Lornes remained in Quebec riding and fishing and sketching, as well as attending some official functions. At the end of August they began the grand tour which took them to Montreal,

Toronto and across the continent to British Columbia by train via Chicago and San Francisco, the same route travelled by the Dufferins. On leaving Victoria they went to California and then across the United States to Charlotte, West Virginia, where they parted on January 24, 1883, Lorne for a state visit to Washington, and Louise to winter in Bermuda (*Lorne Diary*, Jan. 24, 1883). Finally, on April 17, after Lorne had gone to meet her in Boston, Louise returned to Ottawa where, the local newspaper reported in a rather tepid welcome, "The citizens of Ottawa look pleased to have Her Royal Highness once again in their midst. On their behalf we greet her with a cordial welcome, and express the hope that the improvement in her health effected by her Bermuda residence may be permanent" (*Citizen*, April 18, 1883, p. 2). The remainder of their stay in Canada consisted of routine duties and social obligations in Ottawa, tributes and addresses from both houses of parliament, visits to Toronto, Kingston and southern Ontario, and summer in Quebec prior to their departure on October 27 after greeting their successors the Lansdownes in the ancient capital.

These prolonged absences from Canada and from Rideau Hall suggest that more than Louise's health was the cause. Boredom and lack of social graces among Canadians and their politicians may have been contributing factors, as well as threats by Fenians on the life of the princess. Yet it seems clear that Louise was not enamoured of Canada and as a result, as Ponsonby noted in his diary, "Princess Louise is away so much from Canada that she hasn't been a success there" (Epton 116).

Besides, there were other reasons why Louise would not want to spend prolonged periods in Canada. Her days were plagued by misfortune and danger from the beginning. She suffered from neuralgia, a condition which is often aggravated by severe cold; this may account for her preference to spend the winters in Bermuda rather than in Canada. Apart from the weather and the sleighing accident already mentioned, there were incidents that would dishearten anyone already hesitant about life in a new land. One of these is described by David Duff in his official biography of the princess. The occasion was the first dinner for the vice-regal couple on their arrival in Halifax in 1878. "That evening," he writes, "a disaster happened. One of the maids lost the keys to the Princess' jewel case, and Her Royal Highness wished to wear her jewels that night." Finally, her host, Admiral Ingle-field, and Lorne broke the case open as "The unfortunate maid stood by shamefaced and weeping copiously" (Duff 162). Three months after the sleighing accident, a near accident occurred at Montebello, Quebec while the Governor General and the princess were on a train from Ottawa to Montreal. Louise's biographer described the event in terms that rival the most lurid melodrama:

> … the Montreal-Ottawa express was scheduled to shunt off and let the vice-regal "special" through. The express arrived on time and backed down on the points switch.
>
> Scarcely was it clear of the switch when the thundering roar of the special was heard up the line. The points-man tried to close the switch to let the special through. To his horror the switch jammed. He tried to force it, but could not; it was immovable. Three men jumped to his aid and with the help of a crow-bar the four of them strained to shift the switch. Beads of sweat stood out on their foreheads as they grunted and heaved. Louder and louder grew the rumble and clatter of the special, pistons pounding it on to certain destruction. Spectators powerless to help the men panting at the points, stood by fascinated.
>
> Suddenly a man was seen running up the line towards the onrushing special, waving his arms madly, clinging to the hope that the engineer might, by some miracle, see and understand his signals. The miracle happened.
>
> Over the noisy crescendo of the hurtling train was heard the grind of brakes. Rails and wheels screeched, the special slowed, then slid to a stop within a few yards of the jammed switch.
>
> Once again the Princess and the Governor-General had escaped by a hair's-breadth. (Duff 181-2)

Duff tells of another accident in 1882 shortly after Louise's return from her twenty-two months absence from Canada. This time there was a collision between the vice-regal yacht and another boat near Quebec City. Duff describes the incident with his usual flair:

> The Princess was now in excellent health, but a few weeks later she narrowly missed an accident that might well have undone all the good brought about by her holidays in England, France, Germany and Italy. She was returning to Quebec with Lord Lorne from a trip up-river, when their yacht collided with a schooner. The two vessels shuddered at the impact and the bow flag-staff, under which Princess Louise was standing, broke. She was saved by the swift action of Lord Lorne who sprang forward and diverted the staff just in time to ward off the blow. (Duff 191)

Then, on their great western trip later that year, travelling on the as yet uncompleted railway that would link the east and west of Canada, they had another accident which is reported by Duff, complete with the picturesque setting of the event:

> After eighty miles the country opened out, the mountains dwindled away to rolling foothills, bushes appeared, and the coach rumbled along by clear blue streams, pastures on which cattle grazed, and past the log cabins of the men working on the mighty task of linking the Atlantic with the Pacific by railroad. But the coach was beginning to feel the strain; one of the axles broke and its days of usefulness as a means of conveyance were temporarily over.
>
> Lucky indeed were the Princess and Lord Lorne that the accident should happen as the road followed the level land by a lakeside, and not on some giddy mountain ... As it was they had but a three-mile walk to a hostelry on the shores of the lake, where they were informed that there was a steamer available in which they could continue their journey up the Thompson River. (Duff 193-4)

Theatre at Rideau Hall, ca. 1880 (composite).
(NAC PA-013178)

These sometimes comical incidents suggest that given Louise's constitution and temperament she may have had good reason for her absences from Canada. She was not an adventurous person like Lady Dufferin, or a determined one like Lady Aberdeen. Had she been able to accept the hazards and hardships of life in Canada she might have come to appreciate more the people who lived with them all their lives, and might have made a greater contribution to enriching those lives with her own special talents and insights.

For her own benefit as well as that of Canadians in her time, it is unfortunate Louise could not have taken to Canada the way another English gentlewoman did. Victoria Sackville-West was the British first lady in Washington accompanying her ambassador father Lionel Sackville-West while the Lornes were in Ottawa. In her *Book of Reminiscences* she wrote enthusiastically: "We used to go every winter to Ottawa, to stay with Lord Lorne or Lord Lansdowne. And I loved sleighing and tobogganing" (Alsop 241). Alternately, we might wish Louise could have spoken as clearly as Lorne's sister, Lady Frances Balfour, did after her visit to Canada in 1882:

> Lorne is well and intensely happy at being back again, and everything is prospering in this great Dominion. Long may it prosper, but put me on board a steamer with my face homewards, and give me a sight of a heather hill, and a grey mist sweeping over it, and I won't trouble the Land of Ice and Snow again. (Balfour 328)

Later she confessed: "I remember nothing better in (Canada) than the view of our garden through the open door, all decked out in a London Springtide" (Balfour 331). That summary may have expressed Louise's sentiments too, but she was not in a position to say so. Disraeli's bold move to appoint the son-in-law of the Queen as Governor General in order to extend the sway of the Empire did not work out as well as he might have hoped when it came to diffusing the best of British culture in Canada.

Nevertheless, the absences of Louise did not affect the tradition of theatricals at Rideau Hall begun by the Dufferins. The fact that Lorne and Louise had no children probably accounted for the lack of any children's plays during Lorne's tenure, yet the tradition of performances for large and distinguished audiences continued every year he was in Canada except the last, whether Louise was there or not.

Before the first of the theatricals was performed, the Lornes attended a Masque in their honour at the Grand Opera House in Ottawa on Monday, February 24, 1879. Entitled *Canada's Welcome*, it was written and produced by the Dufferins' favourite Canadian playwright F.A. Dixon, with music composed by Arthur Clappé. The musical included soloists representing Canada, an Indian Chief, and the seven provinces that formed the Dominion at the time, as well as a chorus of hundreds of singers who had been rehearsing for several weeks. Canada was represented by an Indian maiden who displaced the Indian Chief and his primeval customs. At first she was afraid of the rough pioneers who settled the land and hid in the forest; but soon she was drawn out by the provinces who all made her feel welcome. She in turn welcomed the vice-regal party in the royal box and invited all the soloists representing each of the provinces to do likewise.

The "Words of Welcome" addressed by Canada to Louise were certainly warm, although their effusiveness may have been too much for the timid princess. The quality of the verse might also have given her pause to wonder about the talent of Canada's literati; it contained as much repetition as the original version of "O Canada":

> Welcome! Welcome, from heart and hand:
> Welcome, fair lady, to our land—
> No stranger thou; no strange land this to thee;
> No stranger to our hearts henceforward be;
> Our royal sister from across the sea
> Welcome! Welcome, from heart and hand:
> Welcome, fair lady, to our land! (*Citizen*, Feb. 25, 1879, p. 2)

The Masque was given extensive coverage in the *Ottawa Citizen*, which began its report with a vivid reminder of the uniqueness of the event being celebrated:

> The production in Ottawa, which—although the capital of half a continent, is still relatively but a clearing in the primeval forests of America—of a dramatic representation such as used to be prepared to do honour to European kings and nobles three hundred years ago, is, by reason of the historical and literary associations recalled, an event of more than mere passing social interest. (*Citizen*, Feb. 25, 1879, p. 2)

The review then gave a history of the Masque in European drama and located Dixon's masque within the tradition. And while it praised the work of both Dixon and Clappé, it had reservations about both. The anonymous reviewer wrote:

> We listened attentively to the music, and were much struck with the brilliancy of the orchestral writing exhibited in the accompaniments. Mr. Clappé's forte seems to lie in taste and originality of arrangement rather than in originality of melodious idea. If the melody of the solos does not cling to us, we must frankly say in justice to Mr. Clappé, that the verses written by Mr. Dixon are not, as a whole, well suited for musical setting, and that while we accord to the works of the solos every praise as literary compositions, and as embodying graceful ideas, we think that, inasmuch as not one word of dialogue appears in the Masque, more consideration might have been given to musical and dramatic requirements, and we think this might have been done without spoiling the allegorical idea. (*Citizen*, Feb. 25, 1879, p. 2)

In spite of these reservations, the review went on to praise both Dixon and Clappé, and to remind the Governor General and his wife of their fate for the next five years:

> To Messrs. Dixon and Clappé, the enthusiastic reception the work of their united talents met with last night, must

have been gratifying, and we have already expressed our belief that the distinguished subjects of the "Welcome" must have left the Opera House last night, not only pleased with the representation, but with a kindly feeling towards the people among whom their lot is cast, and who echo every word of courteous and hearty "Welcome" contained in the Masque. (*Citizen*, Feb. 25, 1879, p. 2)

So popular was the Masque that it was repeated in its entirety in the Opera House the following Thursday night. The reviewer again praised the work of the soloists, but showed deep disappointment with some of the choral music as if the singers had become overconfident after the success of the first performance. He wrote:

The rendering of the music was not however, at all equal to that of Monday evening. Whether the failures in the septette and trio were attributable to over-confidence begotten of previous success, we cannot say. An unsteadiness was observable, also, among the chorus throughout, but the success of each and all was so marked on Monday evening, that we would not say one word of discouragement or disparagement, and simply make these brief comments in the hope that none who were present only last night, will carry the impression that the performance was anything like that of Monday, which was beyond all praise. (*Citizen*, Feb. 28, 1879, p. 4)

Janet Hall, who was never invited to the theatricals at Rideau Hall, did attend the first performance of the Masque and, in her more terse commentary, seemed to agree with the reviewer: "Mon 24th Cold. Went with the Cunninghams to see the *Masque of Welcome*, it was in honour of the Marquis and Princess who were present. The solos were very well rendered and altogether it was very good … " (Hall 97). Lorne's Diary also reported that it was cold on that Monday evening in February—"cold weather (23 below zero)" (*Lorne Diary*, Feb. 24, 1879)—but there could be no doubt about the warmth of the welcome by the citizens of Ottawa for its new residents.

The Lorne theatricals were one way they reciprocated this warmth. They carried on the theatrical tradition at Rideau Hall by presenting at least two plays every year from 1879 to 1882. In their last year in Canada there were no theatricals at Rideau Hall, although the Lornes patronized two special theatricals presented at the Institut Canadien in Ottawa on May 1, 1883. The plays at Government House were all presented in March or April, except for one performance on February 28, 1881. All were duly noted in Lorne's *Diary* along with the number of invitations sent—about 400 for each performance—and the names of those invited were published in the local newspaper. Because of the large numbers invited, each play was performed on two nights and separate invitation lists sent for each night. Sometimes the choice of who should attend the opening night was determined by where the surname came in the alphabet; sometimes those from A to L came on the first night and those from M to Y on the second, although there was also a separate category of dignitaries which included such people as the Prime Minister.

The first of two plays at Rideau Hall in 1879 was presented a month after the Masque of Welcome, on March 15 and 19. *Alone*, subtitled "an original comedy drama," was written by J. Palgrave Simpson and Herman C. Mervale. A complicated story of deception, intrigue, a lost daughter, a recognition scene and the union of lovers, *Alone* was based on an old French tale that had been adapted for the Paris stage by Scribe as *La Lectrice* and later for the London stage by T. Haines Bailey as *The Daughter* before being adapted for the Ottawa stage by Simpson and Mervale. Much of the review consisted of a detailed summary of the plot followed by praise for all six members of the cast. Like all the reviews of plays at Rideau Hall, there was little criticism of the actors; invariably the evening was considered a success in all respects.

The *Citizen* review pointed out the appropriateness of the décor and the hospitality of the Lornes following the performance:

Though unity of time is disregarded in the piece, unity of place is strictly observed, one decoration, a sea-side view by Mr. Dickinson (sic), beautifully illustrating all the three acts. After the play the large audience found their way into the supper-room, where they did ample justice to the hospitality of His Excellency the Governor General and Her Royal Highness the Princess Louise. (*Citizen*, March 17, 1879, p. 3)

A special feature of this performance was a Prologue written by Lord Lorne and recited by one of the actors paying tribute to the Dufferins for their contributions to Canada and to the theatre tradition at Rideau Hall. Consisting of fifty-six lines in heroic couplets, it was an example of Lorne's more respectable verse. The lines honouring the Dufferins' theatricals have already been quoted; the beginning and end of the Prologue are worth reproducing here:

A moment's pause before we play our parts
To speak the thought that reigns within your heart.—
Now from the Future's hours, and unknown days,
Affection turns, and with the Past delays;
For countless voices in our mighty land
Speak the fond praises of a vanished hand;
And shall, to mightier ages yet, proclaim
The happy memories linked with Dufferin's name ...
Green as the Shamrock of their native Isle
Their memory lives, and babes unborn shall smile
And share in happiness, the pride that blends
Our country's name with her beloved friends. (NAC)

Between the acts there was a musical interlude with songs in English, French and Italian, all reproduced in the programme. The *Citizen* review of the second performance of *Alone* noted that it "passed off as successfully as the first" (*Citizen*, March 20, 1879, p. 2)—apparently the cast did not falter on the second night as did the chorus in *Canada's Welcome*—and included a list of all those invited.

The second play of that year, *Woodcock's Little Game*, was presented on Wednesday, April 16 and Saturday, April 19, in Easter week. Although the Ottawa *Free Press* devoted a full column to it, the play received scant attention in the *Citizen*, which noted simply under the heading "Government House": "Another of the series of private theatricals took place at Government House last night. There was a large attendance of members of Parliament and their wives, as well as the elite of the city" (*Citizen*, April 17, 1879, p. 4). The *Lorne Diary* is more informative than usual, taking note of both performances and even straying from its non-committal style to make some critical comment on the play itself. On April 16 it read: "First presentation of 'Woodcock's Little Game.' About 400 people present. Went off very well. Snow nearly gone" (*Lorne Diary*, April 16, 1879). After the Saturday performance it noted: "Not so many present as on Wednesday, but the play was again a great success. Her Royal Highness was unable to be present being unwell. The last performance of the season" (*Lorne Diary*, April 19, 1879).

In 1880 three plays made up the Government House theatricals, one on March 11 and 13, and the other two both on April 6 and 8. The first was *Used Up* by Charles Mathews, of which the anonymous reviewer in the *Citizen* spared us a lengthy plot summary, saying it was so well known that no synopsis was necessary. In fact, much of the four columns devoted to the event didn't speak of the play at all, but described at tedious length the Ottawa winter and the journey and arrival of the guests at Rideau Hall, including the greediness of Ottawa cabdrivers. Where the review was valuable was in its description of the actors and what constituted a company of performers who acted regularly at Rideau Hall. This came out when it spoke of a young woman who was new to the vice-regal stage and who had joined other experienced actors for the play. It is worth quoting at length:

> Place (aux) dames; it is a pleasant task to criticize the fair
> debutante, who has won universal approval in the naive

and attractive part of Mary Wurzel. Mrs. Corbett has proved herself fully competent to sustain the high character of the performances which have made the private theatricals of Rideau Hall justly celebrated and which rendered her position a very difficult one. Comparisons would naturally suggest themselves in which the great and varied excellence of the acting of Lady Dufferin, the vivacity and archness of Miss Fellowes, the natural pathos of Miss Staunton, and the graceful characteristics of many other ladies who have taken part in them would be remembered, but Mrs. Corbett fairly won the hearts of the audience, and there is no hazard in saying that her position as a worthy successor of the accomplished predecessors we have named, is already established. The heavy work fell upon Captain Collins and Captain Chater, who had stage reputations to sustain, and whose performances fully justified our expectations. (*Citizen*, March 15, 1880, p. 1)

After noting the Governor General's hospitality following the performance and describing the departure of the ladies who, "having swiftly donned their wraps, hurried to their sleighs as if they were so many Cinderellas," he concluded with further information on the acting company at Rideau Hall: "We venture to congratulate the noble host upon the perfection and entire success of the arrangements, and we are sure that we express the feeling of the whole audience, when we offer our best thanks to his amateur Troupe" (*Citizen*, March 15, 1880, p. 1).

The *Lorne Diary* made no comment on the quality of the production but it gave us some clue to the rehearsal time put into the plays, and the support received from the princess herself. Thus, on February 18, three weeks before the first performance, we read: "First rehearsal of theatricals," and on March 10: "Dress Rehearsal of 'Used Up' at 8.30—at which Her Royal Highness was present," although on the days of performance the only information we glean is, "about 420 present" (*Lorne Diary*, Feb. 18, March 10, 11, 1880) on opening night. The verbose *Citizen* reviewer gave another estimate of the audience as well as the seating arrangement in the ballroom when he wrote:

> At half-past eight the doors of the theatre are opened, and the seats are soon filled by a throng of more than four hundred and fifty ladies and gentlemen. There is no flurry or confusion. Two rows of chairs are reserved. The first are soon occupied by His Excellency and his suite, and the others by Ministers of the Crown and other dignitaries, and their wives, and their sisters, and their cousins, &c. (*Citizen*, March 15, 1880, p. 1)

On this occasion the guests received a bonus in the form of the first public performance of the "Canadian National Hymn" composed by Lord Lorne and put to music by Sir Arthur Sullivan when he visited Rideau Hall at the end of February that year. It was made up of seven eight-line stanzas with a chorus to be sung after each verse, as follows:

> O bless our wide Dominion,
>   True freedom's finest scene;
> Defend our people's union,
>   God save our Empire's Queen.

The *Citizen* writer gave his impressions of both the verse and music of the anthem, and suggested that Sullivan's melody was not up to the lyrics of the Governor General:

> The stanzas are gracefully turned, and effective in their simplicity, and rhythmic measure as national lyrics must be, in order to catch the popular memory and sympathy. They interpret the highest spirit of Canadian patriotism, of which loyalty is the essence and stimulus. The music was composed by Sullivan, during his late visit to Government House. It is flowing and melodious, but not equal to the words and thoughts that it is intended to illustrate and enforce. The composer, perhaps, felt constrained to fulfil his share of the work while he was here. No man, however gifted, can command inspiration, and we think the music

might be retouched with advantage to its originality and effectiveness. This as a single opinion will probably be in a very marked minority, if round after round of hearty applause may be taken as an indication. (*Citizen*, March 14, 1880, p. 1)

Today's readers may well judge that Canadians are fortunate neither the words nor the music were adopted as Canada's national anthem.

The April theatricals were *Cool as a Cucumber*, a farce in one act, and *Checkmate*, a comedy in two acts, both on the same programme. The *Lorne Diary* noted simply that there were about 330 present for the first performance, and about 450 for the second (*Lorne Diary*, April 6 and April 8, 1880). The *Citizen* reviewer informs us that the Tuesday performance was marked by the first public appearance of Princess Louise since her sleighing accident in February and that she was greeted by "a round of enthusiastic cheers which the restraint of the occasion could scarcely repress" (*Citizen*, April 9, 1880, p. 4).

The theatricals of 1881, presented on Monday, February 28 and on Shrove Tuesday, March 1, while Princess Louise was on her extended absence from Ottawa, did not receive as much attention from the local *Citizen*, but were included in an article under the general heading "Winter Amusements— Theatricals at Government House," which featured a defence of the Ottawa winter and a description of winter sports and dances at Rideau Hall. The plays were a comedy, *Perfection*, and a farce in one act, *Betsy Baker*. *Perfection* concerns the plight of a young man who falls desperately in love at first sight but is told

that the fair and faultless being he seeks, can neither draw, sing nor play, is imperfectly educated otherwise, and, to crown all her other imperfections, has a cork leg. He has already impulsively committed himself by a declaration, and there is no honourable way of retreat.

He leaves her in despair but nobly resolves to keep faith,

meets her again and finds that he has been thoroughly mystified; his charmer draws like Millais, sings like a seraph, and being a native Corkonian, has not only one Cork leg, but two, both sufficiently active for a waltz or a galop with the best, in fact that she dances like a sprite. (*Citizen*, March 2, 1881, p. 1)

Both plays were applauded by the critic, but most of the praise was given to the actors rather than the plays themselves, especially in the case of the second one: "*Betsy Baker* ... had the disadvantage of coming after a very well sustained, bright and lively comedy, almost as light as a farce, but it was also a decided success, perhaps more by reason of excellent acting than the merits of the piece itself" (*Citizen*, March 2, 1881, p. l). He lavished praise on all the actors, most of them familiar to devotees of Rideau Hall theatricals, and in so doing gave us further insight into the company of actors assembled there year after year. Concerning the excellent performance of Miss Stuart, who played Susan in *Perfection*, he tells us that "she comes by it as a direct inheritance from both parents." Evidence of this he gives from *Betsy Baker*, in which Mrs. Stuart played the title role, and he goes out of his way to describe the mother's accomplishments over the years:

> Mrs. Stuart never fails to give spirit and life to any part she undertakes, and she made "Betsy" a character fully as successful as any in the long list in which we have had the pleasure of witnessing her admirable acting. It is not out of place here, we are sure, to express our thanks to her in the name of the many who have been indebted to her year after year for giving them the benefit of talents which are often exercised at much personal sacrifice, and which make her most deservedly, a popular favourite.

One other actor was singled out for special tribute, Captain V. Chater, an aide de camp of Lorne, who was preparing to leave Ottawa and the boards of Rideau Hall:

It was certainly matter of wonder to those who know anything of the arduous duties most thoughtfully performed
that have devolved upon Capt. Chater during the winter
that he found time to study his part so thoroughly and to
prepare himself to render it so well. Everyone will regret
that the time is approaching when he must join his regiment, and he will take with him, wherever he goes, the
kindly wishes and remembrances of hosts of Canadian
friends.

The review ended with gratitude for the "sumptuous supper" served in the Tennis Court room after the plays, and of
the guests'

> pleasant recollections of entertainments for which they are
> indebted to the most courteous and thoughtful of hosts,
> who we trust will pardon us for a feeble attempt to render
> justice to himself and to those who have volunteered, by
> taking part in the theatricals, to second his unwearied
> endeavours to promote our enjoyment. (*Citizen*, March 2,
> 1881, p. 1)

More soberly, Lorne's *Diary* records that on the first night
there were "350 people present" in spite of "Snow all day.
Heavy snowstorm during the night and frost," and on the
second about 342 present with a "Small dinner party" (*Lorne
Diary*, Feb. 28 and March 1, 1881).

The theatricals of 1882, also given in Louise's absence,
were *Old Soldiers*, a comedy in three acts, and *The Area Belle*,
a farce in one act. The performances were noted in two issues
of the *Citizen* on April 19 and 21, the day after each double-
bill; on this occasion the guest list was divided over the two
nights. This *Citizen* account was the shortest of any during
Lorne's term; no plot summary was provided but the talents
of some of the actors were described, notably of Major Short
in *Old Soldiers*, who "ably withstood the temptation to merely make the part that of the traditional stage Irishman." Once
again the Stuarts were prominent, with Mrs. Stuart taking

roles in both plays, Miss Stuart in *The Area Belle*, and Lt. Col. Stuart in *Old Soldiers*. Of his performance we are told, "The Major Fong of Lt. Col. Stuart was played with an ease and finish which bear token that this gentleman must have had considerable experience behind the footlights," a statement that coincides with the comment the previous year about Miss Stuart's inheriting her dramatic talents from both parents. But again it is Mrs. Stuart who receives the warmest praise for her role as "Mrs. Major Moss, widow and woman of the world," in *Old Soldiers*, where she was "the embodiment of an intriguing susceptible widow, and proved what has oftentimes been proved before, that in her Ottawa possesses a comedienne of the highest order."

The reviewer informs us that *The Area Belle* was "somewhat cut down, the business at the supper table being especially curtailed, and the celebrated song introduced by J.L. Toole of 'An 'orrible Tale,' being omitted altogether. This was probably owing to the length of the programme" (*Citizen*, April 19, 1882, p. 1), possibly so that the guests might get to their own supper following the theatricals, although we are not told of any supper party after these performances.

The *Lorne Diary* is particularly laconic describing these nights, noting simply "1st night of Theatricals" and "2nd night of Theatricals," with "about 400 present" on the first night (*Lorne Diary*, April 18 and 20, 1882). The *Diary*, which inexplicably ends on February 28, 1883, makes no mention of any theatricals that year, nor does the *Citizen* describe any in the month of March, April, or May, during which time Parliament sat until its prorogation on May 25 after a session of five weeks and two days, the longest up to that date since Confederation. Since the theatricals under the Lornes were always held while Parliament was in session, it is unlikely they were held at any other time that year. Besides, Lorne and Louise did give two state balls at Rideau Hall in that period, on May 10 and 14, which were described in the local press. Louise returned to Ottawa from Bermuda on April 28, 1883 after being away from the capital for two years and nine months. When she returned to Canada in June 1882 she did not visit Ottawa prior to her trips to Western Canada, the United States, and Bermuda.

It may have been that with the imminent departure of the Lornes from Canada that year, and the many social and political functions they had to attend, including the tributes from both houses of Parliament, they simply did not have time or energy to organize any theatricals. They did, however, lend support to a night of amateur theatricals given at the Institut Canadien on York Street in Ottawa on May 16. The *Citizen* account, obviously by a different person from the flamboyant reviewer of the Rideau Hall theatricals, shows that the type of plays chosen followed the format of those on the vice-regal stage, a comedy in three acts followed by a farce. The headline reads, "The Princess at the Canadian Institute Last Night," although Lorne was there as well; obviously the affection of the *Citizen* for Louise had not been dampened by her long absence from the city. Although the stage manager was a Major Anderson, the performers were not among the familiar members of the Rideau Hall company. The first play, *Married for Money*, is described as "a sparkling comedy, well fitted for amateurs, and ... remarkably well cast." The drawing room of the comedy is described as "the best piece of stage setting ever seen in the building." Among the actresses two Misses Bell are singled out since "Miss Bell's 'Mrs. Mopus' would have done credit to a professional, and her sister's 'Mrs. Simpkins' was equally good." Of the second play we are told, "*That Rascal, Pat* was a really good farce, and well put on. 'Pat,' by himself, was rich and his Irish jig brought down the house. Miss Brymner as 'Nancy' had an unthankful task to perform, but made the best of a trivial part" (*Citizen*, May 17, 1883, p. 4). Both plays were repeated at the Grand Opera House the following Saturday for the benefit of a wider circle of Ottawa theatregoers.

The French Canadian Institute Hall was a favourite of Lord Lorne in Ottawa. He attended plays and lectures there since both he and Louise were stimulated by the French culture they met in Ottawa and by the opportunity to show their knowledge and awareness of French. On another occasion, on March 16, 1880 he attended a performance there of the French comic opera, *Le Farfadet* by Adolphe Adam, with the Lieutenant Governor of Quebec. The opera is described as "a new feature in entertainment of this kind and will be found an agreeable departure from the usual and ordinary programme of amateur concerts." In this article on the day of the performance, the *Citizen* gives us some idea of the size of the theatre in the Institut Canadien—"There are three hundred reserved seats from which a good view can be had to all parts of the stage"—and of the way in which the local paper encouraged and advertized dramatic presentations at that time—"Over two hundred have been sold already, and parties desiring to be present would do well to secure reserved seats without extra charges at Messrs. A. & S. Nordheimer's" (*Citizen*, March 16, 1880, p. 2). We are also informed of the price of those seats—Reserved seats, 50 cents, Parquette and gallery, 25 cents. Lord Lorne's patronage was reinforced by the Governor General's Foot Guard band providing the orchestra for the performance.

Lorne was a seasoned theatregoer. All in all, according to his *Diary* and local newspaper reports, he attended some forty dramatic presentations in Ottawa outside Rideau Hall. This is a remarkable number in view of the fact that he took up residence each summer in the Quebec Citadel and toured various parts of Canada and the United States at other times during his term. Sometimes when Louise was in Ottawa she accompanied him to the theatre; sometimes she did not. When Louise was not with him, we read that the Governor General and his suite attended the performances. His suite ranged from his sister, Lady Frances Balfour, to visiting friends and dignitaries and members of his household. But the frequency of his attendance shows that Lorne had a genuine love of theatre, that he cultivated popular productions from Shakespeare to Gilbert and Sullivan, from pantomime to melodrama and French comedy, and that he had favourites among international and local actors and actresses such as Mary Anderson, E.A. Sothern, Mrs. Scott-Siddons, Mrs. C.J. Watson, and a Mr. Boardman.

Following the *Masque of Welcome*, the dates of Lorne's theatre going in Ottawa extend from March 21, 1879 when he and Louise attended an adaptation of Dickens's *David Copperfield* entitled *Little Em'ly*, to April 24, 1883 shortly before they left Ottawa for good, when both of them went to *The Mighty Dollar* one week after Louise got back from Bermuda. Like most of the plays they attended in Ottawa, these were presented at the Grand Opera House, which had been built in 1874 and was thus quite new on their arrival. Frequently Lorne attended one play per week, sometimes two, and occasionally plays on two or three successive nights. In May 1882, when Sothern was performing in Ottawa, Lorne went to the Opera House three nights in succession to see *Lord Dundreary*, *David Garrick*, and *Rip Van Winkle*, and had Sothern to lunch on the second day (*Lorne Diary*, May 11, 12, 13, 1880). Lorne's choices included French plays such as *Le Gendre de M. Poirier* (on February 24, 1881) and *La Mascotte* (on March 21, 1882). There are few comments on the plays in the *Diary*, *La Mascotte* being among the very few to receive a poor rating for being simply "very badly played" (*Lorne Diary*, March 21, 1882). He had a particular fondness for Gilbert and Sullivan, and saw *H.M.S. Pinafore* (in 1879), *The Pirates of Penzance* (in 1880), *The Sorcerer* (in 1882), and *Patience*, the play which parodies Oscar Wilde in the character of Bunthorne, on March 20, 1882, just two months before Wilde's lecture in Ottawa in the same Opera House. Although Lorne was quite happy to see Bunthorne in *Patience*, he had no desire to see Wilde in person, as will be explained below. Lorne also saw *Pinafore* in Halifax on January 31, 1880 as he waited for Louise's ship to dock on her return to Canada, and *Pirates* at the Academy of Music in Montreal in the company of Louise on May 26, 1880, just one week after he had seen it in Ottawa without her.

Perhaps his favourite actress was Mrs. Scott-Siddons, whose reading he attended on March 9, 1880, and whom he invited to lunch at Rideau Hall the following day. In November that same year he went to hear her again in Ottawa reading the part of Juliet. Lorne may have been partial to her because of the high opinion she had of Canadian audiences. In a speech in Montreal in 1879, he noted, "Only the other day Mrs. Scott-Siddons told me that she found her Canadian audiences more enthusiastic and intelligent than any she had met" (Collins 423). Mrs. Watson's readings he attended three times in Ottawa; in Quebec, in the company of Louise and her brother Prince Leopold, he went to what the *Diary* calls "Mrs. Watson's theatricals" (*Lorne Diary*, May 25, 1880).

Another popular pair was the husband and wife team known as The Florences, whose play *The Mighty Dollar* the Lornes saw twice in Ottawa, once on April 26, 1880 and again on April 24, 1883. Since this was perhaps the last play they saw in Ottawa and since it was so popular there, it is worth quoting the review that appeared in the *Citizen* both for its comments on the play and the performers, and on the welcome and prestige that greeted any play attended by the Governor General:

> Rarely has the Grand Opera House held a larger, and assuredly never a more brilliant, audience than that which assembled last night to see the ever popular Mr. and Mrs. W.J. Florence in *The Mighty Dollar*. Notwithstanding that the prices were slightly higher than usual, it was with difficulty that even standing room could be obtained on the floor of the house. His Excellency the Governor-General and Her Royal Highness the Princess Louise (Marchioness of Lorne), occupied the royal box, and both on entering and leaving, were greeted with a perfect storm of cheers ...
>
> Improbable and exaggerated as the whole play certainly is, it at the same time strikes at the root of a too frequent evil in political life across the line, and perhaps is more popular there than here. If so, the audiences must have some special means of evincing their interest, for more applause than Mr. and Mrs. Florence met here would be difficult to conceive. It is to be regretted that

their engagements do not permit of their giving a second performance, but Ottawa must be content with the hope that they will re-visit the Capital at a very early date. (*Citizen*, April 24, 1883, p. 1)

Lorne's travels in Canada and the United States gave him little opportunity to attend plays, but when he took up summer residence in Quebec he could avail himself of the opportunity to go to the theatre there. Not to be outdone by Ottawa's *Masque of Welcome*, Quebec arranged a *Cantata of Welcome* to greet the new Governor General during his first residence in the city. The music on this occasion, June 11, 1879, was composed by Calixa Lavallée, the composer of *O Canada*, with words by the poet Napoléon Legendre. It was a busy day for the vice-regal couple. In the morning Princess Louise laid the foundation of the Kent Gate, a gift of Queen Victoria to the city. In the evening the spectacular *Cantata* was presented in the skating rink; it closed with the simultaneous singing of *God Save the Queen, Vive la Canadienne*, and *Comin' Through the Rye* (Kallman 137).

But it was almost two years later before we read of Lorne attending any more performances in Quebec. When Louise was there with him, they often spent time painting or riding or fishing, as in the summers of 1879, 1880, and 1882. So it may be that during the one summer of 1881 when she was not in Canada at all, Lorne felt freer to go to the theatre more often. Fortunately, he found plays of great variety and high quality at hand: Madame Janauschek's company in Schiller's *Mary Stuart* and *Macbeth*, and several plays by French companies—Sardou's *Nos Intimes*, as well as *L'Étrangère, Le Sphinx*, and *Les Deux Orphelins*; and in July he went to see the Vokes family (*Lorne Diary*, May 16, 18, 25, June 14, 16, 18, July 11, 1881). On at least three occasions Lorne attended Garrison theatre in Quebec. The first was in 1879, when he and Louise went to an entertainment, presumably including theatre since that was the forte of the Garrison entertainers, by the officers and men of "B" Battery in the Citadel (*Lorne*

Diary, Jan. 30, 1879). The second, in 1881, was *The Pirates of Hog's Back*, the garrison version of the Gilbert and Sullivan musical, presented in the Citadel, after which he "went to the officers' mess for a short time" (*Lorne Diary*, March 8, 1881). The third, unnamed, he attended at the Music Hall in the company of Louise in 1882; it is the only play recorded in the *Diary* during their residence in Quebec that year (*Lorne Diary*, June 15, 1882).

Although they attended balls and other social events in Montreal, the only performance recorded there besides *The Pirates of Penzance* was an entertainment given by the Social and Dramatic Club of Montreal (*Lorne Diary*, May 28, 1880). The *Diary* speaks of them not attending any plays in Toronto, and only two in Western Canada—*The Magic Dole* in Victoria (Nov. 17, 1882), and what seems like the oddest Canadian play Lorne ever attended, "on ship theatricals by the Police Jackets on Board" at Yale, B.C. (*Lorne Diary*, Sept. 30, 1882). One of the two performances recorded during their travels in the United States was in San Francisco, where they went to see the Chinese Theatre Restaurant and Joss House (*Lorne Diary*, Sept. 15, 1882), probably the same one patronized by the Dufferins during their visit six years earlier. The harshest comment made in the *Lorne Diary* was levelled at a production of the Bijou Comic Opera Company in Santa Barbara; it is described simply as "a very bad performance" (Jan. 5, 1883).

If Louise did not have the same enthusiasm for theatre as her husband, it is clear that she had a greater involvement in classical music. She even had a pianist, Mr. Oliver King, with the title "pianist to Her Royal Highness Princess Louise." King was also a composer, and in 1883 won the first prize given by the Philharmonic Society of London, England for writing the best concert overture for orchestra (*Citizen*, April 21, 1883, p. 4).

The Rideau Hall *Diary* notes Lorne's attendance at one of King's concerts in Ottawa in 1880 at St. James Hall when Louise was on her first trip to England (*Lorne Diary*, Dec. 7,

Ballroom, Windsor Hotel, Montreal, ca. 1880, with Lord Lorne and Princess Louise.
(NAC C-001830)

1880). And if there were times when Lorne went to the theatre in Ottawa while Louise stayed home, there were occasions on which Louise went to concerts unaccompanied by Lorne. Their respective cultural preferences are typified in the month of April, 1880 when Louise went to two musical events without Lorne—once to hear the organ at Christ Church Cathedral, and then to the Opera House to hear the violinist Remenyi. A week later Lorne went without her to hear one of Mrs. Watson's dramatic readings (*Lorne Diary*, April 10, 13, 20, 1880).

One singer both of them admired was the Swedish soprano Christine Nilsson, whom they went to hear on several occasions. They attended two concerts she gave at the Grand Opera House in San Francisco on December 12 and 14, 1882. On the 13th of that month we read that Madame Nilsson came to visit Princess Louise and was invited to dinner in the evening (*Lorne Diary*, Dec. 12, 13, 14, 1882). Prior to her concert in Ottawa on March 9 the following year, the *Citizen* anticipated her visit with several articles, announcing on March 1 that the concert "is under the special patronage of His Excellency The Governor-General and Her Royal Highness Princess Louise, who were present at Mme. Nilsson's concert in San Francisco, and at whose request (she has) visited the capital" (*Citizen*, March 1, 1883, p. 3). In a tongue-in-cheek commentary on her visit to Ottawa, the *Canadian Illustrated News* reported: "The Marquis of Lorne is always doing gracious things. One of his aides was in attendance at the Ottawa railway station to receive Madame Nilsson, on Friday, and the gifted lady was a guest at Rideau Hall during her stay at the Capital. Thus is the nobility of art appreciated by a noble mind" (March 17, 1883, p. 162). Nilsson actually resided at Rideau Hall during her Ottawa visit. Louise was in Bermuda at the time but Lorne and his party attended the concert and, the newspaper reported, "seemed thoroughly to enjoy the programme," which included several other performers besides Nilsson (*Citizen*, March 10, 1883, p. 3) The same edition of the paper ran a "Short

Sketch of the Swedish Song-Bird," and even followed her progress two days later when it noted that she was involved in a near tragedy on the train from Ottawa to Montreal. The headline read: "The Diva's Train Wrecked on Its Road to Montreal—Very Fortunate Escape" (*Citizen*, March 12, 1883, p. 4). She seems to have been accident-prone in Canada just as Louise was.

It is difficult to gauge Lord Lorne's taste in music, partly because his *Diary* doesn't give the programme for many of the concerts he attended, and partly because he frequented a variety of groups and performers in a large number of institutions in Ottawa and elsewhere, often for charitable purposes. A list of the halls he visited in Ottawa includes most of the large performing spaces in the city at the time: Gloucester Street Convent, Ottawa Ladies College, L'Institut Canadien, the Grand Opera House, and St. James Hall. Besides the many individual performers he went to hear, Lorne seemed to enjoy musical entertainment provided by such groups as the Jubilee Singers, the Naval Cadets, the Mammoth Minstrels, Haverly's Minstrels, and the Ottawa Choral Society.

With the exception of Quebec City, the Lornes attended more concerts than plays during their travels across Canada. This was no doubt due to the fact that there was more Canadian musical talent at that time than there were companies of actors, since most of the professional drama in Canada, including the plays the Lornes saw in Ottawa, was imported from the United States and Great Britain. Thus, while it seems the Lornes attended almost no plays in Montreal, Kingston, Toronto, Halifax, or Winnipeg, in all of these cities—as well as in Victoria where they went to one play and one concert, and in Quebec where they went to several of both—they did attend concerts by such groups as the Society of Music and the Philharmonic Society of Montreal, the Philharmonic Society of Toronto, and the Philharmonic Society in Winnipeg. In Halifax Louise went to a Promenade Concert at the Gardens, and in Victoria they both attended a concert at the Philharmonic Hall.

Two events the Lornes were definitely not involved in should be mentioned in any account of their cultural activities. The first was the lecture by Oscar Wilde which was given in Ottawa on May 16, 1882 at the Opera House. Although Lorne did attend other lectures there and elsewhere, and often had the lecturer to lunch or dinner at Rideau Hall, he seems to have avoided any part in Wilde's visit to the Capital, which was part of a North American tour in 1882. It is clear that Wilde expected to see Lorne in Ottawa—Louise was abroad at the time—for he wrote in a letter to his friend Norman Forbes-Robertson from Montreal, where he lectured on May 15, "Tomorrow night I lecture Lorne on dadoes at Ottawa" (Wilde 117). He did, in fact, deliver one of the three lectures that night entitled "The Decorative Arts," but Lorne was not there, nor was he interested in seeing Wilde on either of the two days he was in Ottawa. Wilde did dine with the Prime Minister, Sir John A. Macdonald, and had a privileged seat on the floor of the House of Commons where he listened to the debates for half an hour. Lorne preferred to go golfing and riding on the day of Wilde's lecture, and was working on his speech for the prorogation of Parliament which took place the day of Wilde's departure. At that time Wilde was not accepted by the British upper class, and had not written any of the works for which he became famous. Had Lorne attended his lecture, Wilde would have received much more attention and sympathy in Ottawa and in Canada than he did, such was the influence the mere presence of the Governor General had on the people or causes he supported.

Another story that needs clarification is that while in Canada Princess Louise composed an operetta based on life in the Gaspé region, where the Lornes holidayed each summer they were in Canada. It is an attractive story that was repeated as late as 1955 in MacNutt's book on the Lornes, where he writes:

> The Princess, being a lover of the arts, dabbled in the popular pastime and wrote an operetta of her own. The theme

was of the simple fishermen of Gaspesia whom she had met during her summers on the Restigouche and the plot was a modified version of *Enoch Arden*. The suit of the comely widow ended with the return of her husband, who had been presumed lost with the mackerel fleet, and the triumphant gurgles of the baby in the cradle. The ballads were written in the Jersey patois spoken throughout the Gaspé region. (MacNutt 208)

The manuscript of such a drama has not been located, and lest scholars expend time and energy looking for it, they should read the denial of its ever having been written by Annie Howells Fréchette, wife of Achille Fréchette, the French-Canadian poet and translator in the House of Commons, and sister of the American writer William Dean Howells. In an article entitled "Life at Rideau Hall," written during the Lornes's tenure there, she went out of her way in a section on the popularity of the Rideau Hall theatricals to state: "… just here I am reminded to say that the announcement that the Princess has written a play founded upon scenes and amongst the fishermen of Gaspé Bay is quite untrue. No such play has been written, or, at least, not by Her Royal Highness" (Fréchette 219). However one might wish such a play had been written, it seems that in 1881 Louise was more interested in the spas of Germany and Switzerland than in the waters of the Restigouche.

When Lorne and Louise came to Canada, their interest in and practice of art were well known. As a result, one of the first events they attended was an exhibition of water colours especially mounted for Louise in Montreal on December 7, 1878, a few days after her arrival in Ottawa. Louise responded to this and other tributes to her work by sketching and painting in Ottawa and elsewhere. The *Lorne Diary* tells of her sketching in many locations outside Ottawa—at Niagara Falls, Santa Barbara, and especially the Quebec City area, where the banks of the St. Charles River, and even the inside of a canoe, were favourite locations for her work. She even painted apple branches laden with fruit on a Georgian six-panel door which faced into her boudoir in Rideau Hall. "In this work," says Gerda Hnatyshyn, wife of former Governor General Ray Hnatyshyn, "she was very much in tune with the flourishing Arts and Crafts Movement of her day" (Hnatyshyn 57). Now facing into a hallway in the residence for visitors to admire, the door was featured on the Hnatyshyns' 1993 Christmas card from Rideau Hall.

Princess Louise contributed many works of art to Canadian galleries during her time in Canada. On May 26, 1879 Lorne opened the new Art Association building in Montreal, and Louise contributed two paintings for the exhibition. Janet Hall was visiting Montreal at the time and wrote that she "spent a long time viewing the pictures, some of them very beautiful—there are two from the easel of the Princess, one a portrait of the Marquis' Irish Grandmother and the other sketches" (Hall 104). To the Montreal gallery Louise gave a copy of Benjamin West's famous painting *The Death of General Wolfe* as well as a portrait she did of the British painter Clara Montalba, one of two sisters who in 1879 visited the Lornes at Rideau Hall where she sculpted a bust of Lorne which she left there. In Canada Louise sculpted a statue of her mother Queen Victoria which still stands in Montreal outside the Music Building on the campus of McGill University, formerly the Royal Victoria College.

The Lornes made friends of artists in North America, particularly Lucius R. O'Brien of Toronto, and Alfred Bierstadt, the American landscape painter, who visited the Lornes both in Ottawa and Quebec. Symbolically, the last entry in the *Lorne Diary* recorded a visit of both Bierstadt and the Sackville-Wests to Ottawa: " ... drove to the Parliament Buildings with Miss West and Albert Bierstadt—home via Chaudière Falls" (*Lorne Diary*, Feb. 28,1883)—a view Louise loved to sketch, although at this time she was in the milder climes of Bermuda.

The opening of the gallery of the Art Association in Montreal was an important occasion not only for Louise's contribution to it, but also because it showed both her and

Lorne's determination to establish a national association of Canadian artists which later became the Royal Canadian Academy of Art, and formed the nucleus of the National Gallery of Canada. Lorne was aware of the objections to such an association and of the criticism he would receive. But he had confidence in the work of Canadian artists and commitment to the growing number of artists in Canada. He used the occasion of the Montreal exhibition to lay out specific plans for the new association:

> I think we can show we have a good promise, not only of having an excellent local exhibition, but that we may in course of time look forward to the day when there may be a general Art Union in the country; a Royal Academy whose exhibitions may be held each year in one of the capitals of our several Provinces; an academy which may, like that of the old country, be able to insist that each of its members or associates should, on their election, paint for it a diploma picture; an academy which shall be strong and wealthy enough to offer, as a prize to the most successful students of the year, money sufficient to enable them to pass some time in those European capitals where the masterpieces of ancient Art can be seen and studied. (Collins 425)

He went on to describe the subjects for what he envisioned as a distinctively Canadian art:

> The features of brave, able, and distinguished men of your own land, of its fair women; and in the scenery of your own country, the magnificent wealth of water of its great streams; in the foaming rush of their cascades, overhung by the mighty pines or branching maples, and skirted with the scented cedar copses; in the fertility of your farms, not only here, but throughout Ontario also; or in the sterile and savage rock scenery of the Saguenay—in such subjects there is ample material, and I doubt not that our artists will in due time benefit this country by making her natural resources and the beauty of her landscapes as well known as are the picturesque districts of Europe, and that

we shall have a school here worthy of our dearly loved
Dominion. (Collins 426-7)

Lorne's proposal was realized in less than a year with the
founding of the Canadian Academy of Art in Ottawa. It
accepted the three fundamental points contained in Lorne's
Montreal speech: the establishment of exhibitions in different
provincial capitals each year, the donation of diploma paintings by new members, and the awarding of prizes to young
artists to study in Europe. At the opening of its first exhibition in the old Clarendon Hotel on Sussex Street in Ottawa
on March 6, 1880, Lorne made another speech showing how
Canadian art was developing through the efforts of members
of the Academy and with the encouragement and determination of himself:

> It is impossible to agree with the remark, that we have no
> material in Canada for our present purposes, when we see
> many excellent works on these walls; and if some do not
> come up to the standard we may set ourselves, what is this
> but an additional argument for the creation of some asso-
> ciation which shall act as an educator in these matters?
> Now, gentlemen, what are the objects of your present
> effort? A glance at the constitution of the Society will show
> your objects are declared to be the encouragement of
> industrial Art by the promotion of excellence of design, the
> support of Schools of Art throughout the country, and the
> formation of a National Gallery of Art at the seat of Gov-
> ernment. (Collins 439)

Lorne might well be proud of the exhibition of the diploma
work of the twenty-five members that made up the academy
for he had chosen them himself. Besides, Louise contributed
a number of her own paintings, which were widely praised, as
Janet Hall attested in her entry on the new Academy: "there
is quite a large collection, some of them remarkably good.
The Princess has several on view, they are very nice, exhibit-
ing more talent than any I have seen before" (Hall 121).

Lorne's own enthusiasm for the project prompted him to visit the exhibition four times after the formal opening and once again with Louise, who was still recovering from her sleighing accident on the day of the opening. He had made his first major contribution to Canadian culture even in the face of some bitterness and wrangling as we learn from a letter to Sir Michael Hicks-Beach, then Colonial Secretary, in which he spoke of "a marvellous amount of bitterness and bad language ... Half the artists are ready just now to choke the other half with their paint brushes" (MacNutt 137-8). But royal support was able to contain the bitterness. A despatch from Hicks-Beach on June 22, 1880 announced that the Queen had consented that the term "Royal" should be included in the name of the Academy. Lorne was named patron and Louise patroness, with Lucius R. O'Brien President and Napoléon Bourassa of Montreal Vice-President. Perhaps only the efforts and patronage of the Governor General could have made the new academy a success.

According to plan, the subsequent exhibitions of the Academy were held in different cities: Halifax in 1881, Montreal in 1882, and Toronto in 1883 with Lorne present at all the openings. He remained a week in Halifax in July 1881 and attended a "conversazione" (reception) put on by the Academy on the day of his departure (*Lorne Diary*, July 9, 1881). The Montreal exhibition was marked by a more splendid event; two days after the opening Lorne gave a ball at the Queen's Hall and Assembly Rooms at which 600 people were present (*Lorne Diary*, April 13, 1882). Louise accompanied him to the Toronto opening of June 1883 at the Normal School, where he made his last important address on art in Canada in reply to members of the Academy and of the Ontario Society of Artists. He reviewed the accomplishments of the Academy and its artists and once again used a public occasion to suggest plans for the development of art in Canada, including the construction of a proper art gallery in Toronto. He even made a pitch for a project that had been dear to Lord Dufferin, the formation of a national park at Niagara.

And he paid tribute to his wife and her support for the Academy, adding a touching story of her interest in the founding exhibition in Ottawa which she was unable to attend:

> The Princess has taken the deepest interest from its inception in the project of establishing a Royal Academy. When, owing to the unfortunate accident at Ottawa, she was unable to visit the first exhibition of the Academy held in that city, remember she insisted that I should bring up to her room nearly every one of the pictures exhibited, in order that she might judge of the position of Canadian Art at that time. (Collins 482)

The story was greeted by hearty applause. It is one that would lend itself nicely to visual representation by any of the artists present, but there seems no evidence that any of them portrayed the incident in a work of art.

In his speech Lorne pointed out that many local art associations and schools were established after the exhibitions of the Academy were presented in their cities. One of these was the Art School in Ottawa to which Lorne gave his special attention and support. Several times in his *Diary* we read of short visits to the Art School, as well as a donation of $500.00 (*Citizen*, April 24, 1882, Supplement, p. 1). And Louise's first public appearance in Ottawa on her return from Bermuda in 1883 was at amateur theatricals in the Opera House in aid of the Art School. The *Citizen* reports that she received a most enthusiastic welcome from those in attendance and that the plays were "in a high degree successful" (*Citizen*, April 20, 1883, p. 2). The title of at least one of the plays—*A Wonderful Woman*—reflected the audience's welcome; the other was *A Night at Notting Hill.*

Lorne's second enduring contribution to Canadian culture was the Royal Society of Canada, which he inaugurated in the Senate Chamber on May 25, 1882. As in the case of the Academy of Art he had laid the groundwork earlier and looked to chosen advisers for help. His proposal for a literary and scientific society was first touted in the Quebec *Chronicle* in June,

1881 during Lorne's summer residence at the Citadel. The idea was strengthened when he undertook his first trip to Western Canada and met members of the Smithsonian Institute who were collecting artefacts of Canadian Indians for their museum in Washington. On his return to Ottawa in October, Lorne assembled a group of scholars in Montreal under the chairmanship of Principal Dawson of McGill University. This group drew up a constitution for the society which they submitted to the Governor General for approval. Soon the names of proposed members were published and the issue became more heated and controverted than membership in the Academy of Art had been. Newspapers took sides, the Toronto *Globe* calling it "a mutual admiration society of nincompoops" and refusing "to hold the Governor-General responsible for a project so absurd" (MacNutt 139). On a more personal level, Nicholas Flood Davin, lawyer, writer and politician, attacked John George Bourinot, Clerk of the House of Commons, writer, and proposed honorary secretary of the Royal Society, in a pamphlet dedicated to the Governor General under the title, "The Secretary of the Royal Society—a Literary Fraud." Even J.E. Collins, a supporter of many of Lorne's initiatives, wrote critically of the Society shortly after its inception:

> As for the Royal Society itself, it has developed mutual admiration and brotherly love among those who before they had the opportunity, by close contact, of becoming acquainted with each other's great virtues and talents, were filled with contempt for one another. More than this, it has become a court where recognition and applause are given to that higher kind of literary ability which the people of this country have never recognized and are utterly incapable of appreciating. It has in short, to be more specific, become a Temple of Consolation for a number of distinguished persons whose contributions have been beyond the range of the magazines and book-publishers. It need hardly be said that the condemnation of a book by the public is of little harm if the Royal Society takes that book under its patronage; nor on the other hand will it avail a man aught

to write in a manner that the general culture of Canada calls well, or for his writings to obtain an extensive constituency, if its author has neither membership nor recognition in the Royal Society. (Collins 370-1)

In a more jocular tone he wrote of the qualifications for membership:

> The membership was confined to persons resident in Canada or Newfoundland who had "published original works or memoirs of merit, or had otherwise rendered eminent service to literature or science." But such an enormous number had "published original works or memoirs" of surpassing merit, and so large was the body of those who had "otherwise rendered eminent service to literature or science," that the heart of a large portion of the cultured community was fairly broken when the list of those who had been admitted, and thus rendered immortal in the annals of Canada, was published. (Collins 368)

He also wrote of the consolation available to those who were not chosen as members:

> Where there were several thousands of writers from which to select for permanent fame only about two hundred, the task of choosing, without creating jealousy, was beset with difficulties; but a method was judiciously adopted somewhat resembling the manner in which at lotteries one thrusts his hand into a bag and draws the first ticket that gets between his fingers; so that there was no ground for murmurings about "invidious distinctions," while the disappointment was easier to bear by the reflection that if it was not a mark of depreciation to be left out of the society, it was no evidence of distinction to be taken into it. (Collins 369)

More seriously, Dr. Goldwin Smith, one of the leading intellectuals of the day, who became first vice-president of the section of the Society on English literature, said:

The selection of members inevitably involved invidious preferences and rejections which were not ratified by public opinion, while anything like exclusiveness is repelled, and rightly repelled, by the spirit of Canadian society. (Collins 369)

In spite of opposition, and buoyed by support from other quarters, Lorne carried the day with his plan. He made his own defence of the Society in his eloquent inaugural address:

Imperfections there must necessarily be at first in its constitution—omissions in membership and organization there may be. Such faults may hereafter be avoided. Our countrymen will recognize that in a body of gentlemen drawn from all our provinces and conspicuous for their ability, there will be a centre around which to rally. They will see that the welfare and strength of growth of this association shall be impeded by no small jealousies, no carping spirit of detraction, but shall be nourished by a noble motive common to the citizens of the republic of letters and to the student of the free world of Nature, namely: the desire to prove that their land is not insensible to the glory which springs from numbering among its sons those whose success becomes the heritage of mankind. (Collins 472)

The first president was Dr. J.W. Dawson of McGill and the vice-president the Honorable P.J.O. Chauveau, one of the most distinguished men of letters in Quebec. The Society was divided into four sections, each with its own president and vice-president, namely, French literature; English literature; mathematical, physical and chemical sciences; and geological and biological sciences. The esteem with which Canadian literature was held at the time may be gathered from the colonial titles of the first two sections.

The atmosphere that surrounded the second annual meeting in May 1883 was much calmer and the Society was hailed as a noble addition to Canada's growing intellectual and cultural life (*Citizen*, March 25, 1883, p. 4). It was the last meeting of the Society over which Lorne presided, and he

made special efforts to give the members a royal welcome, as
the *Canadian Illustrated News* noted: "... on the second day a
grand reception (was held) in the presence of His Excellency
the Governor-General and Her Royal Highness the Princess
Louise ... On the third day the members ... were entertained
at luncheon by His Excellency, and received at a garden party
by the Princess Louise" (June 2, 1883, p. 338).

Since the Lornes's time the Royal Society has become a
respected and non-controversial part of the cultural life of
Canada. With the establishment of other literary and scientific awards such as the Governor General's medals, and the
Order of Canada, the Society has become one among many
ways in which the talents of distinguished Canadians are recognized. It now holds meetings in conjunction with the Con-
gress of the Social Sciences and Humanities (formerly the
Learned Societies) of Canada's universities, and invites members of these societies to take part in its deliberations.

Many addresses and tributes were made to the Lornes
prior to their departure from Canada in late October 1883.
Several were made when Lorne convened both Houses of Parliament in the Senate Chamber on May 25 to prorogue that
session and to bid farewell to the many members he had come
to know. John A. Macdonald's address was among the more
restrained and straightforward. He lauded the contribution of
the Lornes to the cultural life of Canada while stressing his
belief in the imperial presence:

> The warm personal interest which your Excellency has
> taken in everything calculated to stimulate and encourage
> intellectual energy amongst us, and to advance science and
> art, will long be gratefully remembered. The success of
> your Excellency's efforts has fortified us in the belief that a
> full development of our national life is perfectly consistent
> with the closest and most perfect connection with the
> Empire. (Collins 486)

Frederick Dixon, who had written the *Masque of Welcome* for
the Lornes on their arrival, and had become their close friend,

penned some lines of farewell. Neither these nor any other he wrote won him a place in the canon of Canadian literature, nor membership in the Royal Society, yet they represented the strength of his and of many other Canadians' feelings for the vice-regal couple. The last three of the eleven stanzas are worth quoting:

> No wasted years were these you spent
> We know your rule has made us glad,
> No word you ever spoke but had
> Some kindly aim, some wise intent.
> And you, our Princess, wise as good,
> We hold you dear for all your worth,
> And heart unspoiled by pride of birth,
> And all your grace of womanhood.
> We ever hold you, all will tell,
> True hearted and unselfish friends;
> And Canada this message sends
> "God speed your lives," and so farewell. (Collins 335)

Annie Howells Fréchette was closer to the mark in her assessment of the Lornes's legacy in her article which had appeared two years previously. Looking both ahead and behind she concluded:

> Two years is a short time, but it has been long enough to establish upon a substantial foundation a national academy of arts and several art schools in Canada, and what is, perhaps, still more to the point, to implant a respect for mental superiority in all departments. Like all people who are true to their tastes, and who are happy enough to have the means, they have opened and smoothed ways in which to advance those who are less fortunately placed. They have sent young artists abroad, generously patronized those already before the public, and fostered education in many ways. With this kindly spirit and good work the present Governor-General and his wife will have marked their stay in Canada with a characteristic influence which will be felt for many years to come. (Fréchette 223)

That influence is still felt over a hundred years after the Lornes sailed from Canada's shores. It might have been greater had Louise been in Canada for more of her husband's tenure and had shown as much enthusiasm for Canadian life as Lorne did. But both of them showed a respect for the cultural life of Canada that made the young nation proud of its accomplishments thus far.

Works Cited

Alsop, Susan Mary. *Lady Sackville*. London: Weidenfeld & Nicolson, 1978.

Balfour, Frances. *Ne Obliviscaris/Dinna Forget*. Vol. 1. London: Hodder & Stoughton, 1930.

Canadian Illustrated News (Montreal).

Collins, J.E. *Canada under the Administration of Lord Lorne*. Toronto: Rose, 1884.

Duff, David. *The Life Story of Her Royal Highness Princess Louise, Duchess of Argyll*. London: Stanley Paul, 1940.

Epton, Nina. *Victoria and Her Daughters*. London: Weidenfeld & Nicolson, 1972.

Fréchette, Annie Howells. "Life at Rideau Hall." *Harper's New Monthly Magazine*. Vol. 63, no. 374 (July 1881): 213-23.

The Globe (Toronto).

Gwyn, Sandra. *The Private Capital*. Toronto: McClelland & Stewart, 1984.

Hall, Janet. *The Diary of Janet Hall, 1876-1882*. Ed. Kobus de Boer. Amsterdam: Vrije Universiteit, 1983.

Hnatyshyn, Gerda, and Paulette Lachapelle-Bélisle. *Rideau Hall: Canada's Living Heritage*. Vanier, Ont.: Friends of Rideau Hall, 1994.

Kallman, Helmut. *A History of Music in Canada*. Toronto: University of Toronto Press, 1987.

Lorne Papers. *Diary and Engagement Book*. National Archives of Canada, RG7, G18, vol. 115. Cited as *Lorne Diary*.

MacNutt, W. Stewart. *Days of Lorne*. Fredericton: Brunswick Press, 1955.

NAC (National Archives of Canada. "Programme. Theatricals at Government House, March 1879." MG28, I139, vol. 8).

The Ottawa Citizen.

Stamp, Robert M. *Royal Rebels: Princess Louise & the Marquis of Lorne*. Toronto & Oxford: Dundurn Press, 1988.

Wilde, Oscar. *The Letters of Oscar Wilde*. Ed. Rupert Hart-Davis. London: Rupert Hart-Davis, 1962.

Lord Lansdowne.
Photo by W.J. Topley (NAC PA-026730)

Chapter 4

Lover of Art and Sport:
Lord Lansdowne, 1883-1888

Henry Charles Keith Petty-Fitzmaurice, the fifth Marquess of
Lansdowne, succeeded Lord Lorne as Governor General in
1883. He had not been Queen Victoria's first choice; having
just had a son-in-law as Governor General and a daughter as
first lady, she had suggested her son, and Princess Louise's
favourite brother, Prince Leopold as the next Governor General when the Colonial Secretary, Lord Derby, proposed Lansdowne. When Derby re-submitted Lansdowne's name she
concurred.

Lansdowne was a man of great political skill and tact, and
proved to be successful in Canada. Sir John A. Macdonald,
who was Prime Minister throughout Lansdowne's term of
office, had very cordial relations with him and declared Lansdowne to be "the ablest governor under whom I have served,
with possibly the exception of Lord Lisgar (1868-1872)"
(Wallace 436). It should be noted that Macdonald had not
worked with Dufferin, since he was out of office all the years
that Dufferin was Governor General.

Lansdowne's background and education had prepared
him for the political responsibilities of the Queen's representative in Canada and for giving leadership in cultural affairs,
especially in the realm of art. He was born in Lansdowne
House in Berkeley Square, London on January 14, 1845. In
1866 he inherited the Adam palace of this renowned house
with its 200 or so paintings; with such an inheritance he maintained a lively interest and appreciation of art throughout his
life, even though he had to sell some of the paintings from
time to time to pay the £300,000 in debts he also inherited.

He was educated first at a private school in Reading, and
then at Eton, whence he was removed in his final year so that

he could prepare more seriously for Oxford and avoid the sports and other distractions that his tutor feared would inhibit his education. In spite of the tutor's efforts, outdoor sport—especially fishing and hunting—remained a lifelong indulgence for Lansdowne and often gave him solace and relaxation in Canada as well as Britain in the midst of the political pressures he faced. At Oxford he came under the tutelage of Jowett, the famous Master of Balliol College, but in spite of the latter's encouragement and high opinion of him, he received no better than a second class in "literae humaniores" when he left in 1867.

By that time he had succeeded to the title of the fifth Marquess of Lansdowne after his father's death in 1866. He thus found himself in possession of huge estates and huge debts at the age of twenty-one. While striving to pay off these debts, he took his seat in the House of Lords and began his political career first as a junior lord of the Treasury (1868-1872) and then as Under Secretary of State for War (1872-1874) and Under Secretary of State for India (1880). On leaving Canada he assumed the post of Viceroy of India (1893-1898) and then the Secretaryship of the two sensitive portfolios of the War Office (1895-1900) and the Foreign Office (1900-1905). Later he became the Conservative leader in the House of Lords (1906-1916) and served as Minister without Portfolio in the Coalition Government of 1915-1916.

Lansdowne was married in Westminster Abbey in 1869 to Maud Evelyn Hamilton, seventh and youngest daughter of the first Duke of Abercorn. They had two sons and two daughters, all of whom came to Canada with them. The younger son was killed in action in France in October 1914; Lansdowne's grandson, the seventh Marquess, was killed in action in Italy in August 1944.

While Lansdowne's biographers describe him as a devoted family man and a loving husband, he had a special love for his mother reminiscent of the affection that Lord Dufferin expressed for his mother, Helen Selina Sheridan. This is seen mainly in his letters to his mother which are quoted at length in his official biography by Lord Newton. On his wedding day he wrote her from his home of Bowood in Calne, Wiltshire:

> I shall be very happy here, and no one has more to make him so, but I shall miss you and think of you and wish for the day when you will come—for I know you will. Good-bye, dear dear Mother. I have done so little to repay all your love to me that I sometimes think that you must be sick of me, and think that there is nothing left in me which is not hard and ungrateful. Try and believe that I am not all bad and love me in spite of my unkindness. (Newton 16)

The same feelings of separation and guilt were expressed when Lansdowne accepted the post of Governor General of Canada. He wrote his mother two letters prior to his departure; one was from Bowood on May 18, 1883:

> There is nothing for it now but to look at the matter with all the courage you can command. I am sure that you will do so, and that at any rate you will try to forgive me for having acted on my own judgment and in the teeth of yours.

The other was written from Dublin on July 26, 1883:

> The nearer I find myself to the inevitable moment when the final separation must come, the more I feel how hard it will be to bear the break of so many loved associations. I know, too, how this thought is present to your mind, and I am worried by the consciousness that you think I have brought all this anxiety upon you gratuitously. You must try to forgive me and to believe that I have done what I thought right. I sometimes fancy you do not realize how much it costs me to turn my back upon so much that I am devoted to. (Newton 25)

Before leaving Canada to take up his appointment as Viceroy of India he wrote the following paragraphs in another remarkable letter to his mother dated February 8, 1888:

Lady Lansdowne.
(NAC PA-025641)

I am almost afraid that before this letter reaches you, you may have heard from others the news which I have to tell—that I am to be Dufferin's successor in India. I can imagine to myself the effort which it would have cost me to say this to you, if I had been at home. I can almost picture to myself your reproachful face and your dismay at the step which I have taken ... I can think of nothing but your sorrow and disappointment, and of the demolition of the hopes and expectations which we have both been nursing for so long ...

I need not tell you what a blow it is to me to feel that instead of coming back for good next year—instead of dropping back into my place amongst you all—I am to begin another term of banishment—but I have made up my mind to face it, and if I could only believe that you would forgive me, I would face it with a comparatively light heart ...

And now I must end this wretched letter. I know you will think me very heartless and ungrateful for all your love and kindness, and I have been oppressed with this conviction ever since I saw what was coming. (Newton 50-2)

While these excerpts emphasize the keen sensitivity of Lansdowne, if not his excessive attachment to his mother, the feelings they express do not seem to have come between him and his wife, who were praised as a model pair. What the letters do show is the emotional side of a man who was always proper and even passive in his public life. The impression one gets from photographs and from letters to public figures is that Lansdowne always said and did the right thing with little emotional expression. Perhaps we should rejoice to see this other side of him. It may well explain his life-long preoccupation with art and his fostering it whenever he could. When his mother died in 1895 at her home Meikleour House in Perthshire, he inherited her property as well.

One of the reasons that induced Lansdowne to accept the Governor Generalship of Canada was the possibility of paying off some of his debts. In this connection it is interesting to note the extent of his property when he was appointed in

1883. He was the fourth largest landowner in the United Kingdom, and the sixteenth in the amount of money his lands brought in. This is duly noted in Cokayne's *Complete Peerage* at the end of the entry on the Lansdownes:

> Family Estates.—These, in 1883, consisted of about 11,000 acres in England (worth about £21,000 a year), about 122,000 acres in Ireland (worth about £32,000 a year), and about 10,000 acres in Scotland (worth about £9,000 a year), which last belonged to the Dowager Marchioness. The amount in detail was 11,145 acres in Wilts and 4 in Hants; also 94,983 acres in co. Kerry, 12,995 in co. Meath, 8,980 in Limerick, and 617 in King's County; also 9,070 acres in Perthshire and 1,348 in Kinross-shire. Total (in the three kingdoms), 142,916 acres, worth £62,025 a year. (Cokayne 443)

One of the motivating factors for his accepting the appointment to India was again the prospect of paying off his debts.

The Lansdowne years in Canada were marked by some important events for the country but presented little challenge and no crisis for the Governor General. The North West Rebellion and the execution of Louis Riel took place in 1885; the Canadian Pacific Railway was completed the following year—ahead of schedule, partly because of the support of Lansdowne; there were disputes and negotiations with the United States over the Atlantic fisheries; steps were taken towards bringing Newfoundland into the Canadian confederation; and there was even some discussion of a commercial union with the United States, to which Lansdowne was opposed. These were good years for Canada, and when Lansdowne left in May 1888 he said they "had been upon the whole years of peaceful progress during which the country had progressed in industry, education, and art, as well as in all the conditions essential to the well-being of a great and prosperous community" (Newton 53).

Lansdowne's perception of the tranquillity of those years shows that he did not always appreciate the complexity of

Arch of Welcome for Lord Lansdowne.
(NAC PA-027104)

Canada and especially the effects of the Riel rebellion on the country. He could at times be aloof and simplistic in his analysis of what was of vital importance to Canadians. This is seen in his statements about the uprising in a letter from Rideau Hall to his mother dated March 25, 1885:

> We have got a disagreeable little outbreak among the half-breeds in the North-West and there may be some trouble before it is put down. The rebels are led by Riel, whose name you will remember in connection with the rising in 1870 and who ought then to have been shot if he had his deserts. (Newton 32)

Of more immediate concern to Lansdowne was an incident which took place in Toronto in 1887 when he went there to celebrate Queen Victoria's golden jubilee. Two Irish nationalists, William O'Brien, M.P., and a Mr. Kilbride were sent to Canada to discredit Lansdowne and drive him out of the country because of his land holdings in Ireland and his alleged unjust dealings with his Irish tenants. They were encouraged by the Irish Land League, which had been organized to uphold the claims of tenants. But their arrival in Toronto brought them little sympathy, and their public addresses served instead to evoke a demonstration of loyalty for Lansdowne. In Toronto Lansdowne was protected by the Queen's Own Rifles, while O'Brien barely escaped with his life. The tact with which Lansdowne handled the provocation by largely ignoring it showed his own political and social finesse. On his return to Ottawa he was greeted by huge crowds at the railway station and praised at an overflowing reception in his honour. He wrote of these events from the capital:

> The people of Canada have supported me well and nothing could have exceeded the enthusiasm with which we were received at Toronto and then on our return to this place. I have every reason to feel grateful to Mr. O'Brien whose visit has awakened a great deal of loyalty which might have remained latent. (NAC 5)

Skating at Rideau Hall in Lansdowne's time.
(NAC PA-033915)

Two days later he wrote to Sir Henry Holland of his great reception in Ottawa: "On our return here the whole city turned out to welcome us, the streets were decorated and altogether we were given a reception such as I am told no Governor General ever before experienced" (NAC 1).

Many of his sporting and artistic interests Lansdowne was able to indulge in Canada. To their summer residence near the Citadel in Quebec City the Lansdownes brought furnishings and paintings from Bowood. This house they called New Derreen after Lansdowne's favourite residence near Kenmare, County Kerry, Ireland. At this cottage on the Cascapédia River he was able to enjoy his favourite pastime of fishing. He wrote many letters home telling of the wonderful catches they made. Dudley Barker describes the splendour of that indulgence:

> The fishing ... was first rate. The Governor-General had, ex officio, the use of the Cascapédia River, perhaps the finest salmon stream in the world. Lansdowne built a wooden bungalow there, named it New Derreen, and in four mid-summer seasons of some six weeks each, using fly alone, he and his friends killed 1,245 salmon averaging 24 pounds. Lansdowne reckoned that he never fished better than in Canada. (Barker 147)

In Ottawa the Lansdownes' favourite sport was ice-skating. They embraced this as enthusiastically as they embraced Canada itself, and their two daughters became quite expert at it. Lord Frederic Hamilton, brother of Lady Lansdowne, visited Ottawa on several occasions when the Lansdownes were at Rideau Hall, and he described the skill of the vice-regal family on skates:

> From skating daily, most of the Government House party became very expert, and could perform every kind of trick upon skates. Lord and Lady Lansdowne and their two daughters, now Duchess of Devonshire and Lady Osborne Beauclerk, could execute the most complicated Quadrilles

and Lancers on skates, and could do the most elaborate figures. (Hamilton 247)

Several extant photographs of the Lansdownes in Ottawa show them on the ice rink at Rideau Hall. Once a week they were joined by many citizens of the capital who skated to the strains of a military band and were able to warm themselves by the stove in the ice-palace built for the band so that their brass instruments could be thawed. Lansdowne gave two evening skating and tobogganing parties each year, and Hamilton tells us, "He termed these gatherings his 'Arctic Cremornes,' after the then recently defunct gardens in London, and the parties were wonderfully picturesque" (Hamilton 256). Lansdowne also attended the elaborate Montreal Winter Carnival for which he was loaned the home of a hospitable sugar magnate. This festival included a fancy-dress skating fête in the large, covered Victoria Rink. The Lansdownes took part in style:

> Previous Governors General had, in opening the fête, shuffled shamefacedly down the centre of the rink in overshoes and fur coats to the dais, but Lord and Lady Lansdowne, being both expert skaters, determined to do the thing in proper Carnival style, and arrived in fancy dress, he in black as a Duke of Brunswick, and she as Mary Queen of Scots, attended by her two boys, then twelve and fourteen years old, as pages, resplendent in crimson tights and crimson velvet. The band struck up "God Save the Queen," and down the cleared space in the centre skimmed, hand-in-hand, the Duke of Brunswick and Mary Queen of Scots, with the two pages carrying her train, all four executing a "Dutch roll" in the most workmanlike manner. It was really a very effective entrance, and was immensely appreciated by the crowd of skaters present. (Hamilton 263-4)

In spite of the fact that Lansdowne accepted the Governor Generalship of Canada partly for financial reasons he did entertain lavishly. Gwen Neuendorf attests to this in her study of the British Dominions. Referring to Lord Dufferin's entertainments she writes:

> Subsequent Governors General were less lavish and Lans-
> downe alone afterwards is remarkable for the sumptuous-
> ness of his hospitality, a strange fact in view of his assum-
> ing the position because he was in financial difficulties
> through the refusal of his Irish tenants to pay their rents.
> (Neuendorf 29)

Lansdowne did not look forward to all of his entertainments with the same enthusiasm that greeted the skating parties. In a letter to his mother on January 18, 1884 he wrote:
"To-morrow we have a Drawing Room, an awful ceremony,
but thank heavens there is no kissing. I say this without dis-
respect to some of the fair Canadians" (Newton 29). Still he
must have enjoyed many of them if his reaction to his Ottawa
guests was the same as that of his brother-in-law:

> The Ottawa of the "eighties" was an attractive little place,
> and Ottawa Society was very pleasant. There was then a
> note of unaffected simplicity about everything that was
> most engaging, and the people were perfectly natural and
> free from pretence. The majority of them were Civil ser-
> vants of limited means and as everybody knew what their
> neighbours' incomes were, there was no occasion for make-
> believe. The same note of simplicity ran through all amuse-
> ments and entertaining, and I think that it constituted the
> charm of the place. (Hamilton 245)

Although Lansdowne did not do particularly well as a student, he took from his tutors in Eton and Oxford an enduring
love of the Greek and Latin classics. It is not unusual to read
in his letters an off-handed quotation or phrase in these languages. He once wrote to Mr. Choate, the American ambassador in London, apologizing for using a quotation from Horace
on the ground "that an imperfect knowledge of Horace is
always supposed to be the only intellectual equipment of an
Eton boy" (Newton 486). Speaking of Lansdowne's reticence

and privacy, Barker reveals something as well of his familiarity with the classics:

> Only with an old friend might he occasionally proceed to the intimacy of a discussion of some lines of an Horatian ode, or of the problems posed by particular Greek verses, of which the metrical translation into English was one of his private relaxations. (Barker 139)

In later life, confined by ill health and vilified by many for the Peace Letter he wrote in 1916 recommending a negotiated peace with Germany, he often took refuge in the harmony and peace afforded by the ancient poets. Newton quotes a letter to a Mr. F.W. Hurst on a difficult passage in an ode of Horace (I. 23, 2nd stanza):

> I would allow the text to stand. It is not easy to translate, but I do not think it very difficult to discern what Horace had in his mind.
>
> "Veris adventus" means, I think, "the first breath of spring." "Inhorruit" is dreadfully difficult to render into English. There is, somewhere or other—I think in Virgil—a line in which the words "Inhorruit unda tenebris" appear. The best translation I can suggest is: "Whether, at the first breath of spring, a shudder passes over the fluttering leaves, or whether a green lizard pushes the briars aside," or "shows itself among the briars." The image seems to me to be perfectly conceived, and I do not think Bentley's reading would improve the picture. (Newton 486)

There is evidence here of a fine critical mind. Newton also cites an interesting letter in which Lansdowne confessed to his private indulgence in translating the Greek classics. To Mr. C.W. James, another friend, Lansdowne wrote:

> That was indeed an unguarded moment when I confessed that I had once tried to translate the lament of Moschus over his herbaceous border. I never dreamed that I should be called upon to "deliver the goods," and I am

reluctant to deliver them now; but I cannot resist your appeal, so here they are—for your eyes only.

These attempts only prove to those who make them how hopeless it is to translate the super-poetry of these old writers. This is a weak rendering, which I could criticise as mercilessly as you will:

Alas! Alas! low are the mallows laid.
The fresh green parsley and the anise fade;
    The garden's joy is sere.
Yet for all these is a new life in store,
Still their sap rises as it rose before,
    And waits the coming year.
But for us men, so strong, so brave, so wise,
When once pale death has sealed our mortal eyes,
    There is no second birth.
We sleep the sound sleep which no dawn may break,
The long, long sleep from which not one may wake,
    Within the hollow earth. (Newton 486-7)

From this translation we see that Lansdowne was much too hard on himself for the quality of his translation. In fact, his knowledge of the classics was one of the factors that induced Oxford University to offer him the Chancellorship of his alma mater on two occasions—once on the death of Lord Salisbury in 1903 and again on the death of Lord Goschen in 1907. Both offers he declined, as well as an invitation to be Chancellor of Bristol University.

In his letters it was not unusual for Lansdowne to toss off a Latin or Greek phrase as in his invitation to Arthur Balfour to visit him at his beloved Derreen in County Kerry. Newton refers to the letter: "... he describes it as resembling Ithaca: ut neque planis porrectus spatiis, nec multae prodigue herbae" (Newton 127). In Ottawa, writing to Dr. Dawson, a clergyman who had written him a Reception Ode for the welcome by the citizens of the capital on Lansdowne's return from Toronto after O'Brien's attempts to discredit him, he paid tribute to his family's sense of public duty when he said: "Of their deeds I may say emphatically 'viscera nostra voco'; it is none the less pleasant to find that they are not forgotten" (NAC 1). Lansdowne's sense of language is seen in his carefully written letters from Canada to the nobility, diplomats, politicians, churchmen, artists, family and friends. It is further seen in his comments on a translation of the French-Canadian poet Louis Fréchette by G.W. Wicksteed:

> I have read your translation of Fréchette's fine lines. It has the greatest merit which a translation can have. I mean about fidelity to the original. I can appreciate your success in this respect because I have often been struck with the great difficulty of finding a real English equivalent for a French expression and vice-versa.
>
> I think I have already told you how much I liked the "Jubilate" which has the right sort of ring about it for a National hymn. (NAC 1)

This awareness of what is required in a good translation shows why some of his own translations from Greek or Latin were so effective.

Going beyond the finer points of translation Lansdowne recognized the importance of communication between the two major language groups in Canada when he commended Wicksteed's translations in another letter: "I am much obliged for your kindness in sending me a copy of your rendering of 'Les Ecommunies' [?]. You are doing good service when you make such masterpieces of French-Canadian work the common property of both races" (NAC 1).

There is little evidence that Lansdowne had a serious interest in music, but he was supportive of musicians during his time in Canada, and attended musical performances on several occasions. One of these was on May 14, 1888, ten days before their final departure from Ottawa, when he and Lady Lansdowne attended a musical and dramatic program at the Opera House in aid of the Good Shepherd's Convent. The evening consisted of musical selections, the one-act farce *Betsy Baker* (the same play performed under the Lornes at Rideau Hall in 1881), and the operetta *Les Revenants Bretons*, which was described as "sparkling and tuneful, and the by-play was most appropriate to all concerned" (*Ottawa Citizen*, May 15, 1888, p. 1).

Responding to one petition from the Canadian Society of Musicians, founded in 1885, Lansdowne agreed to be its patron, and shortly afterwards received another petition requesting him to ask Her Majesty to confer on it the name and title of the Royal Canadian Society of Musicians. For some reason this was not supported by the Ontario government, and the prefix was never given to this short-lived society. Had it been a society of artists applying to Lansdowne for the privilege he might have worked more effectively for them. In any case, this did not prevent musicians from courting the Lansdownes' favour. In honour of both of them the Canadian composer W.E. Clarke wrote a *Lansdowne Waltz* in 1883, and John C. Bonner, Hand Master of the Governor General's Foot Guards, dedicated to him *The Queen's Jubilee Polka* in 1887.

A more serious involvement in the arts in Canada was Lansdowne's interest in painting. Mention has already been made of the large collection of paintings he inherited—Rembrandts, Reynoldses, Gainsboroughs, Hogarths and Romneys. In England this involvement was recognized by the fact that he was appointed a trustee of the National Gallery in 1894; one of his great regrets when he became ill with rheumatic fever in 1919 was that he was unable to attend the meetings of the Gallery, "in whose work he took much practical interest" (Newton 485). He had even brought some of his paintings—including some Romneys and Gainsboroughs—as well as some furniture and china to Canada. His brother-in-law commented on the effect of the Canadian winter on the furniture and paintings:

> The intense dryness of the Canadian winter climate, especially in houses where furnace-heat intensifies the dryness, produces some unexpected results. My brother-in-law had brought out a number of old pieces of French inlaid furniture. The excessive dryness forced out some of the inlaid marqueterie of these pieces, and upon their return to

Europe they had to undergo a long and expensive course of treatment. Some fine Romneys and Gainsboroughs also required the picture-restorer's attentions before they could return to their Wiltshire home after a five years' sojourn in the dry air of Canada. (Hamilton 243)

On the practical side Lansdowne showed great interest in and gave constant support to the Royal Canadian Academy of Art founded by his predecessor. This is seen in the ongoing correspondence he maintained in Canada with Lucius R. O'Brien, the first president of the Academy, who held the position throughout Lansdowne's term in Canada. There is a familiarity and warmth and awareness in Lansdowne's letters that show how much art meant to him and how anxious he was for it to take a prominent place in the lives of Canadians. When the RCAA was to meet in Ottawa in 1886, Lansdowne wrote to O'Brien: "My inclination is to give a dinner on the evening of the 2nd and to invite all the academicians who may be in the capital" (NAC 2). Earlier he had offered to donate $250.00 a year to the Academy for the purchase of "a worthy object" (NAC 2). When the Academy decided to house itself in a new building in 1887, Lansdowne increased his donation: "I shall be glad to contribute toward the expense which will be incurred and I will therefore increase my subscription for this year to a total of $500.00" (NAC 2). It is interesting to note that over a hundred years later the RCAA still exists, and in 1987 moved into a newly renovated building, Heritage House, in Toronto.

Lansdowne's appreciation of art and of the exchange necessary to foster the arts in a bi-cultural nation like Canada was shown in an amazingly blunt letter in which he scorned the suggestion of Lord Lorne that the Academy be reorganized into French and English sections along the lines of the Royal Society, likewise founded by Lorne. Again he wrote to O'Brien, this time from his retreat on the Cascapédia River, where the beauty and tranquillity he loved so much may have contributed to the openness of his language:

The analogy which he founds upon the constitution of the
Royal Society is a misleading one. Where two languages are
current in the same country each language will have its
own literature. It was decided, and I think wisely, to create
French and English sections representative of French and
English Canadian Letters and Science. The Fine Arts on
the other hand speak to us in a language which is current
everywhere, and although different races develop different
Schools the works which these produce appeal to and are
intelligible by the whole civilized community. (NAC 1)

Lansdowne's admiration for O'Brien's work is seen in several letters, especially as Lansdowne's term was coming to a
close in 1888. In February of that year O'Brien sent the Governor General some of his drawings and received the following reply and invitation: "I am quite delighted with the drawings some of which I like better than any of yours which I
have yet seen and that is saying a good deal. Will you come
here to luncheon tomorrow and tell us something about them
and the affairs of the Academy" (NAC 1). The very last date
in Lansdowne's letter books from Canada contains a letter to
O'Brien which gives further evidence of his support for art in
Canada and of his affection and respect for the President of
the Academy:

My thanks for your kind words in regard to the interest
which I have taken in the Royal Academy. It will give me
great pleasure if you find time occasionally to let me know
how you are getting on ...
We are overwhelmed with business, and you must
excuse me for using an amanuensis. (NAC 1)

One concrete form which Lansdowne's support of Canadian
artists took was the Colonial and Indian Exhibition in London
in the fall of 1886. He was concerned with Canada's participation before, during and after the event. In fact the one journey he made to England during his tenure in Ottawa was at
that time, and he probably took the occasion of the exhibition

to visit his beloved mother and homes. While Canadian participation was being planned he was in correspondence with O'Brien and insisted that it be of high quality. When he was in England during the exhibition he wrote several letters praising the Canadian exhibits and soliciting support for them from British sources. His letter to Sir Hector Langevin shows an understandable prejudice in favour of the Canadian entries: "I was delighted with the exhibition. The Canadian Courts are a long way ahead of the rest. They are better filled and with 'Exhibits' representative of a civilization far more advanced than that of our competitors" (NAC 2).

A less confident tone appeared in the letters in which he sought support from British critics, two of whom he wrote from Bowood, his estate in Wiltshire. He reminded Sir Frederick Leighton, "The beginnings of art in a young country are beset by very many difficulties and our RCAA founded by Lorne and Princess Louise has to struggle for existence" (NAC 2). When Leighton recommended that the painter J.C. Hodgson write the report that the Governor General wanted on the paintings, Lansdowne appealed to Hodgson a week later: "Will you under these circumstances permit me to throw myself and the cause of art in Canada upon your indulgence and to express a hope that you will be persuaded to do us this act of kindness which will be very deeply appreciated" (NAC 2). In due course Hodgson produced a favourable report, and the Lansdowne correspondence on it, especially with O'Brien, continued when he was back in Canada where he confided:

> I send you a copy of Mr. Hodgson's report which will interest you. The Blue Book of which it forms a part has not yet been presented to Parliament. Be good enough therefore to regard the communication of Mr. Hodgson's report as strictly confidential. You will see that he shows much appreciation of your work. (NAC 1)

So successful was this exhibition at Albert Hall that a permanent Colonial and Indian exhibition was planned, and

Lansdowne was so enthusiastic about Canadian participation that he did not hesitate to write a mildly censorious letter to the Prime Minister, Sir John A. Macdonald, when a misunderstanding over it arose: "I was under the impression that by some means or other it had been intimated that we would give £20,000. We must I think send a formal answer as soon as possible or Her Royal Highness will fall foul of us" (NAC 2). I have not discovered the effect on Sir John A. of this suggestion that Queen Victoria would not be amused.

Back in Canada Lansdowne continued his interest in Canadian art and showed foresight in recommending the purchase of paintings not only for their artistic merit but also for their witness to important events in Canadian history. This is what he urged in another letter to Langevin concerning a painting of Rutherford entitled *The Surrender of Poundmaker*, which was a record of the Riel rebellion:

> The picture is certainly not without faults from a strictly artistic point of view, although it is a wonderfully creditable performance for a man whose business is to use the sword rather than the brush ... (there is) no other picture commemorative of the rebellion. (NAC 1)

Finally, mention should be made of Lansdowne's interest in what he calls "curios," native Indian artefacts that he received from time to time from Canadian friends. He is grateful to a W. Pocklington of McLeod in the North West Territories for sending "the Indian spoils," but is even more appreciative of the memento of a hunt that accompanied them: "Your gift of a mountain sheep's head is however a much greater prize, and I am extremely obliged to you for your kind thought of sending it. These heads are becoming very hard to get and you may depend upon yours being given a good place on my walls" (NAC 2). Lansdowne was as much a lover of the hunt as he was a lover of art. In appreciation to Pocklington he sent a photograph of himself along with $25.00 for the curios.

Lansdowne was not an avid playgoer although there are records of theatricals at Rideau Hall and of his attending plays in Ottawa. Reference has already been made to his presence at the Opera House for *Betsy Baker* and an operetta one week before his departure from the capital. While he does not speak of plays at Rideau Hall in his letters and left no diary with a record of what was presented there, we get some idea of the rather formal atmosphere that existed on these occasions from the writings of Sara Jeannette Duncan, the journalist-novelist who spent about four months in Ottawa covering Parliament Hill for the *Montreal Star* twice a week with a column entitled "Bric-a-Brac" under the pseudonym Garth Grafton, and a weekly Ottawa letter for *The Week*. In one of her columns she described the theatrical evenings at Rideau Hall without speaking of the plays themselves, so that we are not certain if she had actually attended any of them when the column was written. Her tentative "I believe" in the passage which follows reinforces this uncertainty even as she gives us an insider's view of these dinner theatricals. She writes:

> Most exclusive among the entertainments that have at all a general character are the musical and theatrical parties, which are not usually given, I believe, during the session when Their Excellencies' hospitalities consist chiefly of a succession of official dinner-parties. Guests are bidden to these at half-past seven and usually depart pretty promptly at ten, a very few minutes being spent in the drawing-room after dinner ... Dinner-parties at Rideau, in so far as resident Ottawa society is concerned, are usually very formally and strictly regulated. Official position rules. Young ladies, unless they are at the head of the fathers' households, are not asked, nor are widows as a rule, or other irresponsible and disconnected individuals, whatever their social position in Ottawa, who are without the claim constituted by a husband's official position. (*Montreal Star*, March 12, 1888, p. 2)

Although Duncan complains that unaccompanied young ladies and widows were not asked, we see her own name unaccompanied in the list of guests at the last ball given by the Lansdownes before their departure from Ottawa (*Ottawa Citizen*, May 3, 1888, p. 4). Redney, as Duncan was affectionately called, got to know the Lansdownes and met them often after they left Rideau Hall.

Marian Fowler describes the atmosphere in which Duncan and the other guests attended the plays:

> Once inside the viceregal mansion, there was a crush in the hall, then a mad scramble for seats as soon as the doors of the dining-room opened. Everyone wanted to sit directly behind the sofa reserved for the Lansdownes and their party; somehow, Redney always managed it. However she found herself stifling a yawn more and more frequently at these predictable affairs. (Fowler 131)

Redney had apparently got herself invited since her earlier column. The atmosphere was less charged than during the dramas put on by the Dufferins ten years previously. The change was no doubt the result of very different attitudes towards the theatre on the part of the Dufferins and the Lansdownes. In both cases the evenings consisted of a play or plays and then a dinner. For the Dufferins the emphasis was on the play followed by a dinner; for the Lansdownes it was on dinner preceded by a play.

If Lansdowne did not show great enthusiasm for the theatre, there is evidence of his encouraging at least one dramatist who approached him, much as he encouraged painters. The dramatist was Charles Mair, who sent the Governor General a copy of his ponderous play *Tecumseh*. Lansdowne wrote him a polite letter as follows:

> Sir: I have had the honour of receiving from you a handsomely bound copy of your drama *Tecumseh*. You have chosen a subject which lends itself well to such treatment and which deserves commemoration. Without having attempted

to read the play with the attention which it deserves I have already satisfied myself that it contains some vigorously written and striking passages.

Please accept my best thanks, and my assurance that I shall value the book as having been given to me by the author. (NAC 1)

Lansdowne could be as diplomatic when he was writing to a playwright as when writing to a diplomat.

Lansdowne's support for the Royal Society of Canada, another invention of Lord Lorne, was however genuine. He corresponded regularly with John G. Bourinot, the secretary and later president, and acknowledged receiving and reading its reports. He supported its application for funds to the federal government and wrote a letter to announce that its grant was being renewed. He attended its meetings, and in August of his first summer in Canada, 1884, opened a joint meeting in Montreal of the Royal Society and the British Association for the Advancement of Science. This was the first time the British Association had held sessions with another organization. The meeting was no doubt the result of the efforts and prestige of the renowned geologist Sir William Dawson, first president of the Royal Society and Principal of McGill University.

On Lansdowne's departure from Canada in May 1888 to take up the Vice-regency of India after a six-month visit to his mother and his estates, there were many tributes to him. The *Ottawa Citizen* was glowing in its praise:

> Space will not permit us to-day to enlarge on His Lordship's general services to Canada—on his warm interest in Education, particularly Higher Education, in Literature, in the Fine Arts, and in Science; on his efforts to promote among the youth and manhood of the country, healthful out-door Sports and Amusements; and on his sympathetic encouragement of the Volunteer Militia Force. Let it suffice that he has devoted his time and his means to the promotion of all good and deserving works. Socially, his

hospitality has been boundless. (*Ottawa Citizen*, April 14, 1888, p. 4)

Three years after Lansdowne left Canada, historian J.E. Collins wrote:

> Lansdowne possessed in an eminent degree the high traditional qualities of an English gentleman. While in Canada he did honour to the office he filled and left behind him a gracious memory. In appointing him to the Governor-Generalship of India, the Crown fittingly rewarded "a good and faithful servant". (Collins 469)

After Lansdowne's death in 1927 his official biographer paid tribute to his years in Canada:

> During the past half century we have been represented in Canada by many distinguished men, some of whom were remarkable for exceptional personal charm, but it may be confidently stated that not one of them left a more enduring memory of respect and affection amongst the Canadian people than the occupant of this office from 1883 to 1888. (Newton 54)

Closer to our own time and place Carleton University's D.M.L. Farr paid a more sober but not less favourable tribute to Lansdowne's political success in Canada: "Lord Lansdowne maintained dealings with the Macdonald Cabinet which were both competent and harmonious. His tenure of the post entitles him to be described as a model Governor General, whom future holders of the position could profitably emulate" (Farr 56).

The Lansdownes gave a farewell ball at Rideau Hall on May 2, and the Mayor and City of Ottawa gave them a men-only banquet followed by a reception for men and ladies in the elegant Russell Hotel on May 15. At the banquet Lansdowne delivered a long speech reviewing his years in Canada and the progress of the Dominion in that time. With typical hyperbole the *Citizen* described the occasion as "the most brilliant and the most representative social entertainment ever witnessed in Ottawa" (*Citizen*, May 16, 1888, p. 5).

After Canada and India Lansdowne's years in public office were difficult ones—in the War Office and the Foreign Office, followed by the death of his son in the war. His Peace Letter of 1916 and the scorn which resulted came in the last stages of a distinguished political career. The following comments by the less than sympathetic Barker in his chapter on Lansdowne should be read in conjunction with the highly favourable biography by Newton, and the life in the Dictionary of National Biography by Lansdowne's heir and successor:

> Nothing much else happened, except that in his seventy-seventh year the ungrateful Irish burned down his beloved Derreen; and in his eighty-first, although by then he was casting over the river from the insecurity of a donkey-drawn invalid chair, he killed a 21-pound salmon which several sportsmen had previously failed to capture. (Barker 173)

It was on his way to the restored Derreen in 1927 that Lansdowne was struck by an aneurism of the heart and died at his younger daughter's home at Newton Anner, Clonmel, County Tipperary on June 3 at the age of eighty-two.

He was at his prime in Canada and supported the arts and culture with his special skills as a diplomat. Being a private and retiring person he did not often take the lead in fostering Canadian culture, and he was not noted for his interest in the performing arts. But his encouragement of pictorial artists and the Royal Canadian Academy of Art were important for the development of both. The fact that the Academy still exists while other organizations of its time do not attests to the ongoing encouragement given Canadian artists by Lansdowne during the first decade of its existence.

Works Cited

Barker, Dudley. *Prominent Edwardians*. New York: Atheneum, 1969.

Cokayne, George E. *The Complete Peerage, or A History of the House of Lords and All Its Present Members from Earliest Times*. Vol. 7. London: St. Catherine's, 1929.

Collins, J.E. *Canada's Patriot Statesman*. Toronto: Rose, 1891.

Farr, D.M.L. *The Colonial Office and Canada 1867-1887*. Toronto: Univesity of Toronto Press, 1955.

Fowler, Marian. *Redney: A Life of Sara Jeannette Duncan*. Toronto: Anansi, 1983.

Hamilton, Lord Frederic. *The Days Before Yesterday*. London: Hodder & Stoughton, 1931.

The Montreal Star.

NAC 1 (National Archives of Canada, MG27, IB6. Reel A624).

NAC 2 (National Archives of Canada, MG27, IB6. Reel A623).

Neuendorf, Gwen. *Studies in the Evolution of Dominion Status*. London: George Allen & Unwin, 1942.

Newton, Lord, P.C. *Lord Lansdowne: A Biography*. London: Macmillan, 1919.

The Ottawa Citizen.

Wallace, W. Stewart, ed. *The Macmillan Dictionary of Canadian Biography*. Toronto: Macmillan, 1978.

Lord Stanley.
(NAC PA-026736)

Chapter 5

Heir of a Sporting Family, Donor of a Famous Cup: Lord Stanley, 1888-1893

It should not be surprising in examining the life of Frederick Arthur Stanley, 16th Earl of Derby, and Governor General of Canada from 1888 to 1893, to find that his sporting interests were more prominent than his cultural pursuits. Indeed the famous Derby horse race at Epsom Downs got its name from an ancestor, the 12th Earl, and horseracing has been a dominant passion in the lives of most of the recent Earls of Derby with the exception of Edward Henry, the 15th Earl and elder brother of Frederick.

Primary evidence on the early life and interests of the future Governor General is scarce, but two extant letters addressed to him in his youth were prophetic in their emphasis on the role of a military and sporting life in his future. One is from Lord Hardinge dated July 9, 1852, when Stanley was eleven years old and probably thinking of the military career he would embark on after leaving Eton. Hardinge was pleased with Stanley's liking for his Louis Quatorze gun, which had a good range although it was inferior to the long-range Warner gun. The letter also reminded him of a troop review at Woolwich (NRA 1). The other letter was written to the young Stanley from General Sir Harry G. Smith five years later to say he was sending him a milk-white terrier of great tenacity (NRA 2). This bent for things military and sporting continued throughout a life of great tenacity and loyalty to the family and the nation that Stanley loved and served.

The future Governor General was born on January 15, 1841 in St. James's Square, London into the distinguished Lancashire family of the Earls of Derby. He was the younger son among three surviving children of the 14th Earl, who was Prime Minister of Britain three times, in 1852, 1858-1859, and 1866-1868, his last term coinciding with the establishment of Canadian Confederation in 1867. The family's prominence and the grandeur of their country seat of Knowsley, Prescot, near Liverpool, is attested in a biography of the Stanley family published in 1869, the year of the 14th Earl's death:

> Perhaps more royal visits have been made to Knowsley within the last few centuries, than to the seat of any nobleman in England, and, as will be seen from the foregoing sketch, there is no aristocratic family in the country having greater facilities for entertaining royal guests than are possessed by the Earls of Derby. (Pollard 214)

From his father's involvement in poetry and the classics one might have expected that Frederick would have as lively and ongoing an interest in them as his predecessor in Canada, Lord Lansdowne. The 14th Earl had won the Chancellor's prize for Latin verse at Oxford in 1819 at the age of twenty, and continued his involvement with poetry in the publication of *Translations of Poems Ancient and Modern* in 1862, which contained poems from Greek, Latin, French, Italian and German, including Book 1 of the *Iliad*. So successful was the last that the Earl, between terms as Prime Minister, translated into blank verse the remainder of Homer's epic, which was published in two volumes in 1864 to great acclaim. Pollard says of this translation, "If he had never given the world any other proof of his high cultural and literary attainments, his able translation of Homer is sufficient to convince everyone of his elevated intellectual powers" (Pollard 182). Pollard later quotes from an unnamed publication not usually sympathetic to Derby: "Of his intellectual qualities it is unnecessary to speak, as he has long stood in the first rank of English orators. As a scholar he is surpassed by few Englishmen, probably by none who have not made scholarship the whole object of their lives" (Pollard 239). In his life of the Earl, T.E. Kebbel wrote in a similar vein:

> He wrote Latin both in verse and prose with great purity
> and fluency; he has produced one of the best translations
> of the *Iliad* of Homer which our literature can boast, and
> his other translations ... show that he possessed the literary
> faculty in no ordinary degree, and that a great English clas-
> sic may have been lost in him when he devoted himself to
> politics. (Kebbel 182)

In 1865 the Earl awarded a prize to Wellington College,
known as the Earl of Derby's Gift, financed by the profits of
his translation of the *Iliad*. As further evidence of the Earl's
involvement in things cultural, we can read the account of a
speech he delivered in the House of Commons on February
21, 1856 supporting the opening of the British Museum on
Sunday afternoons. He contended, "There need not be any
competition between the Church and the Museum (and the
National Glory)" (Stanley 8).

Members of the Royal Society of Canada were also cog-
nisant of the Earl's translation of the *Iliad*, and referred to it
in glowing terms in an address to his son the Governor General of Canada at the first meeting of the Society over which
Stanley presided:

> We feel that a Society that has the cultivation of literature
> as one of its principal objects has a special claim on Your
> Excellency's attention. All of us remember with the deepest
> interest that your illustrious father, in his youth, won many
> academic honours in the study of the great poets of ancient
> days. In the noted oratorical efforts of his brilliant career,
> he displayed that fire and energy which were characteristic
> of the heroes of the immortal epic he had mastered so well.
> While the political historian will record his triumphs as the
> "Rupert of Debate," men of letters will like best to linger
> on his success in rendering the *Iliad* into matchless English
> verse. (*Semi-Weekly Citizen*, May 9, 1889, p. 4)

These flattering remarks were made at Rideau Hall at a
luncheon given by Stanley to the Royal Society, in which he
always took an interest while he was in Canada.

But poetry was not the 14th Earl's only passion, nor his major one. Horseracing was, and this he passed on to the son who would become Governor General of Canada. It seems, in fact, that poetry was not even his second passion, for Kebbel says:

> Next to racing, Lord Derby's passion was shooting; and though he preserved game very strictly he never heard any complaints about it. He was, indeed, so popular with all classes in his own neighbourhood, that the farmers and peasantry would have endured a great deal rather than interfere with his pleasure. (Kebbel 195)

This interest endures today in the form of a popular safari park at Knowsley maintained by the present Earl of Derby.

The reason for going into the cultural and sporting background of the father of Lord Stanley is to raise the question why, with such a background, he was so interested in the sporting side of his father's life, and hardly interested at all in his cultural pursuits. The answer may explain why he didn't encourage more cultural activity while he was in Canada, and why he did indulge in fishing in the abundant rivers and lakes of his adopted country. A more general reason is given by Disraeli, commenting on the report that Frederick's brother Edward, the 15th Earl, was offered the Greek throne and refused: "(The Stanleys) are not an imaginative race, and I fancy they will prefer Knowsley to the Parthenon and Lancashire to the Attic Plains" (Churchill 11).

One of the reasons for Frederick's not being more involved in cultural activities was that he chose a military career in 1858 after leaving Eton, and became first a Lieutenant and then a Captain in the Grenadier Guards, from which he retired in 1865 to enter politics. The previous year, on May 31, 1864 he had married Lady Constance Villiers, eldest daughter of the 4th Earl of Clarendon. Their marriage was a happy and fruitful one, for they had ten children, eight boys and two girls, born between 1865 and 1878. All but two of them survived to adulthood.

Lady Stanley.
(NAC PA-027153)

Early in their marriage the Stanleys had for their London residence Derby House in St. James's Square, and chose to build a new country residence at the family estate of Wither-slack in Westmoreland, which Stanley's father gave them for a wedding present. This they chose over another of their properties at Bally Kisteen in Ireland.

All accounts attest to the happiness of their family life and to the idyllic days they spent together at Witherslack. Randolph Churchill wrote of the 17th Earl, Stanley's eldest son, "Edward and the other children had an ideal life at Witherslack ... All the family letters and records show that they were a happy family, and that the children were united in love and loyalty to their parents" (Churchill 22). It would be difficult to find higher praise for family life than that paid to the Stanleys on the death of their father: "On Earl Freder-ick's death, King Edward VII paid tribute to 'such a united family,' and the future King George V wrote to his friend, the new Earl, 'I think your family was the happiest and most united one I have ever seen'" (Bagley 207).

This description should be borne in mind when trying to assess the character of Stanley and his contributions to Cana-dian life. We might also remember the opening line of Tol-stoy's *Anna Karenina*, "Happy families are all alike," when we look for distinguishing features in Stanley's life. One problem for the biographer is that Stanley wrote little himself and had little written on him, unlike the Earls his father, his elder brother and his son, who have all been the subjects of sepa-rate biographies.

One of the few estimates of Stanley's character was given by Sett-Smith in his book on the horseracing career of the 17th Earl, Stanley's son. He wrote of the father as "renowned for his shyness but equally for his charm, modesty and habit of never being in a hurry to go to bed" (Sett-Smith 20). The procrastination suggested by Sett-Smith's last comment is confirmed by J.J. Bagley in his recent book on the Earls of Derby in which he explains why Stanley lost the favour of Queen Victoria:

His son, Edward, blamed his father's fall from grace on his ingrained habit of never answering a letter if he could possibly help it. Consequently, the Queen had to bombard Ottawa and Quebec, Stanley's favourite Canadian hideout, with letters and dispatches before she could get a reply from her Governor General. (Bagley 209)

Vincent describes Frederick more bluntly: "He was fat, lethargic, honourable, not too bright, uxorious, without high seriousness, but absolutely straight. He was subject to occasional fits of serious depression, like his brother and father" (Vincent, *Later* 0010).

Putting these assessments together, including the reference to his "favourite Canadian hideout," where he could indulge his love for fishing, we have further insight into Stanley's lack of cultural leadership in Canada. We must remember too the time and energy required in raising and nurturing his large and loving family.

Stanley certainly showed leadership in other ways, both before and during his time as Governor General in Canada. His career in England was marked by a succession of political successes and appointments befitting the son of a Prime Minister. In 1865 he resigned his army commission and was elected successively Conservative Member of Parliament for Preston (1865-1868), Lancashire (North) (1868-1885), and Lancashire (Blackpool) (1885-1886), at which time he was created Baron Stanley of Preston in his own right and took a seat in the House of Lords. He held a number of political appointments before coming to Canada, including civil Lord of the Admiralty (1868), Financial Secretary to the War Office (1874-1877) and of the Treasury (1877-1878), Secretary of State for War (1878-1880) and for the Colonies (1885-1886), where he succeeded his brother, and President of the Board of Trade (1886-1888) until he accepted the post of Governor General.

Throughout these years he looked up to and sought the approval of his brother Edward, who was his senior by fifteen years. We might even say that he lived in the shadow of his brother, and asked for his advice on numerous occasions for both personal and financial reasons. He and his family were to some extent financially dependent on the heir apparent and later Earl, a factor which might also explain Stanley's lack of initiative and leadership in other areas. An example of this is cited by John Vincent in his edition of the diaries of the 15th Earl. He notes that when Stanley was offered the peerage in 1888 he consulted his brother, "in effect seeking permission from the head of the family to take a peerage" (Vincent, *Later* 0072). Although Edward advised him to take the India Office and remain in the House of Commons, Stanley had his own ideas and experience which he followed instead:

> He said he had been over twenty years in the H. of C., was growing weary of it, felt the work harder than he liked, did not feel sure that he agreed with his intended colleagues on many points, disliked Churchill as a leader, and thought he should be more free in the Lords. (Vincent, *Later* 0072)

Still, the financial dependence remained even though Stanley had inherited £125,000 from his father in 1869, had received £80,000 from him earlier, and had minor legacies totalling £50,000-60,000 (Vincent, *Disraeli* 344). By that time he had two sons and a daughter, would have seven more children, and had residences in London and Westmoreland to maintain along with the social obligations of his status. His brother was unmarried until 1870, after he had succeeded to the Earldom, and even then was unlikely to have children by the forty-six-year-old widow Mary Gascoyne-Cecil, who had five children by her deceased husband, the Marquess of Salisbury. The heir apparent was thus Stanley's eldest son, Edward George, and the Stanley family was always aware of their dependence on Uncle Edward.

Yet we are told that Frederick Stanley was never seen at Knowsley, where Edward lived, from 1878-1893, when he unexpectedly succeeded to the Earldom and returned from

Canada to assume the responsibilities that accompanied his inheritance. These years of absence meant that he was out of touch with the substantial collection of paintings at Knowsley, which numbered 479 in a catalogue of Knowsley Hall published in 1875, including works by Rubens, Van Wyk, Gainsborough and Romney (Scharf n.p.). If Frederick had any artistic taste, it was not nourished at Knowsley Hall during those years. He may have had some paintings in his London and Witherslack homes, and he did bring some prints to Canada, as will be noted below.

The sensitivity of the Stanleys to the feelings of the 15th Earl is seen in the choice of Wellington College for their eldest son. He was sent there rather than to Eton, which both his uncle and father had attended, because Edward had been dismissed from Eton, apparently for theft. As the 15th Earl with an unhappy memory, "His whim had to be humoured, for he held the financial purse-strings" (Sett-Smith 18). Still, Edward George enjoyed Wellington College and followed in his father's footsteps by joining the Grenadier Guards after graduation.

The long absence from Knowsley, and whatever effect this had on the artistic awareness of Frederick Stanley, were the result of friction between the wives of the two brothers rather than any long-standing division between Edward and Frederick. The bitterness began, it seems, when Constance, Frederick's wife, who acted as Edward's hostess while he was unmarried and headed the Foreign Office, was replaced by Mary after the latter's marriage to Edward. Bagley says of Constance, "From the beginning she took a dislike to her sister-in-law, and the strained relations between the two ladies led to similar tension between the brothers" (Bagley 206). Vincent speculates on the cause of the rift:

> ... it was something Freddy's wife had said in 1878 that proved unforgivable. We know not what was said, but that something was said, some unbearable slur on Derby, or perhaps on Lady Derby, is certain. The wound was so deep,

that thereafter family meetings at Knowsley were impossible, though Derby managed on one occasion to give them both a luncheon in London before they set off for Canada. (Vincent, *Later* 0011)

The Stanley children's perception of the situation was even worse than the reality, and the 17th Earl "grew up thinking 'that my Father and his brother ... did not speak,' ascribing this 'for the most part to my mother's influence,' and claiming that Mary, Lady Derby, 'and my mother cordially disliked each other, and if there was anything either of them could say against each other they did so'" (Vincent, *Later* 0012).

The subservience of the Stanley family is reflected in a letter the 15th Earl wrote to Constance, probably when she was living at St. James's Square and serving as his hostess at the Foreign Office from 1866-1888. He instructed her: "If we are to give outdoor relief to all these Foreigners, you ought to have a new gown to do it in. Get one" (NRA 3). Thus, it must have been with some alacrity that Frederick and Constance left him for Canada in June 1888 after the Earl gave them that luncheon in London. Indeed, the unpleasant relations between the two families may have been a reason that Frederick Stanley accepted a posting as Govenor General two thousand miles away, from which he would not return until he succeeded his brother to the Earldom in 1893.

The Stanleys arrived in Ottawa with four of their children, the youngest being ten. Stanley's sons made up two of the three aides-de-camp in his party. During their five years in Canada Lady Stanley kept albums of photographs and press clippings which gave an ongoing record of their political, social and cultural activities in Canada. These albums were inherited by their daughter, Lady Isobel Gathorne-Hardy, and on her death in 1964 were passed on to her grandson R. Hobbs of Sussex. They are now deposited in the library of Corpus Christi College, Cambridge.

Lord Stanley proved a popular and impressive Governor General. He had strong imperialist sentiments and he saw his appointment to Canada as an opportunity to promote the expanding British empire in the heady years following Queen Victoria's golden jubilee in 1887. Thus, although he was no orator, Stanley promoted the empire in speeches throughout the Dominion. His retiring manner and his personal charm made him popular with Canadians from coast to coast. Both he and Lady Stanley carried out their official duties with enthusiasm and dignity.

There were no political events of great moment during Stanley's time in Canada, but there were crises of the moment that called for tact and diplomacy on his part. One was the Jesuit Estates Bill, passed by the Mercier government of Quebec in 1888, to compensate the Roman Catholic Church for land taken from the Jesuits in 1760, just after the conquest of Quebec. Besides distributing $400,000 to various bodies of the Church, the bill increased the grant to Protestant schools in Quebec by only $60,000. The bill was condemned in other provinces, especially Ontario, and a motion was raised in the Dominion Parliament of 1889 asking the Governor General to disallow the bill. Only thirteen members voted in favour of the motion, and Stanley declined to intervene. This was not a difficult decision for him, but it emphasized the political neutrality he maintained throughout his time in Canada.

In external affairs Stanley supported Canada's claims to sealing rights in the Behring Sea, and the long-standing and potentially serious dispute between Canada and the United States finally went to arbitration in February 1893, five months before Stanley left Canada. Although he was no longer Governor General when the hearings finished in August, he could take some satisfaction in knowing that the dispute was finally settled in Canada's favour.

Stanley was the Queen's representative in the last days of Sir John A. Macdonald's life and long tenure as Prime Minister. He developed a genuine affection for the man who had led the country for all but six of the years since Confederation, and was deeply saddened at Macdonald's death in 1891. He presided over the transition of leadership to two of the five Prime Ministers who succeeded Macdonald in the 1890s—Sir John Abbot and Sir John Thompson.

Although the Stanleys did not show great leadership in the cultural life of Canada, they took part in cultural activities in a sporadic way. One such occasion was a combined musical and theatrical evening on December 15, 1891 when Rideau Hall hosted the court pianist and cellist to the Emperors of Germany and Austria who played works by Beethoven, Wagner, Schumann and Boccherini. The program included two plays in which members of the Stanley family took part, *Cut Off with a Shilling* and *Dearest Mama* (Hubbard 254). The plays were a revival of a program presented on New Year's Eve 1888 for a small group of family and friends. These were not the elaborate dramas of the time of the Dufferins, but pleasant domestic affairs. Even the commentary in the *Citizen* is somewhat muted in its enthusiasm for the occasion and the celebrations that surrounded it:

> After the performances their Excellencies entertained the guests at supper; and at midnight the gong sounded out the old year and in the new year. Everybody wished everybody else a happy New Year, and the gathering broke up. It was primarily intended as a family affair for the children and the staff and the friends and neighbours of all the household, and the invited guests were few. (*Citizen*, Jan. 3, 1889, p. 2)

There is little evidence of the Stanleys sponsoring or attending plays outside Rideau Hall. The reason for this is suggested in a story on the Stanleys which noted that Lady Stanley declined to be introduced to the actress Lily Langtry in Toronto (*Victoria Daily Times*, Oct. 31, 1889, p. 1). Perhaps she found the theatre a distasteful art, or theatre people an inferior class. The Stanleys did sponsor a series of tableaux on marriage at the Grand Opera House in Ottawa. The "Marriage Dramas", as they were called, were edifying and evoked the following comment from the local newspaper:

Cast of *Dearest Mama*, on stage at Rideau Hall, 1889.
(NAC PA-027143)

> If all the marriage dramas in real life ran their course as
> smoothly and beautifully as did the "Marriage Dramas" on
> the stage of the Grand Opera House last evening, the
> Divorce Committee of the Senate would find time hang so
> heavily on its hands that it would have to go out of busi-
> ness altogether. (*Citizen*, Oct. 11, 1892, p. 8)

Perhaps that was the intention of the Stanleys sponsoring
these dramas. Although they were unable to attend on opening night because Lady Stanley's train was late arriving in
Ottawa, they did attend the following night. They also
attended a variety concert at the new Electric Park in Ottawa
a week before their departure from the capital. One suspects
they attended without great enthusiasm but rather as a gesture of good will towards the city they were leaving. In any
case the citizens of Ottawa were impressed by the show:

> Every feature of the programme was carried out in first-
> class style, Miss Pearce, the sweet soprano, being thrice
> encored; Zamora, the Mexican wonder, receiving hearty
> applause; the musical comedians, Bryant and Saville,
> keeping the audience in merry mood, and the Gorman
> Brothers, astonishing even those who knew their talent, by
> their later specialities in dance and song. (*Citizen*, July 7,
> 1893, p. 6)

The Stanleys did not show the special interest in art the Lansdownes had done, but they did bring to Canada a series of
prints by Piranesi which they hung in Rideau Hall, and then
brought back to England. It is doubtful many Canadians saw
these prints or were influenced by them. Before her departure
from Canada, Lady Stanley wrote of these to her successor,
Lady Aberdeen: "The walls are absolutely bare—we brought
out a large collection of old prints we happened to have ... "
(Hubbard 71). However Lord Stanley did open at least one
exhibition of the Royal Canadian Academy of Art, on which
occasion he had praise for Canadian artists:

He congratulated the members of the association on the
very creditable display arranged around the room, and
expressed the hope that the young artists of Canada would
persevere in their noble calling and make a mark for themselves and be a credit to their country, rivalling in their
works the masters of past ages ... The walls of the academy
would soon be covered with the best works of Canadian
artists, marked by a distinct Canadian type. (*Semi-Weekly
Citizen*, Mar. 14, 1889, p. 4)

Following Lansdowne's tradition, he also awarded prizes to
students of the Art School in Ottawa, was patron of the city's
Art Association, and even donated his own prize at one of its
exhibitions (*Semi-Weekly Citizen*, May 2, 1889, p. 4).

Lord Stanley seems to have had good relations with
members of the Canadian Press Association, and entertained
them at Rideau Hall on at least one occasion. The entertainment included skating and sliding, and was followed by a
fancy ball at the Russell Hotel attended by 500 people. The
Press was even impressed by the speech which the Governor
General gave, and one paper called it "un très beau discours,
plein d'esprit" (*Le Canada*, Mar. 5, 1892, p. 3).

One reason the Press Association enjoyed this Governor
General was that he had a good sense of humour. This was
displayed on many occasions, both in his speeches and in his
actions. Speaking at a dinner for the Medical College of the
University of Toronto, "when he admitted that he, too, was
a 'state-aided institution', there was an unrestrained outburst
of laughter" (*Globe and Mail*, Dec. 2, 1892, p. 2). On another occasion a messenger came from the Speaker of the House
of Commons requesting a set of cards for some guests he was
entertaining in his quarters in the House. By mistake the
messenger had come to Rideau Hall instead of the Rideau
Club across Wellington St. from the Parliament Buildings.
Perceiving the error, Lord Stanley interrupted his dinner to
get the messenger two packs of playing cards, which he
asked the messenger to deliver to the Speaker with his com-
pliments. The local paper remarked, "Needless to say the

blunder has caused considerable hilarity in town" (*Citizen*, July 2, 1892, p. 6).

Besides cajoling students at the many schools and colleges he visited, Lord Stanley seems to have taken his visits to educational institutions very seriously. In Ottawa and in most cities he visited outside the capital, he went to schools and stressed the importance of education for a young country. He seemed particularly fond of McGill University, which he visited on several occasions, and where he opened the new Macdonald science buildings with great fanfare followed by a reception for invited guests (*Citizen*, Feb. 25, 1893, p. 1). The buildings had been donated to McGill by William Christopher Macdonald, manufacturer and philanthropist, who was knighted in 1898 and for many years was chancellor of the university. Lord Stanley also visited McGill on his way to Quebec City when he was leaving Canada to sail home (*Le Canada*, July 12, 1893, p. 3).

On the visit to Toronto during which he addressed the Medical College, Stanley also visited several public and private schools. One of these was Upper Canada College, where he responded to an address in Latin by the head boy, B.K. Sandwell, in the same language. *The Globe and Mail* quoted at length from his 15-minute impromptu speech in Latin, and then summarized the Governor General's subsequent remarks:

> Breaking off at this point into the vernacular again, Lord Stanley said that as it was 28 years since he had spoken a word of Latin in public, and as he had not heard of this Latin address which was to be tendered to him until he reached the college, he hoped they would pardon his somewhat faulty grammatical construction and original pronunciation; he was afraid his remarks had been couched in the "Latinum caninum" or dog Latin style. (*Globe and Mail*, Dec. 2, 1892, p. 6)

However much he impressed his young audience, he certainly left a favourable impression on the *Globe and Mail* reporter, who commented:

> Lord Stanley's impromptu reply in Latin to the head boy's
> address of welcome was in truth a remarkable performance,
> which few, if any, even among college professors could have
> equalled ... He spoke ... slowly and deliberately, but with
> scarcely a falter or any hesitancy for a word, and in gram-
> matical construction and pronunciation the effect was
> marvellously accurate and scholarly. Speaking to a Globe
> reporter afterward, the lieutenant-governor mentioned that
> though Lord Stanley had confessed to small acquaintance
> with the language in recent years, still as a student at col-
> lege and university he spoke and wrote Latin as fluently as
> English, a statement easy of credence after his speech of
> yesterday afternoon. (*Globe and Mail,* Dec. 2, 1892, p. 6)

Stanley was clearly the heir of his father not only in his love
of horseracing, but also in his love for and proficiency in
Latin.

In fact, Lord Stanley did not indulge in the traditional
family sport a great deal while he was in Canada. There was
no thoroughbred racing in Ottawa during his time, so he had
to go to the races while he was in other cities. In Toronto he
dined with the Jockey Club and then went to the races (*Citizen,* May 25, 1892, p. 4); another paper noted that he was
expected in Quebec City to attend the races on September 3-
5, 1891 (*Le Canada,* Sept. 1, 1891, p. 3). Perhaps he was
more sensitive than his successor Lord Grey about his attendance at the races elsewhere being noted by the Ottawa
papers, so that he did not indulge in the sport as much as he
would have liked.

His involvement in yachting and shooting was also limited. He was a patron of the Royal Canadian Yacht Club in
Toronto, which had been founded in 1854, and remained a
patron when he left Canada; besides visiting it when he was
there on his farewell trip to the city, he managed to get for the
yachtsmen of Lake Ontario the Queen's Cup, which was
competed for annually on the first of July (*Globe and Mail,*
June 8, 1893, p. 5). He gave a $500.00 prize and badges to
members of Canada's Bisley team on one occasion (*Citizen,*

Sept. 3, 1892, p. 8), and went on a duck hunt to Port Dover, Ontario on another (*Le Canada*, Sept. 30, 1892, p. 2).

The Stanleys entertained lavishly on special occasions, the most special being the ball they gave at the Citadel in Quebec City to mark the second visit to Canada by Prince George, later King George V, whose father had been a boyhood friend of Stanley. They also travelled widely throughout Canada, most notably on a tour of western Canada in 1889, for which a special railway car called "Victoria" was built. Lady Stanley kept a journal of this trip along with a C.P.R. timetable for 1889, which are in the National Archives of Canada (NAC).

The Stanleys' love for the outdoors was most frequently indulged in Quebec in fishing on the Cascapédia River, and in their newly built home Stanley House at New Richmond, Quebec, in the Gaspé region on the Bay of Chaleur. This house was used by two subsequent Governors General, Aberdeen and Minto. In 1962 it was donated to the Canada Council, which organized seminars and retreats for artists and academics there until 1984 when it became another victim of government cutbacks in the arts. It was maintained but not used by the Council from 1984 to 1996 when it was sold for private use. In 1994 the building was declared a heritage property.

Stanley House was, however, well used by the Stanleys. The property was purchased and the eleven-room country house built in 1888, the first year of Stanley's tenure in Canada. It was nine miles from the Cascapédia River where the Governor General and his family and friends most frequently fished during their annual vacations in the region, usually in June and July. They then moved into the Citadel in Quebec City where they resided until October. Stanley obviously delighted in the fishing, and was rewarded by copious catches. One diplomatic gesture he usually made on these trips was to send a large salmon he had caught to the mayor of Quebec. When M. Mercier was mayor he received a 46 lb. salmon from the Governor General (*Le Canada*, June 26, 1890, p. 3);

Sleigh and toboggan slide, Rideau Hall, ca. 1890.
(NAC PA-033954)

his successor M. Frémont was rewarded with a "superb salmon" two years later (*Le Canada*, Aug. 2, 1892, p. 3).

There is one memento of the Stanleys that is not in danger of being sold off, and that is the Stanley Cup, awarded annually to the team that wins the playoffs in the National Hockey League. Hockey was being played in Ottawa in Stanley's time, occasionally at Rideau Hall, and the Governor General donated the most coveted of Canadian sports trophies, presented for the first time to the Montreal Amateur Athletic Association team in 1893, the year Stanley left Canada. Typically, the announcement of the new cup for hockey was made, not by Stanley himself, but by one of his aides, Lord Kilcoursie. Speaking at a dinner of the Ottawa Amateur Athletic Association on March 18, 1892, he read a note from the Governor General: "I have for some time been thinking that it would be a good thing if there were a challenge cup which should be held from year to year by the champion hockey team in the dominion of Canada" (McKinley 19-20). Stanley's sons Arthur and Edward had turned their father into a hockey fan in Canada, and even popularized the sport in England. One of the few hockey games Stanley attended in Canada took place in Montreal between the Royal Scots of Montreal and the Rideau Hall Rebels, for which his two sons played (*Le Monde*, Feb. 27, 1893, p. 1). The game for which the Cup was first awarded was played on February 18, 1893 between Ottawa and the Montreal Amateur Athletic Association team, which won 7-1. Lord Stanley's departure from Canada came just five months after that first Stanley Cup was won.

The Stanleys continued the tradition of skating and tobogganing parties at Rideau Hall, followed by dinners on the curling rink there with the band of the Governor General's Footguards performing for the guests. Their efforts were certainly appreciated by the guests, as the local paper reported of one of these "at homes", as they were called in the invitations: "Their Excellencies Lord and Lady Stanley, and the members of the Vice-regal household were unremitting in their gracious attentions to their guests, who one and all will certainly entertain the most pleasant recollections of the joyous evening spent at Rideau Hall" (*Citizen*, Mar. 2, 1891, p. 4). Back in England Stanley was reminded of his support of skating in Canada when he was asked to write the preface to a book by George A. Meagher, who in 1891 in Montreal was presented by Stanley with a medal as the World's Champion for Figure and Fancy Skating. Writing in 1895 from Knowsley, Stanley recalled vaguely a performance Meagher gave on the rink at Rideau Hall:

> He was, if I recollect rightly, at that time skating on the public rinks and afterwards at Government House, Ottawa, and was always most kind, not only in giving a display of his own powers but also in instructing (en amateur) those who were novices in the art of which he is a master. (Meagher 6)

The short preface, one of the few writings of Lord Stanley, is marked by a tentativeness and hesitancy that were part of his character, but it does show his willingness to support athletic activity, even while his name was being used to sell the author's book.

Lady Stanley's main interest and contributions to the social and cultural life of Canada were in her work for hospitals, mainly in Ottawa. From the outset she tried to improve the conditions of the capital's hospitals, even at the risk of falling out of line in her recommendations. One of her causes was the establishment of a children's hospital. For this purpose she joined and was made president the Ottawa branch of the Ministering Children's League which in 1888, the year of the Stanleys' arrival in Ottawa, bought a property on Wurtemburg St. near the Protestant hospital, which could accommodate 47 children. Lady Stanley made the mistake, in those fiercely sectarian days, of recommending that the hospital be non-denominational. The Protestant community, and especially the Anglican bishop, were furious, and Lady Stanley was forced to resign from the presidency and from the Ministering Children's League itself. As a recent article on hospitals in the Ottawa area put it describing the incident: "This is an Anglican institution. Papal babies need not apply" (*Citizen*, Dec. 14, 1995, p. E3). The nearby General Hospital was owned and operated by the Grey Nuns. However shocked she may have been by this behaviour of late nineteenth-century Ottawa, she was not deterred later from sending a letter to the Protestant hospital advocating the establishment of a maternity ward (*Citizen*, Feb. 3, 1892, p. 2).

Nor was Lady Stanley deterred from taking an ongoing interest in hospitals and medical care in Ottawa generally. She spearheaded a campaign to establish a training institute for nurses at the corner of Rideau and Wurtemburg streets, next to the Protestant hospital, which became known as the Lady Stanley Institute, of which she was elected Honorary President. She was active in sponsoring public concerts to raise funds for the institute, which was formally opened by her husband on May 21, 1891. The headline of the local paper read: "Lady Stanley Institute. Formal Opening by His Excellency the Governor-General On Behalf of the Lady Patroness". The Lady Patroness was surely amused by the headline, and by the account which followed: "He felt proud that one so near and dear to him had been associated with such a movement. In conclusion Lord Stanley said Her Excellency dearly loved and would never forget those with whom she had been associated in Canada, and they would thank them one and all for their many kindnesses" (*Citizen*, May 22, 1891, p. 1). A memento to her hospital work is a condominium, Lady Stanley Place, recently built on the site of the former Lady Stanley Institute and beside the former Protestant hospital, now a heritage building called Wallis House.

Further evidence of Lady Stanley's concern for the sick in Ottawa was her involvement with an organization called the Women's Humane Society. On November 28, 1890 she presented to the mayor and council of Ottawa what was called an "ambulance waggon". Her words of presentation consisted of six lines. Her husband made an odd response to the mayor on her behalf, indicating that she was truly uncomfortable speaking in public:

> His Excellency remarked that Lady Stanley asked him to accompany her on the ground that she was not able to speak for herself. She did not take any part in those public utterances which were so frequent just now, and she had told him the same thing so long that he drew perhaps the same subtle distinction which theologians and casuists were allowed to do between what was their article of faith and their article of pious belief; and as an article of pious belief he was therefore under the impression that she was unable to lift up her voice in public. (Laughter.) She therefore wished him to express her very great satisfaction in having been able to take a part, however humble, in this good work. (*Citizen*, Nov. 29, 1890, p. 4)

This further example of Lord Stanley's humour shows that it was not always of the most felicitous kind. In any case, Lady Stanley's successor as first lady at Rideau Hall—Lady Aberdeen—would never be upstaged by her husband at a celebration of the good work she performed. On a more personal level, Lady Stanley's compassion made her ready to return home in the last year of their appointment in Ottawa when her son Arthur became seriously ill. In fact, in February 1893 she went as far as New York to get a ship to England to be with her son, but received news before her departure that he was much improved, so she returned to Ottawa. In the meantime several social events at Rideau Hall were cancelled because of her expected absence.

It is interesting to note the time spent in Canada by Stanley's eldest son, Edward George, who would succeed him as the 17th Earl. Edward did not accompany his parents to Canada in 1888 for the very good reason that he would marry Lady Alice Montagu, youngest daughter of the Duke of Manchester, seven months later on January 5, 1889 at the Guards Chapel, Wellington Barracks, London where he was following his father's initial career. Oddly, his parents did not return from Canada for the wedding, although a large segment of the British aristocracy did attend, including the Prince and Princess of Wales, Princess Louise, and other members of the Royal family. Six weeks after the wedding he sailed for Canada with his bride to join his father's staff as an aide-de-camp for the next two years. He took an active part in Canadian life, accompanying the vice-regal party on their Western tour of 1889, which visited Winnipeg, Calgary and Banff. Randolph Churchill reported on the young Stanley's enjoyment of the sporting life in Canada, especially the summers at the Citadel, fishing on the Cascapédia, and playing hockey in the winter (Churchill 30).

When Stanley's brother Edward died unexpectedly on April 21, 1893, he succeeded to the Earldom of Derby and its large estates. Although he had been planning to leave Canada in September or October, he changed his plans and left in July for home to assume his responsibilities. His estates totalled about 69,000 acres, mostly in Lancashire. One can sympathize with his concern for the family estates, but his early departure from Canada was typical of his approach to the Governor General's office: he enjoyed the position and he performed his functions conscientiously, but his heart was not totally in it; when a more pleasing prospect presented itself, he soon left to pursue it. This lack of commitment suggests why he did not leave a greater legacy in Canada, and why the trophy by which he is best remembered is for a sport he never played himself.

Whatever regrets Stanley had on leaving Canada, he apparently did not regret leaving Rideau Hall. Early in his time here, one paper reported that he was disgusted with his Ottawa residence and would ask Parliament for money for a new one (*Manitoba Daily Free Press*, Oct. 4, 1889, p. 1). In Montreal, before his departure from Canada, but after his departure from Ottawa, he recommended that the Governor General have two official residences, one in Ottawa and one in Montreal (*Le Canada*, July 14, 1893, p. 3). Perhaps no one had told him that he already had a second official residence at the Citadel in Quebec City, where he had been living every summer.

When he finally left Canada from Quebec City on July 16, 1893 he received a fond farewell and grateful speeches, especially from the people of Quebec. Even the Catholic clergy in Quebec regretted his departure. He delivered a farewell speech in English and French, and was praised for his ease in speaking the French language. One Ottawa paper noted: "The regard in which their Excellencies were held by the people of Quebec, was the reason why so many gathered today to say farewell and God speed to one of the most popular governors Canada has ever had" (*Citizen*, July 17, 1893, p. 1). Editorials in French newspapers were even more generous in their praise:

> At four o'clock this afternoon these noble ones will leave, perhaps forever, Canadian soil. Rarely since our defeat has the departure of a governor been the occasion of so much homage and best wishes for the future which Providence will bestow upon them. With all our hearts we join to them the best wishes of the people of Quebec, our readers, and our own [my translation].
>
> Bon voyage et glorieuse carrière! (*Courrier du Canada*, July 15, 1892, p. 2)

On Stanley's departure from Montreal a few days earlier, the local French paper also paid homage to him, but reminded its readers of the political status of Quebec and of Canada as a whole: "As long as England sends us such representatives of the Crown, it will be easier for us to forget that Canada is not independent, and that its governor comes from a foreign country" [my translation] (*Le Monde*, July 13, 1893, p. 2). This is indeed a tribute to Stanley's political acumen in that he was able to serve as Queen Victoria's representative in Canada for five years all the while maintaining good relations with the province of Quebec.

When Stanley inherited Knowsley he inherited the large number of paintings in the house. One wonders if he enjoyed them, even though we are told that at that time there were few fine paintings, except for a Rembrandt depicting Belshazzar's Feast. The huge house was neither an architectural masterpiece nor one of extreme comfort, and the furniture is described as solid but unexceptional (Sett-Smith 21). The staff of the house was large, and included some forty grounds-keepers, so Stanley would have much to occupy his attention on his return from Canada.

Stanley held no subsequent government posts, but he did involve himself in local affairs, as many of the Earls of Derby had done. He accepted an appointment as first Lord Mayor of greater Liverpool from 1895 to 1896 at a time of major expansion for the city, and he served as Guild Mayor of Preston in 1902. In 1903 he was appointed the first Chancellor of Liverpool University when it was raised from the status of a university college, of which he had succeeded his brother as president in 1893. He remained Chancellor until his death, just as he remained Lord Lieutenant of Lancashire from 1897 until his death. In 1904 his prominence as an imperialist was recognized in his appointment as President of the Empire League. In 1893 he also succeeded his brother as Sloane Trustee of the British Museum, and in 1904 served as President of the Royal Agricultural Society. He was active in philanthropic work, and accepted the presidency of the Franco-British Exhibition of 1907 in London.

Stanley's social and sporting life continued, with his old friend King Edward VII a regular guest at Knowsley. Spurred on by his eldest son and heir he resumed the involvement of the family in horseracing, which the previous Earl had assiduously shunned. He was elected a member of the prestigious Jockey Club the year he succeeded to the earldom, and soon revived the Derby fortunes on the track. He remained a familiar and prominent figure of the Liverpool racing scene until the end of his life.

Stanley died suddenly of heart failure after returning from a walk during a visit to his estate at Holwood, near Beckenham, Kent on June 14, 1908, from which he was returned to his beloved Knowsley for burial. His large estates were now yielding some £300,000 per year in rent. Appropriately he is remembered locally rather than nationally, in a marble statue in St. George's Hall, Liverpool, unveiled in 1911, and in a bust in the Preston town hall.

His son, the 17th Earl, followed his father's example in donating much of his time and energy to local concerns. Thus it is appropriate that Randolph Churchill's book on him is entitled *Lord Derby: 'King of Lancashire'*, the epithet by which he became known. Nevertheless he did hold two cabinet posts, and was ambassador to France at the end of the First World War. His own passion for horseracing made him one of the best known horsemen in England. His cultural activity included indulging his wife's and his own interest in the theatre, a pursuit little known to his father. In April 1885, early in his military career, he recorded in his diary that he attended nine plays that month (Churchill 24). Later in life he explained his decision to buy another residence in Stratford Place in London after selling his house in St. James's Square: "Lady Derby must have somewhere to go when she comes up from Coworth to go to the theatre" (Sett-Smith 37).

The 17th Earl of Derby was succeeded in 1948 by his grandson, who applied the business acumen of the Stanleys to the demands of the mid-twentieth century. From the 1950s he was a successful entrepreneur in the television industry. To meet the financial pressures and taxes on the landed gentry, he opened Knowsley Hall to paying visitors and then closed it when he could afford to reconstruct the aging building. He even sold some of the family heirlooms, including a Van Dyk painting and some Elizabethan and Stuart miniatures. He opened the safari park on 600 acres of Knowsley Park, and remained involved in the family tradition of horseracing. He died in 1994.

It was with their horseracing tradition that this survey of the sporting and cultural activities of Lord Stanley and his family began. The continuation of that tradition throughout the lives of the Stanley family, with the exception of the 15th

Earl, indicates where the real interests of Lord Stanley lay. He did not have much opportunity to satisfy it while he was in Canada, so his sporting was confined to fishing and giving support to the indigenous sports of skating and ice hockey. He was not particularly interested in culture and the arts, and so he did not much boost them while he was Governor General.

Perhaps Disraeli was right when he described the Stanleys as unimaginative; for the most part they were unimaginative in cultural matters. Fortunately Canada would not have long to wait for someone with artistic imagination, for Derby's successor, Lord Aberdeen, and his energetic wife would soon be arriving.

Works Cited

Bagley, J.J. *The Earls of Derby 1485-1985*. London: Sidgwick & Jackson, 1985.

Le Canada (Ottawa).

The Citizen (Ottawa).

Churchill, Randolph S. *Lord Derby: 'King of Lancashire;' The Official Life of Edward, 17th Earl of Derby, 1865-1948*.London: Heinemann, 1955.

Le Courrier du Canada (Quebec).

The Globe and Mail (Toronto).

Hubbard, R.H. *Rideau Hall: An Illustrated History of Government House, Ottawa, from Victorian Times to the Present Day*. Montreal and London: McGill-Queen's, 1977.

Kebbel, T.E., M.A. *Life of the Earl of Derby, K.G.* London: W.H. Allen & Co., 1890.

Manitoba Daily Free Press (Winnipeg).

McKinley, Michael. *Hockey Hall of Fame Legends: The Official Book*. Toronto: Viking Studio Books, 1995.

Meagher, George A. *Figure and Fancy Skating*. London: Bliss, Sands & Foster, 1895.

Le Monde (Montreal).

NAC (National Archives of Canada MG27 IB7 Reel A-673).

NRA 1 (National Register of Archives, London, England 12033. I/106/31). Original in the Autograph Collection of Letters of Lady Constance Villiers at Corpus Christi College, Cambridge.

NRA 2 (National Register of Archives, London, England 12033. I/106/35). Letter dated May 7, 1857.

NRA 3 (National Register of Archives, London, England 12033. I/106/7). Letter dated April 14, n.y.

Pollard, W. *The Stanleys of Knowsley: A History of That Noble Family including a Sketch of the Political and Public Lives of the Rt. Hon. the Earl of Derby, K.G., and the Rt. Hon Lord Stanley, M.P.* Liverpool: Edward Howell, 1868.

Scharf, George, S.F.A. *A Descriptive and Historical Catalogue of the Collection of Pictures at Knowsley Hall.* By Authority of the Earl of Derby. London: Bradhung, Agnew & Co., 1875. n.p.

Semi-Weekly Citizen (Ottawa).

Sett-Smith, Michael. *A Classic Connection: The Friendship of the Earl of Derby and the Honourable George Lambton 1893-1945.* London: Secker & Warburg, 1983.

Stanley, Edward George. "Lord Stanley's Speech delivered in the House of Commons, February 21, 1856, in favour of opening the British Museum, etc., on Sunday Afternoon," in *The National Sunday League to Obtain The Opening of the British Museum and Other National Institutions on Sunday Afternoon.* London: J. Kenny, 1865.

Victoria Daily Times

Vincent, John, ed. *Later Derby Diaries: Home Rule, Liberal Unionism, and Aristocratic Life in Late Victorian England. Selected Passages.* Bristol: University of Bristol, 1981.

———, ed. *Disraeli, Derby, and the Conservative Party: Journals and Memoirs of Edward Henry, Lord Stanley 1849-1869.* Hassocks, Sussex: Harvester, 1978.

Lord and Lady Aberdeen, 1898.
Photo by W.J. Topley (NAC PA-027918)

Chapter 6

Theatre and Spectacle Under the Aberdeens, 1893-1898

Lord and Lady Aberdeen's main contribution to the social and cultural life of Canada lay in the historical tableaux and balls they organized to give Canadians a sense of their own and of British history, and in the organizations to which they gave their moral support and administrative skills. Theatre in the ordinary sense was not a principal interest of theirs; they were more interested in musical performances and in fostering intellectual activity for the public through lectures and readings, and for their own staff through the Household Club they formed.

In fact, the Governor General, John Campbell Gordon, 7th Earl of Aberdeen (1847-1934), was more involved in sports than in culture. John Saywell says he was "perhaps the best skater and curler ever to reside at Rideau Hall" (Saywell xv). While this may have endeared him to many Canadians, it did not please his wife; Saywell describes his athletic prowess and her reaction to it in some detail:

> While his wife lamented the preoccupation with sports in Canada, because it took people away from more worthwhile pursuits, he entered into them with enthusiasm. He was an expert curler, a proficient skater, and a superb horseman. He enjoyed his apprenticeship on a bicycle and spent an evening with a log-running crew on the Gatineau. He commonly attended hockey and lacrosse games and earnestly entreated the athletes to keep the game clean. (Saywell xxvi)

Lady Aberdeen's broad-mindedness and enthusiasm are shown by the fact that she actually came to appreciate this part of life in Canada herself (Saywell xxvi).

The Aberdeen Family.
(NAC PA-027852)

Lady Aberdeen (1857-1931) was born Ishbel Maria Marjoribanks and married the future Governor General in 1877. They had four children—Haddo, Marjorie, Dudley, and Archie—two of whom (Marjorie and Archie) lived with them during their tenure in Canada. Lady Aberdeen's chief interests lay in the organization of services for the benefit of the needy, both material and spiritual. She was president of the International Council of Women when it moved to Canada, became first president of the National Council of Women of Canada, and founded a local council of women in Ottawa. Her commitment to the National Council of Women was ongoing, and was perhaps her greatest contribution to the quality of life in Canada. As Doris French wrote in her book on Lady Aberdeen: "The National Council of Women of Canada would continue to grow and flourish under her skilled guidance—while she sent her private secretary, Miss Teresa Wilson, to Europe to keep up contacts for the ICW" (French 158).

Lady Aberdeen also established the Victorian Order of Nurses in Canada, and founded the May Court Club in Ottawa for the aid of hospitals. She had already founded the Aberdeen Association for the distribution of literature to farmers in the West who would not otherwise have worthwhile reading material. Both she and her husband gave their energies to organizations for the relief of suffering abroad, such as the Indian Relief Fund, and to soliciting money and clothing for the poor of Ottawa.

Throughout her tenure at Rideau Hall, Lady Aberdeen kept a journal from which we can read of these humanitarian activities and of her cultural pursuits. She wrote of this important document in a book of reminiscences: "During our residence in Canada we sent home very full journal letters about our varied experiences to our respective families, 3 or 4 copies of these being prepared for circulation ... and the originals long afterwards collected and bound up into several portly volumes" (Aberdeen 46). Like those of Lady Dufferin and Feo Monck, the Canadian portion of these journals has been published. She had in fact begun keeping a journal at the age of fourteen and made her last entry on April 14, 1939, four days before her death. Her contributions to Canadian life and culture were duly recognized while she was in Canada, and nowhere more glowingly than in the words of the Dominion Archivist, George Johnson, who described her in "A Canadian Tribute to Lady Aberdeen" as "Canada's Lady Bountiful", and wrote:

> Her bountifulness has been limited by no considerations of creed, or race, or condition. It has been as varied as the nationalities which form the social make-up of the Canadian people, and as broad as the lines of latitude and longitude within which Canada is embraced. It has risen to include the least advanced of our people. It has met the wishes and desires of the most advanced. The Indian in his wigwam; the city girl and boy in their imitation sports of lacrosse and snow shoeing; the disciples of Esculapius; the devotees of Terpsichore; the patrons of the theatre; the lovers of music; the organizers of charities, like the Perley Home for Incurables; the churches, with their varied appliances for spiritual and social development; the literary societies of the land; the historians who are seeking to recall the past for the benefit of present and future generations; the teachers who are training lively "Young Canada" in more than 18,000 schools—all these have felt impulses for good directly traceable to Lady Aberdeen. (Johnson)

It is mainly as patrons of theatre that I am examining the contribution of the Aberdeens to Canadian life, and if that contribution is limited compared to the energetic work of the Dufferins, for example, the reason is that they put much of their energy into related cultural activities. Notable among these other endeavours was their work with the Household Club, a cultural and educational organization of the staff at Rideau Hall modelled on the Haddo House Club they had organized at the family estate in Aberdeenshire, Scotland. Although they were sometimes criticized for their involvement with the staff in this way, the criticism was probably

Haddo House, Scotland, view from the west.
(National Trust for Scotland)

the result of envy and snobbishness towards a vice-regal couple ahead of its time. The Club met weekly, usually on Thursday nights, and included music, lectures, readings, plays and discussion. The Aberdeens were able to offer their staff the expertise and knowledge of distinguished guests, and they received praise from many for their efforts. W.T. Stead, the English author and journalist, wrote of the Club after a visit to Rideau Hall: "Members of the household and visitors take part in a medley of music, speech-making and discussion. There are besides classes held in connection with the club and lantern lectures given. On the whole, the experiment is one full of hope and worthy of imitation" (Stead 60b). In her journal for February 22, 1895 Lady Aberdeen described the democracy and efficiency with which the Club was run: "Annual Club Meeting to-night went off very well—Committee elected by ballot—various songs, recitation by Mr. Campbell, guitar & banjo by Marjorie & Archie & reading from the Bonnie Brier Bush by H.E. (His Excellency)" (Saywell 200). The Aberdeen family were all involved in the venture.

Many cultural and theatrical events that took place at Rideau Hall in the Aberdeens' time were associated with the Household Club. One of these was a reading by the poetess Pauline Johnson, which is described on January 24, 1894:

> This evening at our Club Social Miss Johnson, an Iroquois chief's daughter recited pieces of her own composition very successfully. She was dressed in Indian costume & one of her pieces describing an encounter of an Indian chief with some white settlers, the Indians shot dead & the wild lament, imprecations of the daughter on those who had robbed her people of their land was v. telling. (Saywell 62)

On the same program was a lecture on Canadian history by "Grant," presumably Principal Grant of Queen's University in Kingston, who was a friend of the Aberdeens. Their interest in Canadian literature is seen in another entry on May 17, 1895, in which Lady Aberdeen described "An Evening

The Chapel at Rideau Hall in the Aberdeens' time, 1898.
(NAC PA-028012)

with the Canadian Poets," which consisted of readings by the leading poets of the time to a meeting of the Royal Society of Canada:

> An immense crowd turned out—the hall was packed & much interest was shown. Dr. Clark made a capital chairman with plenty of go about him, Principal Grant read a composition of Miss Macharis, Mr. Lampman one of his own about the surroundings of Ottawa & one of Bliss Carman's; Mr. Wilfrid Campbell his "Pan the Beast;" Mr. Duncan Campbell Scott read a charming production very badly—Mr. Edgar M.P. read a beautiful little sonnet of John Reid's (Robert Reid?) & Miss Pauline Johnson recited some of her poems in her Indian dress & with much dramatic power. Altogether it was a success. (Saywell 224)

She was not so impressed with a reading by Mark Twain of his own work in Victoria on August 21, 1895:

> ... we had to go to hear Mark Twain to-night. We took all the children, thinking he was a character they should see.
> I am not v. sure if I liked him ...
> He described buying a buck-jumper & his first experiences v. graphically, but the best bit was about a boy, Huck Finn ... He ended with an essentially stupid ghost-story. We saw him for a few minutes afterwards. He has the strangest slopingish sort of head at the back with long hair about his neck. (Saywell 276)

Another way in which the Aberdeens showed their interest in Canadian culture was through their attendance at university gatherings in Ottawa, Toronto, and Montreal. Their welcome at the University of Ottawa reminds us of the bilingual nature of that university as well as the inconveniences the vice-regal party had to suffer at some of the entertainments they attended. This mixed program on December 12, 1893 included one of the few references to drama they attended in Ottawa outside Rideau Hall:

Reception to welcome us at Ottawa University. Archbishop Duhamel present—the rector an Irishman—only recovering from influenza. About 500 students. A very nice programme. Good singing of a song of welcome—band—recitations, dialogue between Brutus & Cassius etc. A large company present. Two addresses in French & English presented in middle of evening, His Ex. responding in both languages. Great draught from stage in front & the "Welcome" in electric lights straight in front of us all the (time) somewhat dazzling. (Saywell 40)

An entry from Ottawa on January 10, 1896 shows how they were ahead of their time in supporting extension programs at universities: "This evening went with H.E. to the first series of University Extension lectures by Prof. Cappon on English literature—Browning. It was well attended" (Saywell 307).

The Aberdeens maintained a special interest in Irish life and culture during their time in Canada. There were several reasons for this. Although both were born in Scotland, Lady Aberdeen's mother was Irish. Besides, Lord Aberdeen spent six months as Lord Lieutenant of Ireland in 1886 and supported the Home Rule Bill. Its defeat along with the defeat of Gladstone's government that year ended the Aberdeens' first term of office in Ireland. He was appointed to the post a second time in 1906 and remained in Dublin until 1914 to see the passage of the Home Rule Bill of 1912. Lady Aberdeen worked for many Irish causes both in Ireland and abroad. In fact, Aberdeen's appointment as Governor General of Canada came about when Gladstone, on his return to power in 1892, proposed him for another term in Ireland but was dissuaded by the foreign secretary, John Morley. Aberdeen was then offered four other posts, from which he chose Canada. Of their 1886 stay in Ireland, R.H. Hubbard says: "The Aberdeens won such a measure of popularity as no occupant of Dublin Castle had enjoyed for many years" (Hubbard 74).

It is not surprising, then, to read of their attendance at Irish concerts and lectures, and to learn that Lady Aberdeen lectured on Irish literature. They attended concerts in

Canada to mark St. Patrick's Day, one of which in Ottawa
Lady Aberdeen described on March 18, 1895:

> Went to St. Patrick's Concert to-night at Opera House, got
> up in a hurry by the St. Patrick's Literary Society. Senator Sul-
> livan from Kingston was the orator & was to deliver an
> address on Irish Literature, but we did not learn much on
> that subject anyway. The singers & the "athletes" did not do
> badly, but the chairman was nervous & did not keep the
> thing in hand & the audience encored everything so we were
> rather tired of the performance before it ended. (Saywell 211)

Her displeasure with Senator Sullivan's speech on Irish literature may have been the reason she decided to give lectures on
the topic herself in Canada. A friend of Lord and Lady Gre-
gory, she was quite knowledgeable on the subject, and lectured on it at least four times in Toronto, Ottawa, and Montreal. She seems to have enjoyed the task of informing Canadians of the nineteenth-century renaissance in Irish writing.
On May 24, 1895—the Queen's birthday—she wrote in
Ottawa: "I stayed at home and worked at my paper on Irish
literature & enjoyed myself" (Saywell 224). She gave the
speech a week later in Toronto, and the event seems much
more successful than the Ottawa concert she attended. Her
husband was also on the program, of which she wrote:

> In the evening a Meeting in the Massey Music Hall which
> holds 4000 people, & where there were gathered about
> 2500 I should think, in connection with the Catholic
> Young Ladies Literary Society, to whom I had undertaken
> to lecture on "The present Irish Literary Revival," Mr. Tor-
> rington arranging a charming musical programme of Irish
> music & songs.
>   The Archbishop presided & was very kind. H.E. gave
> a capital reading from Mrs. Tynan Hinckson's "Cluster of
> Nuts" & I confess I enjoyed the evening. The audience
> was very responsive & it was a great delight to get some-
> thing different from the Council of Woman subjects.
> (Saywell 228)

For an event to overshadow her interest in the Council of Women it had to be very dear to her.

On March 17, 1898 she gave a lecture entitled "Old Celtic Legends" at the Russell Theatre in Ottawa as part of a concert presented by the St. Patrick's Literary and Scientific Association. Her address was the last item on the first part of the program (NAC). It is interesting to note that one of the songs in the second part was *The Irish Emigrant* by Lady Dufferin, the mother of the former Governor General, sung by a Miss Mackenzie. A newspaper account of the address had the headline: "A Scholarly Address by Her Excellency—One Full of Interest to Erin's Children," and gave the address in full, which "was listened to with marked attention and punctuated at short intervals with loud applause" (NAC). Her daughter Marjorie's list of domestic and social events included another address on an Irish topic on March 31, 1898: "Mother's lecture on Irish castles" (NAC). And on the voyage home on November 19, 1898 Lady Aberdeen told of an address she gave at Windsor Hall on their farewell visit to Montreal. The subject this time was the Irish statesman Horace Plunkett, then living: "I tried to tell them about Horace Plunkett's work as well as about the industrial and literary movements—& they seemed much interested & not a soul stirred" (Saywell 481).

The Aberdeens presented some children's plays at Rideau Hall in the new year as did some of their predecessors, but there was not much mention of them in their books and journals. Marjorie would have acted in the plays. In her life of her mother, in a chapter entitled "Pioneering in Canada," Marjorie suggested much dramatic activity but is not very specific about what this involved. She wrote: "Indoors the Christmas holidays as usual were busy with rehearsals. Ishbel had found that acting gave the family a favourite occupation and, she fondly hoped, a training in the art of public speaking" (Pentland 109). The emphasis on the practical advantages of theatre for the children confirms the utilitarian bent of Lady Aberdeen's character. Unlike Lady Dufferin, she would not revel in theatre for its own sake. She reinforced this impression herself when, on February 27, 1897 she mentioned a Christmas performance among other good works of the Household Club. The meeting at which this was reported took place on an important night in the life of the capital. She said:

> Then just before we left (for the United States) came the Parliament Buildings Fire on Feby 11th. We were holding the Annual Meeting of the Government House Club most successfully that evening—there was a good report from H.H. & we here were able to show quite a good year's work on this side too, including the working up of the Christmas performance, the warm clothes etc. made for poor immigrants by working-party & the raising of a subscription in the household for the Indian Famine. (Saywell 381)

The one Christmas performance she named was *David Copperfield* in a passage in her journal on January 18, 1894. Like so many of their cultural activities at Rideau Hall, it was a presentation of the Household Club. She went into some detail on the benefits of acting for children and described the children's performances as well as her own and the Governor General's. The passage is worth quoting in full because we have so little record of plays at Rideau Hall in their time:

> Chief event of the day was the performance by the children of some scenes from David Copperfield's childhood which was planned out by Miss Wilson & which they have been practising diligently under her direction. It is extraordinary how fond they all are of this kind of thing & how they none of them grudge either time or trouble in learning their parts or in rehearsing them & how little nervous they are about the actual acting … I am sure the practice they thus obtain in speaking out before an audience both as regards the management of the voice & also as the unselfconsciousness before an audience will prove of great value to them besides the stimulus it has given them to take interest in the historical events they have represented & now in Dickens's works. On this occasion the parts assigned to each seemed

to suit them to perfection. Archie made an ideal David Copperfield, except that he could not be persuaded to look sufficiently woe-begone. Dudley was really inimitable as Mr. Dick, & entered with real understanding into the part. Marjorie made a charming Aunt Betsy dressed in one of Nurse's gowns & with a high old cap & black ribbon on— her volley of threats hurled after the retreating figures of Mr. and Miss Murdstone were specially relished both by herself & the audience. Then Haddo was delighted with his part of Mr. Murdstone & with having to flog Archie—he supported the part with great dignity & looked quite grown up in his long black coat & high collar & stock— Miss Wilson took the part of Miss Murdstone, Mr. Stogdon that of Mr. Creakly. His Ex. brought down the house as Mr. Micawber & at the last moment I was inveigled on the scene as "Janet" to drive away the donkeys off Aunt Betsy's green. Altogether it was a success. The audience consisted of a very full meeting of the Club—& in addition Sir John & Lady Thompson & their little Frankie & Lady Grant & her little girl. (Saywell 59)

This is one of the most joyful family scenes in the journal. The play has brought them all together and we regret that Lady Aberdeen did not describe more scenes from their plays in Ottawa.

Hubbard says that another play, *Pride and Prejudice*, was presented that year but there is no mention of it in the journal. Their youngest son, Archie, who was nine at the time, played the role of Mrs. Bennet in the play. The experience he gained at Rideau Hall no doubt encouraged him in his acting during his school days at Winchester and Oxford. Photographs of some of his performances there are contained in the book published to commemorate him after his fatal traffic accident in 1909 at the age of twenty-five (*Archie Gordon*). The fact that there is no mention of other children's plays by name, or of any adult plays performed at Rideau Hall in the time of the Aberdeens may be explained in part by the fact that "at about this time the permanent stage was replaced with moveable panels so that the space could be used as an extension to the ballroom" (Hubbard 80). The importance of theatre presentations at Rideau Hall was declining in spite of Lady Aberdeen's protestations as to their value for the children.

The type of theatre that appealed more to the Aberdeens was theatre that required this extra space and involved spectacle and the participation of all those for whom it was presented. This we see particularly in the two great balls organized by the Aberdeens, but also in two children's masquerades that were presented in Quebec City and Ottawa respectively in the winter of 1894. The first took place in Quebec on February 2 and is described in some detail with emphasis on the roles and costumes of Marjorie and Archie:

> Children's masquerade in Skating Rink at 3—Marjorie headed the procession of girls dressed as a Highland girl in her own kilt, Haddo's jacket, plaid & ornaments—Archie headed the boys dressed first as an Irish boy with swallow-tail coat, red waistcoat & Corduroys & then came off & changed into a red hunting coat, velvet cap etc. to represent an English hunting gentleman. The chicks did their part very creditably even at the head of all these Canadian children & did not come to grief once. Archie had a choice of young lady partners & made his little bows to them v. prettily. About 250 children took part in the masquerade in every manner of costume. (Saywell 66)

The event was organized by Sir Henri Joly de Lotbinière, Premier of Quebec from 1878-1879, and the Aberdeens were especially impressed by the scene depicting the storming of an ice fort on the last day of the carnival. They described it with relish:

> The spectacle was the prettiest thing conceivable. The Ice Fort and ramparts, with the two little outlying forts, were first illuminated from within in every shade of lovely colour shining through the glistening ice, making the

whole scene a fairy creation. Then slowly the snowshoers, to the number of some 1500, filed down in their brilliant blanket costumes, each with a torch, and encamped without the Fort and laid siege to it with a very torrent of fireworks of all descriptions: the Fort answered back. This went on for some time, sending the children crazy with delight at every new shower of fiery missiles. The Ice Palace looked ablaze with fire, and then gradually melted down to a dull, dead, desolate gray, when with shouts and cheers and songs of triumph, the snowshoers and the artillery, who had been pressed into the service, filed up on to the ramparts and invested the Fort, Sir Henri Joly himself mounting the tower and running up the flag. (*Aberdeen* 52)

Eleven days later another masquerade took place in Ottawa, and we see that this one was not confined to children although it resembled the Quebec one. It was described in the reminiscences of the Aberdeens:

On one of these evenings we had a masquerade at the skating rink, which was announced under the name of "Dame Marjorie's School." All our Staff and Lord Ava dressed themselves as village schoolgirls in green Kate Greenway dresses and poke bonnets, with pink sashes and ribbons, and muslin pinafores and fans, Marjorie following as a demure school mistress, dressed in black, with poke bonnet and white kerchief, school-book and birch rod, and hair powdered. The effect was comical. Dr. Shirres made a very good but huge girl. He and Mr. Munro Ferguson shaved off their moustaches for the occasion. (*Aberdeen* 51)

This delight in spectacle was again satisfied in three special events during the viceregency of the Aberdeens: tableaux vivants and historical scenes in Montreal in 1895, the Historical Fancy Dress Ball in Ottawa in 1896, and the Victorian Era Ball in Toronto in 1897. They were indeed theatre on a grand scale, and the Aberdeen books and journals go to great length in describing the preparations and particulars of each one of them. The link between the children's plays and the tableaux historiques was made by the Aberdeens themselves:

> Our children had always been in the way of getting up some little play at Christmas time, generally based on an historical novel, so it was quite natural for us to turn our thoughts in the same direction, and a programme was arranged of "Tableaux historiques". (*Aberdeen* 53)

In fact, the performance was divided into two parts: the wordless tableaux, and the historical scenes. The Aberdeens were more involved in the latter.

Both parts were given on two successive evenings, Tuesday and Wednesday, January 15 and 16. Since these days were part of the Christmas holidays the family spent in Montreal that year, they were able to give much time to the preparation of their scenes. Lady Aberdeen spoke of three rehearsals, which included the Governor General doing some of the directing. Thus, on Friday, January 11 she wrote:

> Mostly consumed in further preparation for our Canadian Historical Scenes. H.E. went to rehearsal this afternoon.
> After dinner went to M. Wiollord's rehearsal for tableaux vivants—150 people employed & he thinks all will go well—but tableaux vivants must always be dull. (Saywell 186)

Despite her harsh but honest judgment on the tableaux, everyone involved worked furiously to put the show together. On Saturday they spent

> a long afternoon at the Queen's Theatre trying to get up the scene of Confederation. H.E. had got Mr. McGee, the Clerk of the Privy Council down from Ottawa, & he coached them all, Lord Monck & Chief Justice Draper, & Sir John Macdonald & all the rest of them to do their part properly for the swearing in. Archie makes a most admirable representation of Sir John Macdonald & plays his part well. (Saywell 187)

With no rehearsal on Sunday, they were back at work on Monday. Lady Aberdeen's description shows their work was like that of many theatre groups on the eve of opening night:

> Today has again been mostly given up to the rehearsal of the historical scenes at the place where they are actually to be given. We were to begin at three, but the Hall—a beautiful place—is scarcely finished & workmen were in possession & women were scrubbing & dusting, & the scenery were not finished off, & some of the costumes did not turn up. But finally things got into shape & we must hope for no hitches to-morrow. (Saywell 187)

On opening night her relief was like that of many theatre people as well:

> The day of the grand performance of Tableaux vivants & historical scenes from Canadian trouble (sic) to which we have been devoting so much time. We are thankful that all has gone well ... M. Wiollord managed the first part of the Tableaux Vivants & they were truly excellent—well conceived, well put on & the dresses magnificent. (Saywell 187)

Understandably, she went into more detail in describing the historical scenes in which all four of her own children participated. Her words on the origin of the scenes, the exuberance of Marjorie's acting, and her own reaction to the scenes are worth quoting at length:

> The second part of course interested us personally the most as it had all been worked up in the house & somewhat in defiance to advice. Miss Wilson adapted the scenes from various old books & generally managed affairs, while Mr. Varney acted as a most efficient & energetic stage-manager & Mr. Sheppard was beyond praise, in the management of the musical part, as well as in helping in the acting. The young people who took part, & there were over 200 of them, belonged to all the leading families (both English & French) in Montreal & this in itself has produced a nice feeling.

Marjorie's acting, sustained by Dudley and Archie & M. Paul Lacoste, son of the Chief Justice, in the Mlle de Vercheres scene is something to remember. H.E. & I got quite creepy over it, & people were much surprised. She quite forgets herself on the stage & throws herself into her part con amore. She acted in French as if she had never spoken any other language, & Dudley & Archie in their quaint little old red & white costumes of young seigneurs, did charmingly. The Evangeline scene was also liked, though most of the McGill students acting were rather wooden. Haddo & Marjorie did their sentimental part quite satisfactorily & did not butt one another as they did in their earlier rehearsals.

Both Brock & Tecumseh & the Confederation scenes were successes. Mr. Varney took Brock & Dr. Barclay's son Tecumseh. It was astonishing to note the absolute silence during the Confederation scene & the interest taken in all the formalities of the swearing-in of Lord Monck. Archie really looked exactly like Sir John Macdonald & some of the others were very good. (Saywell 188)

The moral uplift and educational opportunities were an integral part of these events for the Aberdeens, as we read: "H.E. went on to the stage and gave the children a little talk about patriotism in general & especially as exemplified in Sir John Thompson's life" (Saywell 188). The Prime Minister, who had died a month earlier while dining with Queen Victoria at Windsor Castle, had been a good friend of the Aberdeens.

The second night of the tableaux, tickets were sold and the money given to the mayor of Montreal for the benefit of the poor. Lady Aberdeen was also pleased with this performance, and even more so by the fact that their high purpose was grasped by an editor of the *Gazette*. She wrote: "We are much pleased with an editorial in the *Gazette* to-day written by Mr. T. Reade, interpreting our motives in having the Tableaux v. accurately. From all we can hear, these objects have been understood aright & we are very thankful & very much relieved" (Saywell 189).

Cover for book on Historical Fancy Dress Ball, Ottawa, 1896.
(NAC)

Perhaps it was the success of the historical scenes in Montreal that persuaded the Aberdeens to present an even greater spectacle in Ottawa along similar lines a year later: an Historical Fancy Dress Ball on February 17, 1896 in the Senate Chamber on Parliament Hill. The event was attended by over a thousand guests, each of whom represented a character or group in Canadian history. Nine groups presented scenes from Canada's past and performed dances characteristic of the period they enacted. The ball was a resounding success; Marjorie, who took part in one of the dances, quoted with triumph an Ottawa newspaper: "The critical Ottawa press admitted this to have been 'the most interesting society function yet seen in Canada: the Aberdeens have scored'" (Pentland 126).

The event was conceived with the same high purpose that characterized so much of what the Aberdeens did. Lady Aberdeen spoke in this vein in one of the two long entries on the ball in her journal:

> To tell the honest truth, we started this idea of having a Ball representing the outstanding periods of Canadian history, with the hope that it might lead to the young people reading up a bit & that it might divert Ottawa gossip at least into past times, away from all the painful & humiliating episodes of the present political situation & the everlasting discussion of hockey & winter sports varied with Ottawa society scandal. It was a sort of forlorn hope, but actually it appears to be succeeding. (Saywell 317)

She then gave an outline of all the periods and dances represented, as well as the names of the ladies who organized the dances, concluding with her own:

> 1. The Vikings first discovering Canada—A.D. 1000 … a Scandinavian dance …
> 2. Cabot leaving Europe with his party on his voyage of discovery … (Dance—pavane).
> 3. Jacques Cartier taking farewell of the Court of Francis I en route for Canada … Dance.

Agar Adamson as Napoleon at
Historical Fancy Dress Ball, Ottawa, 1896.
(NAC PA-138384)

4. The early French & English settlers in Acadia ...
Dance—(Quadrille danced slowly).
5. The days of Maisonneuve & the founders of Montreal
... Dance—Bourée.
6. New France in the days of Louis XIV ... Dance—
Gavotte.
7. The days of Montcalm & Wolfe ... (Dance—Farandole).
8. Acadia in the Days of Evangeline ... Acadian peasant
dance.
9. The U.E. Loyalists ... (Dance—Sir Roger de Coverley).
10. Our own Vice-Regal Court of 1896. (Saywell 317)

It was generally agreed that the dances were the most successful part of the performance, and Lady Aberdeen described
them in some detail:

> The dances are to take place in sequence, each having a
> banner of their own, representing Scandinavia, Venice,
> France or England as the case may be. Then at the close of
> the dances, each period is to come up to be presented
> announced by heralds, preceded by their standard-bearer,
> & announced by their ancient names. And then we process
> into supper. (Saywell 318)

That entry was written prior to the ball. It is clear that the
Aberdeens saw the event as theatre for we read in the entry
after the ball, on February 22: "We had a rehearsal on the Saturday night previous, which was found to be a most necessary
part of the performance. From the first moment, one could
not help feeling that the thing was 'going'" (Saywell 322).

Her own children took part in the first number, which was
prepared by Ebba Wetterman, the children's Swedish governess.
In fact, all four of the children took part in the scene since
Haddo and Dudley were in Canada on holidays at the time.
But the most impressive group of all seems to have been the
Acadian peasant dancers. Lady Aberdeen described them for us:

> Pavanes, gavottes, minuets, quadrilles etc. followed, but the
> favourite dance of the evening was that arranged by Mr.

Peter White consisting of thirty girls, nearly all M.P.s'
daughters dressed as Acadian peasants, executing a very
pretty peasant dance, concluding with a dance round the
Maypole beautifully & accurately done. We encored them.
(Saywell 322)

There were some hitches in the evening's performance, but
one of them merely added to the entertainment:

One of the figures consists of the dancers going in couples
under the uplifted arms of other couples. Mr. Erskine
being so tall managed to knock off his winged helmet &
wig, amidst the cheers of the gallery. The wig was deposited at my feet & he looked very handsome without it &
received quite an ovation. He made an ideal Viking. (Saywell 322)

The other hitch was not so entertaining, but the principals
seem to have carried the scene off without the audience
noticing:

We had asked each lady responsible for a dance to select a
leader to bring up his party & to announce them, & these
gentlemen did not do their part well—they mumbled, they
did not give the full titles & sometimes got stuck. However each passed with bow & curtsy & the onlookers were
satisfied. (Saywell 323)

Lady Aberdeen paid tribute to Dr. John George
Bourinot, then Clerk of the House of Commons, for suggesting all the characters that should be represented at the
ball. Bourinot himself wrote a book to commemorate the
event, and included the photographs and names of the participants in each of the groups. The author of an earlier book,
The Story of Canada, he gave here an overview of Canadian
history with emphasis on the scenes represented at the ball. In
embellished Victorian prose, he too emphasized the importance and success of the event as theatre:

And now another Governor-General and his accomplished Countess have assembled, as it were, on the stage of a National Theatre—on the floor of the National Legislature—all the principal actors in the historic past of Canada, and have given vividness to the narratives of those authors who have been the first to take up a branch of literature of whose value and interest the majority of Canadians were for years themselves as ignorant as that famous Governor and High Commissioner who exposed so ably Canadian grievances and laid the foundations of the responsible system of Government which the Dominion and Provinces of Canada now enjoy.

No language can give a reader an adequate idea of the brilliant spectacle which the Senate Chamber presented on the night in question. No pen can recall the music or the dance, or paint the brilliant and varied costumes of the personages that were represented on this eventful occasion. All that the writer can venture to do is to recall "the storied Past"—some of the features of that memorable procession which walked, as it were, out of the shadow and darkness of the Centuries that are now immured in history, and attempted to assume once more the life and vigour of beings of the Present. (Bourinot 9)

Those lines were written seventy-three years before the opening of the National Arts Centre, but they express some of the sentiments that gave rise to the building of a national theatre in Ottawa. Bourinot gave further details of the historical accuracy and effectiveness of the group scenes:

The flags and banners which preceded each group also bore true historic emblems. The raven of the Norsemen, the lions of St. Mark, the red cross of England, as well as her "meteor flag," the white flag of France sprinkled with fleurs-de-lis, appeared in their proper place in the procession as it advanced, group after group. Each of these groups had its own dance—the most characteristic and pleasing feature of the spectacle. In every case, these dances were made, as far as possible, a reflex of the social condition of the time and people represented. For instance, the dance of the Norsemen showed much of the spirit of the sea rovers of old, just as the Minuet with its stately movements, illustrated the dignity and grace of courtly circles. (Bourinot 21)

He concluded with a glowing reinforcement of the high purpose of the spectacle:

> The writer has endeavoured only to show that the pageant must be regarded as having been conceived and carried out with a far higher aim in view than the mere amusement of a few hours. It was intended—and who can say that it will not accomplish the object?—to force the careless student of our history to recognise its great charm and varied interest, and to feel a deeper pride in this "Canada of ours," now commencing to wear the habiliments of a nation. Though "its lights are fled and its garlands dead," yet the educating influences of the historic ball must remain. (Bourinot 21)

Lady Aberdeen had chosen her collaborator well.

The local newspapers were more sober in their many articles on the ball, but they all agreed it was a great success. Both the *Citizen* and the *Evening Journal* gave directions for the participants prior to the ball, and glowing, detailed reports of it with the names of hundreds of those who attended. In an editorial entitled "The Ball this Evening," the *Citizen* compared it favourably with the spectacles put on by an earlier Governor General, saying it "will be one of the most brilliant spectacles, if not the most brilliant, ever seen in Canada. Nothing of the kind has been known in Ottawa since Lord Dufferin's time, and the best effort of that period would not compare with this evening's fête" (*Citizen*, Feb.17, 1896, p. 4). Theatre under the Aberdeens had moved outside Rideau Hall, and beyond the confines of the proscenium arch.

* * *

Ladies and gentleman in costume
for Victorian Era Ball, Toronto, 1897.
(NAC)

In surpassing the spectacles of the Dufferins, the Aberdeens were moving away from the tradition of theatre at Rideau Hall begun by the Dufferins. They were also moving their spectacles from Ottawa, and the next big event took place in Toronto on December 28, 1897 in the form of a Victorian Era Ball to commemorate the Diamond Jubilee of Queen Victoria's reign. It was an even bigger event than the Historical Ball in Ottawa; this time there were some 2500 guests, with four hundred taking part in historical dances to represent various aspects of life in the Victorian era. As in Ottawa, Lady Aberdeen wanted the ball to have a focus, and she turned for advice to Dr. George Parkin, headmaster of Upper Canada College. He suggested

> a scheme taking various features such as Literature, Art, The Drama, Victorian Sports, Victorian Costumes & so forth with one dance to illustrate the Empire. This suggestion at once commended itself to the preliminary meeting of Toronto great ladies whom I summoned to consult & advise. They threw themselves so heartily into the idea of the Ball from the outset that there was never any doubt of its success & instead of there being only one dance to illustrate each period there had to be four or five included in each group. (Saywell 446)

In the final arrangements, the historical scenes consisted of six groups: 1) The Empire; 2) Victorian Costumes; 3) Literature and Music; 4) Science and Inventions; 5) Art and the Stage; and 6) Sports and Amusements (*Book* 45-7). The ball was held in the Toronto Armouries, which was the size of a football field. The reminiscences of the Aberdeens described it as

> an enormous gaunt building, 300 feet long by 150 feet broad, the height being 50 feet, and the cubic space 1,800,000 feet. It was divided into two portions, one for dancing, the other for supper, and a most effective plan of decoration in pink and green was devised, with a pillared

> marble balcony outside a palace at one end. The two thou-
> sand five hundred guests could all be seated to watch the
> historic dances, which were most beautifully got up and
> perfectly executed. (*Aberdeen* 58)

Lady Aberdeen even revealed the cost and numbers per sitting
at the dinner: "It came to $2,100. for 2500 people. Five hun-
dred people could sit down at once at round tables & there
were 100 waiters so nobody was kept waiting & there was
plenty up to the last" (Saywell 447). At a cost of about $1.00
per person the meal was a bargain, even given the inflated
prices Canadians pay for banquets today. The whole event
came off more smoothly than the ball in Ottawa, including
the introduction of the performers, as she wrote:

> there was never a hitch which was certainly more than we
> expected when we had the rehearsal the night before &
> when all seemed dire confusion. One dance finished & the
> next came on like clockwork & between each all the par-
> ticipants were introduced by their real & their assumed
> names by their respective heralds, the standard bearer of
> the group standing opposite us & we standing on the low-
> est step of our broad stairs below the throne. (Saywell 448)

She did not go into detail describing the dances but rather
outlined three highlights, which were centred on the vice-
regal presence and participation, possibly a sign of their desire
to impress the people of Toronto and to emphasize the
importance of the monarchy and its representatives:

> 1. Our procession into the room down the centre & up to
> the dais to *God Save the Queen* ...
> 2. The Empire March when formed into a St. Andrew's
> Cross & again when it filed up to be presented.
> 3. And above all the moment when His Excellency stepped
> to the front of the dais after the Empire march &
> announced that he had informed the Queen about the Ball
> which was to take place & that he had that afternoon
> received a telegram which indicated that Her Majesty's

thoughts were with us—he then suggested we should all unite in singing *God Save the Queen* & as with one sponta- neous impulse all rose to their feet & sang. It was an impressive moment, as all present felt it to be & one of those moments which do much to seal a nation's loyalty. (Saywell 448)

Queen Victoria was not so pleased with his announcement. Lord Aberdeen's sense of the dramatic in revealing the Queen's telegram for the occasion got him into some trouble, as Lady Aberdeen revealed:

> … we were surprised to hear through Chamberlain that the Queen thought A. was not warranted to use it as he did, but further explanations & the emphasizing of the fact that this was no private entertainment but a final public cele- bration of the Jubilee year has made it all right, we under- stand. Anyway we cannot regret the message being given for the effect was all for the good. (Saywell 449)

Her own delight at achieving the desired effects of the ball made her downplay the embarrassment caused by reading the telegram publicly. As so often in Canada, the Aberdeens knew what they wanted and got their way in spite, even, of the Queen's wishes.

The Victorian Era Ball was a great success, and "was described in all the papers as the biggest social function that had ever taken place in Canada" (*Aberdeen* 56). Its impact as theatre seems to have left less of an impression on the Aberdeens; perhaps because it was so large it was unwieldy and failed to achieve the right dramatic impact. A large vol- ume entitled *Book of the Victorian Era Ball*, with some open- ing remarks by Lady Aberdeen and an introduction by Parkin, was assembled to commemorate the event; it was "entered according to the Act of Parliament of Canada in the year 1898 by James Mavor, Professor of Political Economy in the University of Toronto" (*Book*). James Mavor was the grandfather of Canadian playwright, director, actor, teacher, memoirist and arts administrator Mavor Moore. A copy in the Robarts Library of the University of Toronto was presented to that institution by his daughter, Mrs. Dora M. Moore. Some twenty artists were commissioned to contribute eighty-seven drawings of all six themes which made up the dances. They were followed by a list of the ladies and gentlemen who took part in the sets. This was the last great ball organized by the Aberdeens before their departure from Canada on November 12, 1898.

The Aberdeens' penchant for spectacle overshadowed their interest in more traditional theatre; they do not speak of attending any plays in Ottawa, and of few elsewhere. This may have been due in part to their Puritan outlook on the triviality of mere entertainment. It may also have been due to their view of Ottawa society and cultural life as inferior to that of other cities in Canada. Like many of their predecessors they arrived in the nation's capital with low expectations, and often found them realized. This view of Ottawa we see at various places in Lady Aberdeen's journal, as on their return to the city on January 30, 1895:

> As the *Montreal Star* put it this evening, we have left Montreal for Siberia ... We are very sorry to leave Montreal, even though the house here is of course much more comfortable. But it is of no use to try to compare Montreal & Ottawa—we must do our best here—& see if we cannot work things up to a little higher level at any rate. But Ottawa means exile emphasized, accompanied with a feeling of helplessness. Happily, Ottawa does not mean Canada, nor does it represent Canada. (Saywell 194)

The capital also compared unfavourably with Halifax—"We always feel a sort of shock at Halifax, as everything is so smart & proper & we have to be on our ps & qs instead of being left severely to ourselves as we are in Ottawa, where no propriety or smartness would have any effect" (Saywell 415)—and with Toronto, although Lady Aberdeen had some reservations about Toronto's view of itself:

... flying visits of a week or so are of no use in a place like Toronto, which considers itself the centre of the Dominion, although in truth it is very provincial. We should certainly advise our successors to try to spend a few weeks at Montreal & at Toronto with the object of entertaining & getting to know the people as soon as they possibly could. It is in these two places that the men of substance & weight & education reside principally & if once one can get into personal touch & relations with them, one can do so much more for the country. Shut away at Ottawa, we never get a chance to see these people. (Saywell 409)

Here we see more clearly why they so wanted to impress Toronto with the Victorian Era Ball.

Two experiences added to Lady Aberdeen's low estimation of Ottawa. One took place at the first entertainment they gave after arriving in the capital. She described both it and the ensuing debacle in the cloakroom:

We had our first regular entertainment to-night, consisting of a concert, to which we invited the élite of Ottawa. About 350 present—we received in ante-room & passed them on to ball-room where we had arranged platform at further end, & the supper was in tennis-court ... We think people enjoyed entertainment & they do not seem to have had regular concert before. The ladies behaved somewhat boisterously in cloak-room & quite upset our calculations by vaulting over table arranged for giving out the cloaks & insisting on going for their bundles themselves, & as no reasonings or entreaties would make them abstain from this of course there was dire confusion. We think of sending out a little printed note explaining cloak-room arrangements next time with the invitation. (Saywell 42)

The impression left by this scene was strengthened by the advice she received later from Lady Thompson, wife of the Prime Minister:

> Long talk about Ottawa society & its ways & its wishes.
> Lady Thompson sums up its chief demand in saying "feed
> them, feed them, feed them—nothing else will satisfy
> them." However it would be waste of time to write down
> anything about the demands or the tone of Ottawa society
> in detail. (Saywell 213)

However, like many of her predecessors, Lady Aberdeen did
become fond of Ottawa, partly as a result of the May Court
Club she founded for young women. One is inclined to think
that her founding the Club was prompted by the unruliness
of the ladies in the cloak-room; she might have hoped to ele-
vate their manners and taste as she did the members of her
Household Club. Be that as it may, she wrote from the ship
that was taking her back to England:

> ... our dear May Queen girls ... have made a great differ-
> ence in our feelings towards Ottawa during the past few
> months, for through them we seem to have come so much
> nearer to the people in society generally, & I must own to
> beginning to feel quite a sneaking fondness for the place
> itself, in spite of its shabby old Government House put
> away amongst its clump of bushes & in spite of dirty old
> tumble down Sussex St., to drive over which always needed
> an effort, although it was an effort almost daily repeated.
>   Perhaps this fondness is not altogether unconnected
> with a scheme for a grand improvement of Ottawa which
> lies very near our hearts & which if carried out would make
> her one day a very queen of capitals. (Saywell 478)

This last estimate is one that many would endorse today after
all the improvements that have been made to Ottawa since
1898, partly as a result of the efforts of the Aberdeens.

If the Aberdeens did not attend many plays in Ottawa,
this social climate may have been part of the reason. However, they did show some interest in opera, although usually in
a censorious way—which shows once again their distinctly
moral bent and their insistence that theatre and music must
be useful. Of the three productions Lady Aberdeen spoke of,

one was Gounod's *Philomen and Baucis* seen by Archie, Captain Urquhart, chief aide-de-camp, and a Mrs. Ferguson at the Opera House on January 15, 1894. Her comment was simply that they "thought it well done" (Saywell 59).

The other two involved church congregations, and in both cases the Aberdeens saw fit to censure the works. The first was given shortly after their arrival; the ensuing controversy was described by Lord Aberdeen himself on November 14, 1893:

> Excitement yesterday & today in Ottawa society because we refused patronage to an amateur reproduction of *La Mascot* (sic) by the congregation of Grace St. Church in aid of the Old Men's Home. Some of our staff went to see the opera at Montreal & said it was quite unfit for us to attend. So although it has been modified patronage was refused, partly because of the character of the play and partly because there was a division in the congregation on the subject. Many of the leading ladies of Ottawa belong to the congregation & the papers are v. amusing in the fuss they make over this storm in a tea-pot. We are glad that this opportunity of showing our attitude should have come so soon. (Saywell 29)

The *Ottawa Citizen* headlined a story on the storm thus: "Morality of *La Mascotte*; It Is Again Discussed in Church Circles; Refusal to Accord Vice-Regal Patronage Displeases Prominent Ladies of Grace Church Guild", while it gave clear though restrained support to Aberdeen's stand in an editorial in the same issue: "But even those who fail to see any objection to this opera will recognize the propriety of one placed in authority, and whose objections therefore have weight, marking his sense of the claims of morality upon the stage and upon all public performances" (*Citizen*, Nov. 13, 1893, p. 4). Three days later it invoked the authority of the *Montreal Herald* by quoting its stand in support of the Governor General under the heading "The Mascot Incident" (*Citizen*, Nov. 17, 1993, p. 7). Such was the diplomacy

Aberdeen had to exercise in the first year of his tenure in Canada.

This desire to show moral leadership was also seen in Lady Aberdeen's description of one opera they did see in Ottawa entitled *Dorothy*. The objectionable parts here caused her to write the Catholic Archbishop, as she did on March 22, 1895:

> This evening we went with Mr. Ferguson & Dr. Macken-zie to see the opera *Dorothy* played by amateurs on behalf of the organ of the Sacred Heart Church. Well got up—v. creditable for Ottawa but some by-play might have been omitted with great advantage more especially when one remembers that the object was a charity & the actors were amateurs. I have taken it upon myself to write & tell the Archbishop this saying that we were anxious to be v. par-ticular not to encourage anything the least doubtful & that all the main part of this was good—that knowing the piece was given by his sanction (or rather that the actors were allowed to play it) we had no fear—but would he not send someone to see & report to him. (Saywell 211)

The recommended action for church authorities would not need much encouragement in nineteenth-century Canada.

There is some record of the Aberdeens attending plays outside Ottawa, in Toronto, Montreal, New York, and Boston. The first of these mentioned by Lady Aberdeen is Sophocles' *Antigone*, performed by the students of the University of Toronto on February 15, 1894. Although the play included serious questioning of the role of authority in socie-ty, it received no censure in the journal:

> We went to-night to the *Antigone* given by the students of Toronto U. ... Very well done—acting & dresses & music all good. Two girl students acted the parts of Antigone & Ismene—but they were both perhaps a little shy & too sub-dued & they certainly did not walk gracefully. Creon the King was a magnificent looking man & Haimon his son did v. well & they said he pronounced the Greek the best.

> The Chorus effectively dressed & went through a variety of dances & choruses with success. (Saywell 75)

The other two plays seen in Toronto on that visit both starred Henry Irving, who, along with Ellen Terry, dined with the Aberdeens after one of the plays on Monday, February 20. Lady Aberdeen's description of Tennyson's *Becket* does not enlighten us about the quality of the play or the performers, but it does give some idea of the popularity of Irving on tour and of the warm reception accorded the vice-regal couple at the theatre. The lengthy passage makes us regret not having more of her comments on theatre during the Aberdeens' time in Canada:

> This evening went to see *Becket* played by Irving & Ellen Terry. Crammed. There has been quite a craze here on the subject the last few days & the sale of tickets has been v. brisk. This morning there was an auction sale of tickets by speculators much to Mr. Irving's disgust. The highest price for one seat was $13.00.
>
> Mr. Irving & Miss Terry & their manager (Mr. Stoker) took supper with us afterwards. He much pleased with his reception—likes Canadian houses better than American ones—more responsive. To-night there were a number of Toronto Univ. students in gallery who made things v. lively. When we came in they started *God Save the Queen* vociferously singing against the music of the orchestra. The conductor having played the National Anthem once for the Lieut.-Governor, did not understand what was up & persisted, though in vain, to drown the voices of the singers. Then they began steadily to shout "speech, speech"—so it was with relief that His Ex. saw the curtain rise. They insisted on a speech from Irving at the close—a ceremony which he evidently found more difficult than acting—but he came forward, recovered from his murder & still in the Archbishop's attire & gave reiterated thanks for "the *sweetness* of your welcome, which has made our hearts beat very quick." (Saywell 80)

She tells us that the Governor General went to see Irving in Leopold Lewis's *The Bells* the following night, while she went on to Chicago to see about a store opened there for products of the Irish Industries Association. Her remarks on that play emphasized the generosity of Irving: "H.E. has been very busy—went to see Irving again in *The Bells* on Tuesday, in which he delighted ... Mr. Irving gave $250. for unemployed" (Saywell 80).

The following Saturday Irving was performing in Montreal and the Aberdeens, having just returned to Ottawa, went on to see him there. Marjorie and Archie attended a matinee of *The Merchant of Venice*, and she had some touching comments about the significance of that performance in her recollections of her brother:

> Archie & I were taken from Ottawa to Montreal to see our first play *The Merchant of Venice* acted by Sir Henry Irving and Ellen Terry. We had looked forward to this for weeks, & watched the play with intense excitement & delight. This scene came back to Archie's mind a few hours before he died. (*Archie Gordon* 3)

Their parents went by train to Montreal for the evening performance of *Louis XI* by Dion Boucicault. Even though they arrived late, Lady Aberdeen was deeply impressed by Irving's acting and wrote her most spirited lines about any play she saw in North America:

> ... we went there straight from station & came at beginning of 2nd act of *Louis XI*. Irving acted splendidly—terribly—the part of the wicked, cruel, selfish, hypocritical old wretch—& his terror of death & efforts to evade it & the final death-scene one will never be able to forget. (Saywell 82)

It is unfortunate she did not record more personal reactions like these to the plays she attended.

On the two plays she saw in New York and Boston in 1897 there was virtually no comment. After returning to

Ottawa she wrote of the New York production: "We went to
see a piece called *Secret Service* at the Garrick Theatre, a scene
from the Civil War & then resorted to our old friend the
Plaza Hotel. Next day Marjorie & I shopped successfully,
went to see the Cinematograph" (Saywell 391). The comment on the forerunner of the movies is interesting, but here
again she did not elaborate. Of the play seen in Boston she
simply said: "In the evening we went to Anthony Hope's *Prisoner of Zenda* & enjoyed it very much. He was in Boston
himself" (Saywell 432). There is a record of the Aberdeens
attending the Passion Play at Oberammergau after they left
Canada. A whole chapter of their reminiscences, "Ober-
Ammergau in 1899," was devoted to the excursion (*Aberdeen*
109-14). We can only wish they had gone into as much detail
on the plays they saw in North America.

Somewhat tangentially related to the Aberdeens' involvement in theatre was their attendance at several local agricultural fairs in Ontario in September, 1896. Besides reflecting
the flavour of these fairs and the entertainment included in
the Grand Stand shows, Lady Aberdeen's entries told how
wearing such a tour could be, as she wrote on September 18:

> It is a weary grind, this process of being received at the sta-
> tion by Mayor, Aldermen & perhaps a guard of honour—
> then a solemn drive round the town—presentation of
> addresses, interminable luncheons & if there is a Show on,
> we are taken to the Grand Stand as the first business not
> very likely to inspect a parade of cattle & horses but prob-
> ably to witness a "programme of attractions"—tumblers,
> conjurors, dancers, fireworks & the like which are always
> now considered a necessary adjunct to these Shows, in
> order to increase the attendance of sightseers, amuse the
> farmers' families & bring in money. (Saywell 363)

Speaking again of these fall fairs, her sense of the comic and
of her need for comic relief was shown in another entry written in Ottawa:

Here again after another week of "progress" as it is called, through Ontario—that is, being bucketed from one place to another by night & going through the round of being received at the station, addresses presented, a procession round the town, reception at the Fair grounds, an attempt to go round the exhibits in the midst of a huge crowd, a long luncheon, with nothing possible to eat, & visits to various schools, hospitals, convents & other institutions. We live our days to the tune of *God Save the Queen*, from the moment the train stops till it departs, & one sometimes wonders inwardly whether the moment will not arrive when instead of keeping up an inane smile, we will not seize someone & turn them round & shake them or do something desperate to make at least a change. (Saywell 385)

As we read through the four hundred and eighty-four pages of her journal, we wish she had written more like this, and more on the plays she saw. Indeed, had she seen more plays, the whole journal of this somewhat dour, businesslike lady might have been enlivened.

That the Aberdeens did not show more interest in theatre at Rideau Hall or elsewhere meant a decrease in theatre production there that would eventually bring about the dismantling of the theatre itself. Their early attempts to continue the tradition of children's plays at Christmas time gave way to the more spectacular efforts of their tableaux historiques and historical balls outside Rideau Hall for which their theatre activity will largely be remembered. They were aware that Rideau Hall had been underused in this and other ways in their time as a gathering place for Canadians, although they were pleased they had more guests than their two immediate predecessors, Lansdowne and Stanley. Lady Aberdeen lamented that more cultivated and older people did not come to Rideau Hall but was unable to do much about it. She wrote:

More than double the number of people write their names now at Government House than was the case when we arrived and since the Lansdownes' time it has trebled and trebled. And yet there are a number of the nicest and most cultivated people in Ottawa who never write their names at all, looking upon Government House entertainments as mainly intended for young men & maidens who dance and skate. Except for the dinners the older people come but rarely & the Ministers are very hard to catch ... The younger Civil servants & a few unattached society people run the whole show. (Saywell 452)

It is unfortunate the Aberdeens did not follow more closely the example of the Dufferins, whose entertainments followed by dinner were so attractive to the very people the Aberdeens wanted to attract. A more active involvement on their part in cultural and theatrical life at Rideau Hall besides the Household Club might have overcome some of these problems.

Lady Aberdeen was resigned to her failure at Rideau Hall, and hoped her successor could solve the problems. She wrote: "Perhaps our successor will be able to devise better methods which will make Government House more of the use it should be" (Saywell 452). Outside Rideau Hall, in the Parliament Buildings in Ottawa, in Quebec City, Montreal, and Toronto the Aberdeens had indeed been cultural leaders in Canada. In the intimate setting of the Household Club they had also succeeded. But with the more general population of the nation's capital they had not. Lord Minto would make valiant efforts to overcome the shortcomings of the Aberdeens, and would succeed in some of them, but they would not be enough to save the social and cultural traditions at Rideau Hall.

Works Cited

Archie Gordon. Album of Recollections. Privately printed. Christmas, 1910.

Book of the Victorian Era Ball. Toronto: Rowsell and Hutchison, 1898.

Bourinot, J.G. *Historical Fancy Dress Ball*. Ottawa: John Durie & Son, 1896.

French, Doris. *Ishbel and the Empire: A Biography of Lady Aberdeen*. Toronto and Oxford: Dundurn Press, 1988.

Hubbard, R.H. *Rideau Hall: An Illustrated History of Government House, Ottawa, from Victorian Times to the Present Day*. Montreal and London: McGill-Queen's, 1977.

Johnson, George. "A Canadian Tribute to Lady Aberdeen." National Archives of Canada, DA816A2J8. From newspaper clipping, n.p., n.d.

NAC (National Archives of Canada, *Lord Aberdeen Papers*, MG27 IB5, Vol. 12A, Reel C-1355A).

The Ottawa Citizen.

Pentland, Marjorie. *A Bonnie Fechter: The Life of Ishbel Marjoribanks, Marchioness of Aberdeen and Temair*. London: Balsford, 1952.

Saywell, J.T., ed. *The Canadian Journal of Lady Aberdeen*. Toronto: The Champlain Society, 1960.

Stead, W.T. "Lord and Lady Aberdeen: A Character Sketch," *Review of Reviews*. CIHM microfiche series, no. 13920. s.l.: s.n., 1894?: 41-60.

"We Twa," Reminiscences of Lord and Lady Aberdeen. Vol. 2. London: W. Collins, 1925. Cited here as *Aberdeen*.

Lord Minto as Viceroy of India, 1906.
Photo by Albert Jenkins (NAC C-017270)

Chapter 7

A Sporting Family at Rideau Hall: The Mintos, 1898-1904

Aberdeen's successor at Rideau Hall was Gilbert John Elliot-Murray Kynynmond, fourth Earl of Minto. He was appointed in part to tone down the excesses of the Aberdeens as seen in the activities of the Household Club and in extravaganzas such as the Historical Balls and the Victorian Era Ball. These and other events made the Aberdeens the butt of jokes at home, and had often distressed the Queen, as we have already seen. It is not surprising, then, that when the Mintos were invited by Queen Victoria to Balmoral shortly before their departure for Canada, she gave Lady Minto advice which clearly referred to the Aberdeens. Lady Minto recorded it some years later: "You must never be persuaded to give your name to any new venture which might be criticized but only to those above suspicion" (Mary, Countess 234). This advice may explain the modest entertaining done by the Mintos at Rideau Hall, although it did not deter them from going to the theatre and to concerts, as well as indulging their fondness for skating, skiing, hunting, shooting, riding, cycling and other popular sports during their time in Canada.

Minto was born in London on July 9, 1845, the eldest son of William Hugh Elliot, third Earl of Minto, and Emma Hislop, daughter of a baronet. Although the senior Minto won three out of five elections between 1837 and 1857 he preferred athletics to politics, and in this he set an example which his eldest son would emulate throughout his life. The Governor General's later appointment as viceroy of India was foreshadowed both by his great grandfather, the first Earl, whose tenure as viceroy of the subcontinent lasted from 1806-1813, and by his grandfather on his mother's side, who commanded the Deccan army in India in Hasting's Pindari and Maratha war.

His mother was a highly intelligent, literate, and sensitive person who edited the letters of the first Earl, and who kept a diary in which she showed great awareness of life around her and a talent for writing. She was especially revealing in what she said of the eldest of her four sons, the future Governor General. She was honest in assessing his limited intellectual capacity but was aware of other qualities that often compensated for this deficiency. He was, in her view, "a little slower to quicken than the others" (Buchan 6), and, she said:

> His learning will never be deep nor his energy great, nor is he remarkable either for originality or quickness, but he is sensible, easily interested, likes history, poetry, and drawing, and will, I think, as I have always thought, learn more when his learning is of a kind more to his mind. (Buchan 7)

She also commented: " ... he is not intellectual, but he has plenty of good sense, a singularly fair and candid mind, and a will strong enough to be unconscious of itself" (Buchan 17).

The learning that was "of a kind more to his mind" was the lore and love of nature he acquired from a boyhood spent in the Roxburghshire hills of the family estate at Hawich in the border area of Scotland. Minto learned and loved all he could of nature, and in this he was the heir of both his parents. Carman Miller described the father's influence: "Small, tough, and competitive, Gilbert shared his father's passion for sports, games, and outdoor life. Both preferred horses, masculine company, manly sports, and adventure to debates, drawing rooms, and polite conversation" (Miller 8). In the mother's diary we have an almost mystical description of the hills around their home, showing a view of nature which undoubtedly influenced her son:

> The White Rock this afternoon was much more like a holy place to me. Nothing could be more peaceful, and we all sat there for some time listening to the wood pigeons, and

watching some boys wading in the river, probably following a salmon. I think sometimes if we would let God draw
us to Him my means of the natural agencies with which He
has surrounded us, instead of insisting upon it that we can
only get at Him by violent and distasteful efforts of our
own, by singing without voices and preaching without
brains, we should be more religious people. And certainly
no sermon I ever heard can speak to one's heart so forcibly
as do the scenes and associations of an old family house like
this, where tender memories are in every room, like dried
flowers between the leaves of a book. (Buchan 14)

The healthy irreverence she showed in this passage was shown
by her son in Canada when he confided to his journal the dis-
gust he often felt at the sermons he heard. It was also one of
the reasons he was quite casual in his church attendance in
Canada.

Minto learned more from nature than he did from books,
and his boyhood experiences prompted him to confide to his
journal on February 5, 1882, when he was thirty-six years old:

The more I see the more I look down upon the learning
obtained from books alone. The ordinarily accepted clever
men and women of the world have drawn most of their
knowledge from reading. Goodness knows, I know well
enough the help, even the necessity, of information only to
be obtained from books. At the same time those whose
character is formed by such means alone can bear no comparison to the man who is naturally first-rate, has no book
learning, but has gained all his experience in the school of
a world of many sets, societies, and adventures. Combine
the book learning and the experience of the world, and you
get something very rare. (Buchan 61)

His mother died in April of that year, and in recounting her
death Buchan emphasized her influence on her eldest son:

... no mother and son were ever in more frank and intimate
accord ... His mother's combination of a keen critical mind

> with the happy glow of romance and the warmth of love made her influence supreme, and her personality when alive, and after death her memory, were the chief shaping forces in his life. (Buchan 64)

In fact it was she who served as his teacher before he went to Eton in 1859, and "She established a well-balanced curriculum of history, geography, biology, geology, languages, theatre, painting and ... the adventurous border tales popularized by Sir Walter Scott" (Miller 10). Gilbert would continue to have a broad range of interests throughout his life, including theatre and painting, but when he underwent his formal education at Eton and then Cambridge, it was his interest in sports that engaged most of his energies. He attended Eton from 1859-1863, enjoyed the shcool and its social life, was active in sports, and popular among his classmates, but failed two years in a row so that he was withdrawn at his mother's insistence at the age of eighteen. What he did bring from Eton was the nickname Rolly, which would remain throughout his life, and under which he would later race as a gentleman jockey.

The autumn and winter of 1863 he spent with a tutor in Dresden, and part of the summer of 1864 with another tutor on the Isle of Wight. If he did not learn much at school in these years, he was gaining experience of the wider world. He spent Christmas of 1864 with his family in Rome where his mother wrote of him leading "a very lively life, hunting twice a week, and going out constantly in the evenings to dinners, opera, balls, parties, and private theatricals" (Buchan 18). His journal during his two undergraduate years at Cambridge recorded his attendance at balls and amateur theatricals as well as his insatiable love of sport. Indeed, when he graduated with a Bachelor of Arts from Trinity College in 1866, he wore jockey clothes under his academic gown since he was to take part in a steeplechase race at Cottenham immediately after the ceremony—a race he won by a head. In fact, his greatest achievement at Cambridge was to gain a reputation as a horseman, unlike his more studious classmate, Lord Lorne, who was also destined to be a Governor General of Canada. Minto's next appearance in the Senate House at Cambridge would be to receive an honorary doctorate of laws in 1911.

His formal education over, Minto was free to pursue a career of "peripatetic jockeydom" as Buchan put it (Buchan 24). This career was partially interrupted by three years as an ensign in the Scots Guards when his parents bought him a commission. He sold the commission in 1870, or, as the *Dictionary of National Biography* said, he "retired" (Roberts 172). He was then able to continue his jockeying more earnestly; he competed in the Grand National several times, and won the Grand Steeplechase de Paris in 1874. Although he never won the Grand National, he had a severe fall in 1876 which, according to Buchan, broke his neck (Buchan 28), but in the view of more recent commentators caused only a severe neck injury. This, however, ended his career as a jockey, but it did not dampen his appreciation for the sport or his ability to learn from life's experiences rather than from books. Many years later, at a farewell banquet given him by the Turf Club in Calcutta at the end of his term as Viceroy of India, he summed up these lessons:

> I do not regret my racing days, gentlemen; very far from it. I learned a great deal from them which has been useful to me in later life. I mixed with all classes of men, I believe I got much insight into human character ... the lessons of the turf need not be thrown away in after life. The lines to George Ede, and the old racing instruction "Wait in front," mean much in this world's struggles. Don't force the pace, lie up with your field, keep a winning place, watch your opportunity, and when the moment comes go in and win. (Buchan 29-30)

About the same time Minto confided to a friend that he wished he had been a trainer (Buchan 26).

The years between the selling of his commission and his appointment as military secretary in Canada to Lord

Lansdowne in 1883 were not all sporting ones. They were also years of military adventure and travel in a variety of lands, and only after they were over did he marry in 1883 at the age of thirty-two. In 1871 he and two of his brothers witnessed for three days the uprising of the Paris Commune. In 1874, as correspondent for the *Morning Post*, he spent a month with the Carlist army in northern Spain. In 1877 in the war between Russia and Turkey he became an attaché to the Turkish army under Colonel Lennox, and again served as a representative of the *Morning Post*. On this occasion his health suffered in the climate and he was forced to return home. Undeterred he took part in the Second Afghan War on the staff of Sir Frederick Roberts. In that conflict he was slated to accompany the ill-fated Cavagnari and his staff on their mission to Kabul but was recalled home on private business; otherwise he too would have lost his life with other members of the expedition. In 1881 he accompanied Roberts as private secretary for an expected battle in South Africa, but the war was settled before their arrival. 1882 saw him serving in the mounted infantry in the Egyptian campaign and, although wounded, he led the regiment in the march into Cairo, for which he was honoured.

Meanwhile Minto had published his first article on military matters, a reply to Archibald Forbes in the March 1880 issue of *The Nineteenth Century*, in which he defended new military rules to regulate the work of the press. It was the first of many articles and reports he would write on military affairs. Between these military operations, and then after 1882, he worked with the volunteer forces in the Border country surrounding the Minto estate. During these years he occasionally went to the London theatres. Miller says cryptically, "He also enjoyed the theatre, both the play and the players" (Miller 22), and suggests that the play he most liked was *The Merry Duchess*, in which a Duchess falls in love with a jockey.

At the same time the ex-jockey was courting the lady who would one day be his own countess, Mary Caroline Grey

Lady Minto.
(NAC PA-028149)

(1858-1939), an attractive and intelligent woman thirteen years younger than he. They were married in St. Margaret's Church, Westminster, on July 28, 1883. She was the fourth and youngest daughter of General the Honourable Charles Grey, second son of Charles, the second Earl Grey, Prime Minister of England and author of the Reform Bill of 1832. Her father was also private secretary to Prince Albert and, after Albert's death in 1861, to Queen Victoria, so that Mary and the other children were raised in St. James's Palace in London. One of her brothers was Albert Grey, who would succeed his brother-in-law Gilbert as Governor General of Canada in 1904. Mary was fluent in both French and German as well as English for, she tells us, her mother spoke to her in both these languages and rarely in English (Mary, Countess 224).

The Mintos had five children, the first of whom, Eileen, was born in Ottawa on December 13, 1884, when her father was serving as military secretary to Lord Lansdowne. Sir John A. Macdonald was dining at Rideau Hall the night she was born, and proposed a toast to "la Petite Canadienne." Three of the children—Ruby, Violet, and Larry—were born at St. James's Palace, where Lady Minto's mother was allowed to live after her husband's death in 1870 until her own death in 1890. Queen Victoria served as one of Larry's guardians (by proxy) at his baptism in the Chapel Royal. The last child, Esmond, was born in 1895 and was thus three years old when the family became principal residents at Rideau Hall.

The later lives of the Minto children show how closely the British aristocracy and the families of several Governor Generals of Canada were connected, and how the First World War touched so many of them. Violet married Charles Nairne, the younger son of Lord Lansdowne, who was killed in action in 1914; Esmond was killed in Flanders in 1917; and Larry, who succeeded his father as the fifth Earl, served as aide-de-camp to the Duke of Devonshire, Governor General of Canada, in 1918. All the children, like their father, excelled in horsemanship, while Eileen included acting among her talents, and Ruby proficiency at music. We shall see later how they developed these and other talents while in Canada.

Buchan described the Minto marriage with his usual superlatives: "Melgund was fortunate in many things, but his marriage was the crowning felicity of his life. He won a wife who was to be a comrade and helpmate as perfect as ever fell to the lot of man" (Buchan 69). The Minto family was an active and happy one which revelled in many activities and found much to challenge their energies in Canada. In later life Lady Minto served as lady-in-waiting to Queen Mary for twenty-six years although two of her own children—Eileen as well as Esmond—died before her own passing in 1939.

Three months after his marriage, Minto was appointed military secretary to Lansdowne. The appointment was not surprising because Minto had some military experience from his expeditions abroad, had worked enthusiastically with Volunteer Forces at home, and was a schoolmate and friend of Lansdowne. He came to Ottawa three weeks before Lansdowne and prepared for the new Governor General's arrival. In the Riel Rebellion of 1885 he was General Middleton's chief of staff and took part in the battle of Fish Creek; a rumour even circulated in Ottawa at the time that he had been killed at Batoche. During his tenure as Governor General he revisited the battlefields, where he recalled his comrades in arms with great fondness.

But on the whole both he and his wife found his work and life as military secretary in Canada uninteresting and, in spite of the social and sporting life he enjoyed as a member of the Montreal and Toronto Hunt Clubs, he resigned his appointment at the end of 1885, much to the annoyance of Lansdowne. His father's illness at home was an added reason for his departure. In an attempt to retain his services in Canada, and as a tribute to the impression he had made, John A. Macdonald offered him the command of the North West Police, which Minto also declined. Shortly before Minto left, Sir John A. made the prophetic remark: "I shall not live to see it but someday Canada will welcome you back as Governor General" (Buchan 82).

That would not be for another thirteen years of relative calm and peace for Minto as he reared his young family at their estate in Roxburghshire. The calm came after the election of 1886, in which he was a Liberal Unionist candidate in the borough of Hexham, Northumberland. He ran mainly on a platform of opposition to Irish Home Rule, which he described as "the surrender to an organized rebellion repeatedly denounced by your present Ministers" (Buchan 85), and was consequently defeated by the Home Rule candidate by 967 votes. He had chosen this riding on the advice of his brother-in-law Albert, the future Governor General, who ran in the nearby borough of Tyneside and also lost.

Minto then settled down happily to raise his family and run the estate, where he exercised his talents as an expert landscape gardener. His interest in the past induced him to organize the family archives, a task which foreshadowed his later encouragement of a public archives for Canada. Straightened financial circumstances forced him to cut staff, eliminate some of his large herd of cattle, and sell some paintings along with one of his London houses.

He got involved in local and county work, especially in promoting the efficiency of the Volunteer Forces. Since he was still a brigadier and respected for his military expertise, he was often asked to be a judge at military manoeuvres, take part in military discussions, and write on military affairs. He continued to enjoy fishing and hunting on the estate, while both he and his wife developed their proficiency at ice skating, and passed tests to become members of both the London and Wimbledon Staking Clubs. He also led his growing family on long bicycle trips in the Border countryside and abroad.

Minto's life would change again when his father died on March 17, 1891 and he thus became the fourth Earl of Minto. Instead of running in the election of 1892 he took his seat in the House of Lords and made his maiden speech in June, 1893 on the employment of discharged soldiers.

London was the centre of the Mintos' social and cultural life, although there is no evidence that the fine arts were an important part of it. In his eyes the social season consisted of "A great deal of rot, a great deal one likes, and a great deal to learn: interesting people to meet, and the centre of every-thing, charity and devilry, soldiering and politics" (Buchan 109). Each spring they spent a month on the Continent, including a trip to Spain where, Buchan said, they "saw the pictures of the Prado, and stayed during the Easter revels of bull-fights and fairs in the beautiful palaces of the Duc d'Al-ba in Madrid and Seville" (Buchan 111).

Macdonald's prediction came true on July 26, 1898 when Joseph Chamberlain announced that Minto would suc-ceed Aberdeen as Governor General of Canada. Minto had sought and received the support of influential friends and rel-atives, particularly Lord Wolsely, to gain the appointment, and was delighted to accept it even though two other candi-dates had turned it down. He was fifty-three and anxious to get involved in public service work again. The appointment was the occasion for a summing up of his life to that point; in his journal he wrote:

> With me it has been as a boy athletics, then steeplechase riding, then soldiering, till the love of a military career became all-absorbing. But through it all I have gathered a good deal of experience of other men in many countries, and the older I grow the stiffer has become my rule of doing what I thought right in the line I had taken up as a soldier and country gentleman. This, with a certain amount of reading, a little writing occasionally for reviews, and a good deal of intercourse with those people who are helping to make, or are interested in, the world's history, both men and women, has helped me to where I am. It does not seem much, and yet it has often meant hard work, and the sacrifice of many social engagements and other things which to the society world may often have seemed inexplicable, as there was little to show for it. (Buchan 114)

His single-mindedness reflected here had paid off for him; the Minto family—father, mother and five children—sailed from England on November 3, and arrived at Quebec nine days later. They were met by the Aberdeens, and the new Governor General immediately took the oath of office.

The most serious political event in Canada during Minto's vice-regency was the country's participation in the Boer War. He worked diligently to raise and send Canadian troops to South Africa, "a policy for which the governor-general was directly responsible" (Roberts 173), wrote one biographer. Looking back at the event some forty years later, Lady Minto insisted that he "always considered that the decision to send a Canadian contingent to the South African was the most momentous decision ever taken in the history of Canada" (Mary, Countess 237). It was certainly a cause for which his military background had prepared him and one which he embraced with enthusiasm and energy.

Two less happy situations during his term of office also involved military matters. They were the dismissal of two military commanders from the leadership of the Canadian militia. The first was Major-General Edward Hutton, who was appointed to the command in 1898. Minto was clearly sympathetic to him; they had been fellow pupils at Eton, had served together in Egypt, and had both been advocates of mounted infantry forces. But Hutton ran afoul of both Laurier, the Prime Minister, and Borden, the Minister of Militia, and was, to Minto's chagrin and embarrassment, dismissed from his post of General Officer Commanding in Canada. Hutton's successor in 1902, Lord Dundonald, also ran afoul of the government, and was similarly dismissed. However, Minto had learned from his previous experience, and did not support Dundonald as he had Hutton. In fact, the last order Minto signed as Governor General was Borden's bill for a Militia Council, which ensured that the G.O.C. would thereafter be a Canadian.

Minto strongly supported the Canadian position in the Alaska boundary dispute and, when Lord Alverstone's vote on the tribunal turned its decision in favour of the Americans' claim in 1903, he pleaded for reconciliation and Canadian acceptance of the award. Minto was not always so conciliatory. He got embroiled with Laurier over who should receive official honours from the crown; these differences surfaced especially during the 1901 visit of the Duke and Duchess of Cornwall and York (later George V and Queen Mary), and revealed a certain rigidity and insensitivity to Canadian concerns on Minto's part. The same insensitivity was evidenced in his award to Laurier of the Fenian War Medal in 1904, which came as a complete surprise to the Prime Minister at the Governor General's annual levee. Laurier had actually served in the Arthabaskaville Provisional battalion in 1870. Minto's military background had not developed his sense of tact.

On issues limited to the city of Ottawa Minto showed more common sense and foresight. Finding Rideau Hall inadequate for his large family and staff, he arranged for the construction of what came to be known as the Minto wing at the east end of the building. Like other viceregal families, the Mintos looked forward to the day when a new residence would be built. Ironically it was the Minto wing which caught fire in 1904, and from which Lady Minto, recovering in bed from the broken leg she suffered skating four days earlier, had to be carried on a screen.

Unlike other Governor Generals who merely lamented the appearance of the city in which they were forced to live, Minto made recommendations for the enhancement of the nation's capital to the Ottawa Improvement Commission, which came into existence in 1899, early in his term of office. It was the first of three federal planning bodies which would contribute significantly to the development of Ottawa, its successors being the Federal District Commission in 1927, and the National Capital Commission in 1959.

The Mintos were sensitive to the divisions between French- and English-speaking Canadians, and made efforts to bring the two groups together. Besides his official and social activities during the family's residence in Quebec City, Minto often stayed for days at a time in Montreal where he had many friends, and where he held special functions to bring English and French together. Lady Minto's excellent French, and Minto's serious attempts to converse in the language, endeared them to French-Canadians and set an example for English-Canadians. Miller wrote of these efforts in December, 1902 to bring the two Montreal communities together: "He called to his office several prominent Montreal citizens— Dr. William Peterson, Senator George Drummond, and Louis Lavergne, to ask them to help him to improve French-English relations" (Miller 177). Although Miller said these efforts had no long-range effects, they showed Minto's awareness and concern to improve communication between Canada's two founding European cultures.

The Mintos were more selective than the Aberdeens in the people they invited to Rideau Hall, and did not entertain as lavishly as their immediate predecessors. They were criticised for catering too much to the sporting people with whom they felt a natural affinity. A disappointed Martin Griffin, librarian of Parliament, exaggerated when he complained in a letter to Lady Aberdeen: "The skating people seem to be the only ones their Excellencies care for" (NAC 1). In time Griffin would see that they also catered to curling people, horsey people, shooting people, hockey people, and theatre people. They would also seek out and invite to Rideau Hall prominent world figures in these and other fields.

A favourite was Guglielmo Marconi, who visited Rideau Hall several times, was supported by Minto in his experiments with wireless telegraphy, and in return invited Minto to send the first official message across the Atlantic in 1902. Lady Minto recalled fondly Marconi's visits, and called him "one of the world's greatest geniuses," referring to his famous telegram "from Glass (sic) Bay to England (Cornwall)" (Mary, Countess 246). She may be forgiven her misspelling of the Cape Breton city since she was writing this memoir in England some thirty-six years after the event.

Although the Mintos had several American friends, and Lady Minto frequently visited New York, Newport, and Washington during her husband's term of office, Minto made only one official visit to the United States in that time. The reason for this was a regulation that made it necessary for him to receive permission from the Colonial Office to leave Canada, and even then he had to appoint a deputy who would serve in his absence. Lady Minto noted this restriction, but added, "This ban has long since been removed" (Mary, Countess 236). The one occasion was a visit to Theodore Roosevelt, then Governor of New York State, in October, 1899 at Oyster Bay, N.Y., to attend an international yacht race between the Columbia and the Shamrock (Mary, Countess 236).

Although less flamboyant in their support of worthy causes than the Aberdeens, the Mintos gave their patronage and active support to several. Minto organized the Canadian Association for the Prevention of Tuberculosis at a time when, for political reasons, support from politicians was not forthcoming. He chaired several of its early meetings, which were held at Rideau Hall. Lady Minto succeeded Lady Aberdeen as Honorary President of the Victorian Order of Nurses, and raised some £20,000 to help the nursing profession in Canada (Mary, Countess 255). On March 17, 1904 the Governor General chaired the annual meeting of the VON, the last during his tenure in Ottawa. A special address was given to his wife for her work, and Minto added his own praise in the privacy of his diary: " ... she certainly has done wonders" (NAC 2, Mar. 17, 1904). But Lady Minto wanted to make her own mark, and so she came up with schemes to help "cottage hospitals," medical clinics in small communities. This commitment came after a trip to western Canada which made her realize the isolation of many areas of the country, and the heroic work being done by nurses in these areas. She used many occasions to raise funds for her cottage hospitals, including concerts, plays, and even the death of Queen Victoria. Buchan once again is fulsome in his praise for her good works:

> Lady Minto's energy was unflagging, and her tact infallible. She busied herself with every form of social work, interesting herself in the charities already established, and raising a fund in memory of Queen Victoria which was devoted to establishing cottage hospitals in outlying districts. She accompanied him (Lord Minto) everywhere and everywhere made friends. (Buchan 181)

However it was sports that had priority in Minto's life in Canada. Reading his journal and the travel diary kept by Lady Minto, one gets the impression that his official duties were interludes in the round of athletic activities that he so avidly engaged in. His preeminence as a horseman, a hunter, a shooter, a cyclist, and a skater before coming to Canada has already been noted. All of these activities he was able to indulge in while in Canada, and he was quick either to take part or at least an interest in almost every other sport available to him—canoeing, skiing, ski-jumping, fishing, hockey, baseball, football, snow-shoeing, curling, and golf.

Many times in his and his wife's journals we read accounts of their travelling to Montreal or Toronto mainly to attend horse shows. He also attended horse races and was a favourite of the Ontario Jockey Club in Toronto. He even watched some trotting races in St. Stephen's, New Brunswick on a tour of the Atlantic provinces in 1901 (Mary Minto, Aug. 2, 1901). At times he would go from Ottawa to Montreal and back the same day for a horse show, as he recorded on May 8, 1902: "To Montreal by 8.30 train for Horse Show—good show—back at 10 p.m. to Ottawa" (NAC 2, May 8, 1902). In January 1903 a delegation sought and received his support for a race-track in Aylmer, Quebec, across the river from Ottawa. On that occasion he wrote: "Skead and ... a Mr. Cameron ... came to see me as to organization of a race course on the Aylmer road. I said I thought idea excellent, and delighted to do what I could" (NAC 2, Jan. 15, 1903). Many photographs at Rideau Hall show the Minto family on horseback, and they were frequent riders in

Capital Lacrosse Team, with Duke and Duchess of Cornwall and York (later King George V and Queen Mary), in the pavilion, 1901.

Photo by Pittaway (NAC C-033329)

and around their official residence. On one ride, Minto survived a fall by his horse, and wrote of it at some length in his diary (NAC 2, Oct. 28, 1902).

Hunting was no less dear to his heart, and he got away from Ottawa almost every fall for about two weeks to shoot moose, and even fox at St. Ann's, Quebec. These trips with some of his male friends were a source of great exhilaration to him, and he devoted several pages of his journal to an account of these happy days, as he did in a description of the hunt at Kipawa, Quebec, near the Ottawa river in 1903 (NAC 2, Sept. 30-Oct. 9, 1903). In a long description of a hunt near Montreal, he wrote joyously: "What recollections of the old days!" (NAC 2, Nov. 20, 1902). He was able to revive some recollections at Rideau Hall on a January night in 1903 when he watched a magic lantern show of a hunting trip in the North West the previous year (NAC 2, Jan. 11, 1903).

Shooting duck was another of Minto's favourite sports, and for this he went to Poplar Point, Manitoba at various times. At the end of his three-month tour of the North West in 1900, he remained several days at Poplar Point to shoot with Senator Kirchoffer while his wife proceeded to Ottawa (Mary Minto, Oct. 8, 1901). In 1901 he joined the Duke and Duchess of Cornwall and York there for some shooting as their extensive tour of Canada was coming to a close. In a letter to the Duke's father, King Edward VII, he described the shoot and the difficulty he had arranging it:

> I met them on their return from the West at a place called Poplar Point, in Manitoba, where we had two days' duck shooting, which I believe the Duke enjoyed. I think that eleven guns got about 700 duck in a day and a half's shooting, and a detached party of four guns got about 200 more. I had great difficulty in arranging this shoot: my Ministers were opposed to any shooting at all, and I finally had to insist on it on the ground that it really was absurd to say that H.R.H. should not be allowed a day and a half's relaxation. (Buchan 186)

Running the Timber Slide on the Ottawa River, with the Duke and Duchess of Cornwall and York (later King George V and Queen Mary), 1901.

Photo by W.J. Topley (NAC C-007205)

From September 24 to October 14 the following year the Mintos travelled to Manitoba and Saskatchewan, where they shot duck, prairie chickens, and geese for a grand total of over 1,000 birds (Mary Minto, Oct. 14, 1902). Eight days later the Governor General left for three days' duck-shooting at another favourite spot, Long Point, Ontario, to which he returned the following year for a week, although on this trip he complained about not doing well (NAC 2, Nov. 2, 1903). Although Lady Minto did not accompany him on the second excursion, she went hunting pheasant herself for four days with the Seward Webbs at their Shelburne Farms in New York State, from which she returned "with terrible tales of the dangers of pheasant shooting" (NAC 2, Oct. 21, 1902). There are many photographs in Lady Minto's travel diary of the Mintos and their retinue proudly displaying their abundant harvest of birds.

As we might expect, Minto's enthusiasm for shooting carried over to international contests. He gave his impression of one of these at Rockliffe in Ottawa for the Palma Trophy, which featured British, Canadian and American teams, as "the most exciting match I ever saw," although the British team was first and the Canadian team last (NAC 2, Sept. 13, 1902). He also wrote of the luncheon and speeches at the Dominion Rifle Association clubhouse afterwards.

There was ample opportunity in Canada for Minto to indulge in his second favourite sport, fishing, especially on the Cascapédia River, where he used Lansdowne's cottage, New Derreen. But times had changed since Lansdowne's day, and Minto voiced a complaint about American fishermen who had invaded what was once the exclusive fishing grounds of the Governor General. As Buchan wrote:

> It was a great grief to Minto that the fishing on the Cascapedia was no longer the perquisite of the Governor-General; for the enjoyment of this sport he had to be beholden to private owners, or to accept the hospitality of the American clubs who had purchased the fishing of many Canadian

Lord Minto and friend skating on the Ottawa River.
(NAC PA-033800)

rivers. The luxury of the newcomers seemed to him to sub-
urbanize the sport. "Very hospitable, certainly," the journal
notes, "but an unworkmanlike look about them; very smart
sporting clothes, looking as if they never had been and never
would be rained on. X— himself in a grey hat and white
puggaree, variegated waistcoat, new puttees under white low
gaiters, and brand new leather boots. He would have startled
them on the Tweed. (Buchan 196)

Canoeing and cycling Minto enjoyed regularly in
Ottawa, although usually as a social and recreational pastime
rather than the vigorous sports they were for him back home.
While he often spoke of going out with members of his family, his most frequent partner in Ottawa was Lola Powell,
whose relationship with Minto is explored in a chapter of
Gwyn's *Private Capital* entitled "Minto's Folly", a sobriquet
often applied to Lola herself. On one memorable occasion the
Mintos ran the timber slides in the Chaudière Falls near
Ottawa in the company of the delighted Duke and Duchess
of Cornwall and York (Mary Minto, Sept. 23, 1901).

No prodding was needed to initiate the Mintos into the
joys of winter sports in Canada. Both were already accomplished skaters when they came to Ottawa, and they were
determined both to increase their own and their children's
skills and to introduce Canadians to the finer points of the
sport. One of their most popular social events was a weekly
skating party at Rideau Hall. To improve their skills they
induced the American champion George Meagher to spend
time in the capital almost every winter, to give them lessons,
to display his own skill, and to judge skating competitions.
The arrangement with Meagher was spelled out by Minto in
one journal entry: "Meagher came at 3 p.m. and skated all
afternoon ... we have made a bargain with him for a month"
(NAC 2, Jan. 12, 1903). This was the same Meagher who had
persuaded Lord Stanley to write a preface to his book on skating, although Stanley was scarcely a skater himself. In the
Mintos, Meagher found enthusiasts and friends. He praised
them, too, especially "the impetus which has been given by

Her Excellency the Countess of Minto ... one of the most graceful lady skaters in the world" (Mary, Countess 253). Minto often arranged for Meagher to skate privately with him and with his wife. In February 1903 Minto gave a long description of the skating competition at Ottawa's Rideau Rink; Meagher was one of the judges, and Ruby and Eileen with their respective partners tied for first place in the doubles events. Minto took this occasion to note: "It is marvellous how skating at Ottawa has improved ... but they are still here a very long way behind the 'old country'" (NAC 2, Feb. 9, 1903). This is a timely reminder for Canadians who think that ice-skating, like ice-hockey, was invented in Canada. To ensure that skating would continue to flourish in the nation's capital, the Governor General was instrumental in forming the Minto Skating Club, which has been the home of world champions and competitors, and remains an important training ground for Canadian skaters today.

Lady Minto even had the misfortune of breaking a leg while skating in Ottawa in 1904. Her own enthusiasm for the sport was seen in the fact the she was skating on an outdoor rink on March 30, a very late date to be skating outdoors any year. She recorded simply: "My skate caught in some bad ice and I fell breaking my leg" (Mary Minto, Mar. 30, 1904). Lord Minto gave a much longer description of the accident, including the arrival of a Dr. Powell at the rink with a splint (NAC 2, Mar. 30, 1904). The unfortunate aftermath for the injury-prone Minto family was a fire in the Minto wing at Rideau Hall four days later, on Easter Sunday, while Lady Minto was recuperating in her room. She had to be carried on a screen to another room. But minor misfortunes could not deter the exuberant Mary Minto who, in her 1938 memoir, boasted that she still skated at the Westminster Skating Club, and at seventy had skated with an old partner, Alex Adour (Mary, Countess 254).

Another misfortune associated with the skating activities of the Mintos was the drowning in the Ottawa River near Rideau Hall of two people who were either members of the

Mintos' party or followers of their skating group on December 6, 1901. (See Gwyn 321-6.) The two were Bessie Blair, the nineteen-year-old daughter of the Minister of Railways and Canals, and the twenty-nine-year-old Henry Albert Harper, the Assistant Deputy Minister of Labour. When the newly formed ice gave way beneath Bessie, and she plunged into the freezing water, Harper dove in to save her, but both were drawn under the ice by the current, and drowned.

Whether or not Minto felt guilty for setting a bad example of skating on the river so early in December, he was very solicitous toward both the victims and their families. He and Lady Minto attended Bessie's funeral while his Military Secretary represented him at Harper's funeral on the same day. Harper was the dear friend and room-mate of Mackenzie King, who was then, at twenty-eight, Deputy Minister of Labour. In Harper's honour King arranged for a statue of Sir Galahad to be erected on Wellington St. in Ottawa, in front of the Parliament Buildings, with an inscription from Tennyson's *Idylls of the King*: "Galahad cried, 'If I lose myself, I save myself.'" The statue still stands as a reminder to passers-by of Harper's heroism, and of the loss of two young lives. Although Minto had departed Canada a year prior to the unveiling of the monument in 1905, he needed no monument to remind him of the tragedy that had attended him on one of his best-loved outdoor activities in Canada.

In describing the involvement of the Mintos in winter sports, Buchan showed that skating was not their only activity:

> There would be an occasional tramp with the Snow-shoers in their picturesque costumes to the rhythms of French-Canadian songs. Minto also took up skiing with enthusiasm, and with Lady Minto and the children was often seen careering over the snow-clad hills at Fairy Lake. (Buchan 196)

Minto wrote of watching ski-jumping at Rockliffe Park, and noted with pleasure the increase in popularity of skiing in Ottawa. They were as well lovers of winter carnivals and ice-palaces. In February 1902 they went to Quebec City for a carnival and were forced to cross the St. Lawrence River from Lévis to Quebec in a canoe when the ice-bridge broke up (Mary, Countess, Feb. 3, 1902). In 1903, they went to Montreal for Ice-Racing (Mary, Countess, Feb.7-8, 1903), and in 1904 attended an Ice-Carnival at Ottawa's Lansdowne Park at which, Minto noted, "Polly, Eileen, Vi and self (dressed) as Hungarians—a great success—an enormous march led by Polly and self" (NAC 2, Mar. 14, 1904). Many photographs of the event attested to the authenticity of the costumes and the massiveness of the ice-palaces.

Since Minto was a Scot, it was natural he should take an interest in curling while in Canada. In fact, he donated a prize for a match played annually at Rideau Hall, and he invariably invited the curlers to lunch at the rink. When a group of Scottish curlers visited they were given a luncheon in the ball-room (NAC 2, Jan. 19, 1903). Although Minto left one competition to go to the theatre, he returned to the match which was still going on after the theatre, and was rewarded with "some magnificent play" (NAC 2, Feb. 5, 1903). He also gave a trophy for lacrosse, the Minto Cup; in 1901 the Duke and Duchess of Cornwall and York witnessed the final match for the cup and the duke was so taken with it that he was given the ball as a souvenir (Hubbard 103). Minto didn't speak of playing golf in Canada but he was induced to open the new Ottawa Golf Club on the Aylmer Road in Quebec, and duly recorded the occasion: "Drove Eileen out to open the new Golf Club ... all Ottawa there ... a very pretty Club House" (NAC 2, May 17, 1904).

Minto was a willing spectator at almost any sporting event. In Toronto he went to a baseball game between Toronto and Baltimore, "the latter winning" (NAC 2, May 7, 1903), but he said nothing of the impression the game had on him. He did have some comments on the football game he attended between Ottawa Rough Riders and Ottawa University for that year's championship: " ... had never seen one of these big matches before ... thought it about the most deadly/dull entertainment I ever attended" (NAC 2, Nov. 7, 1903). But he was a most enthusiastic hockey fan; he even played the game at Rideau Hall with members of his staff, family and friends, both men and women. He frequently attended hockey games in Ottawa, and occasionally in Montreal, and several times dropped the puck for official face-offs. His journal included lengthy descriptions of games; the winners were invariably recorded, as in the case of the match between Ottawa and the Montreal Victorias on January 4, 1902, which Ottawa won 5-4, "a most exciting match" (NAC 2, Jan. 4, 1902). A year later he described a game between Ottawa and Montreal as "the most exciting match I ever saw," and then testified to the violence of the sport even then when, "at the close of the match one of the Montreal match (sic) hit Murphy, who was sitting next me in the face ... apologies" (NAC 2, Jan. 17, 1903). One of his most vivid descriptions was of a game between Ottawa and the Victorias on February 5, 1903, won 7-6 by Ottawa; it describes how he went with Polly, Eileen and aides to Montreal "for ice racing (skates) and hockey match in the evening ... Dined in our car and then to arena for match, Ottawa v. Victorias—former winning by 7 to 6 ... a tremendous match ... Ottawa led all the early part of the game easily, but tired and went to pieces towards the finish til it became 6 all—Ottawa gaining the winning point in the last few minutes" (NAC 2, Feb. 7, 1903).

When he didn't attend one particular game played in Montreal between Ottawa and the Montreal Athletics, he followed it on radio, and gave the score at intervals in the course of writing in his journal, until the final report at 11:30 p.m.: " ... last news just in—Ottawa wins 3-1—Three cheers!" (NAC 2, Feb. 21, 1903). At the end of 1903 and the beginning of 1904 he recorded a series between Ottawa and Winnipeg for the Stanley Cup, which may seem strange to fans today accustomed to seeing the final series played in the month of May or June. Minto attended two of the three games at the new rink at Lansdowne Park. The first game "Ottawa won easily but played ... very foul" (NAC 2, Dec.

30, 1903). The second was played on New Year's day when Minto held his annual levee on Parliament Hill; he did not attend the game although several people from Rideau Hall did. When he heard that Winnipeg won 6-2, he wrote in the vein of a seasoned fan: "I rather doubt Ottawa having done their best—they probably want to have the third match" (NAC 2, Jan. 1, 1904). That match he did attend three days later, and recorded the result with enthusiasm: "Everyone to see hockey match, the last of three, Ottawa v. Winnipeg, the former winning by 2 to 0—a tremendous match" (NAC 2, Jan. 4, 1904). From these and other entries, one can't help feeling that the annual trophy for professional hockey in Canada should more appropriately be called the Minto Cup rather than the Stanley Cup, named after Minto's sedentary predecessor. But lest we feel sorry for Minto, we should remember that he did have a lacrosse cup named after him, as well as a curling tournament, a skating club, and an annual skating show, the Minto Follies.

After Minto's vigorous participation in sport we might wonder if he had time and energy left for involvement in culture in its artistic expression. In fact, various writers on Minto have dismissed his cultural contributions to Canada as of no significance. Stevens and Saywell, for example, in their book-length introduction to Minto's Canadian papers, commented: "He was not a philistine, but neither was he interested in literature, art or music" (xix). Miller stated flatly, " ... he did little or nothing for the arts and letters" (54), and later elaborated on this, saying, "He had neither the passion nor pretence to pose as a patron of the arts and letters, although he always performed his duties ... He seemed more at home at horse shows" (190). The last comment is certainly true, but a close examination of Minto's interest in the arts makes it clear that he was a frequent theatregoer, that he had a liking for certain types of music, that he did attend art shows, albeit often at his wife's bidding, that he had a deep concern for preserving native Indian artefacts, and did much to establish a Canadian archives and to encourage the study of Canadian history.

While not an avid reader, Minto often recorded books that he read, mostly biographies or historical papers. These included a life of Macdonald, which he opted for over a skating event; he wrote: "Large party to Rideau Rink tonight— stayed at home, reading life of Sir John Macdonald" (NAC 2, Jan. 5, 1903); another time he chose a memoir over a night at the theatre: "Everyone to the play tonight—Stayed home and finished Sir H. Rumbold's *Recollections*" (NAC 2, Mar. 20, 1903). At times he wrote of reading all day long, as in the case of *The Creevy Papers* (NAC 2, Feb. 7, 1904) or his friend Lord Wolsley's *Life* (NAC 2, May 8, 1904), both days being Sundays. Once on a hunting trip in the Mattawa district of Ontario, he brought along a book of short stories, as he recorded at the camp: "Have been reading the *Under Dog*, a very good collection of stories" (NAC 2, Nov. 23, 1903).

Such entries are rare. What is not so rare are the references to theatre both at Rideau Hall and elsewhere in Ottawa, mostly at the elegant Russell Theatre. Several notable theatricals were presented at Rideau Hall under the Mintos, all of them written and produced by Captain Harry Graham of the Coldstream Guards, one of Minto's aides-de-camp. Graham was a lively and talented actor, producer and lyricist who described himself as "a Scotchman by birth, an Englishman by occupation, a dilettante with a turn for writing inferior doggerel, a taste for literature, an ear for music, a retentive memory and a prodigious thirst" (NAC 3). Although Miller described both Graham and Lascelles, another ADC, as "two jovial, frolicking school boys, bent on a lark, who were brought out for their decorative and entertainment value rather than any practical talent" (Miller 57), Lady Minto called Graham "a gifted dramatist and musician ... whose *Babes* took Ottawa by storm" (Mary, Countess 235). Referring to his skill as a director she said, "Harry Graham's unquenchable zeal for theatricals and music drew out the talent in each of them" (Mary, Countess 252). In a similar vein Buchan wrote, "There were ... many dramatic performances brilliantly stage-managed by Captain Harry Graham"

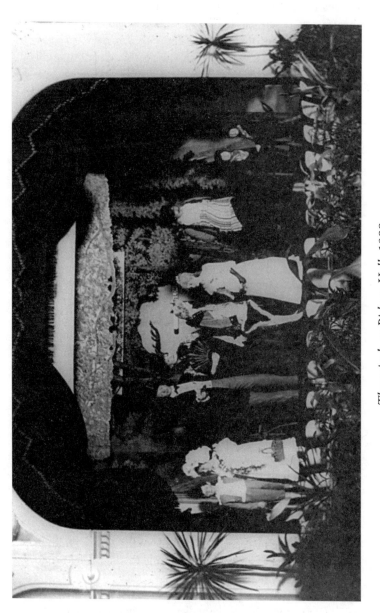

Theatricals at Rideau Hall, 1899.
(NAC PA-027930)

(Buchan 18). On the programs printed for these events the theatre was described as "The Theatre Royal, Government House." The first of these was *The Babes in the Woods* produced in March 1899, of which the acerbic critic Amaryllis wrote in *Saturday Night*, "The local hits were capital, especially that little play on our Canadian idiom, 'on' instead of 'in' Sussex Street" (Gwyn 317). In January 1900 he produced his next pantomime, *The Princess and the Pauper*, which included the Mintos' friend Lola Powell in the cast, and which Minto called "a tremendous success" (NAC 2, Jan. 14, 1900). The next and last play of Graham at Rideau Hall was produced in April 1904. The reason for the hiatus in theatricals between the two last dates was that Graham left Minto's staff during the royal tour in 1901 and only returned in 1903, at which time Minto mused in Toronto, "Harry arrived this a.m. and took up his duties as ADC—so glad to have him back again ... curious that he left us here during the Royal Visit and rejoins us here" (NAC 2, May 8, 1903).

In January 1902, during Graham's absence, the Mintos held one of their few balls, and the occasion drew comment that showed both the importance of the theatricals and the sensitivity of Minto: " ... the first (ball) we have given except the state balls ... about 300 people ... our theatricals under Harry's management have hitherto taken the place of balls, and the latter are after all difficult and full of possible heartburnings when many must be left out who think they ought to come" (NAC 2, Jan. 31, 1902). From this we see that the Minto theatricals were very much the inspiration of Graham, who produced one more for them in April 1904, *Bluebeard: A Musical Melo-Farce in Two Acts*. It featured both Graham, as Captain Frivolo, and Lola Powell as Zisboombah, Bluebeard's favourite niece, as well as three of the Minto children. Graham's whimsy came across not only in the play, but also in the Notice in the program:

> During the entr'acte the audience is requested to fall into a troubled sleep for about ten minutes. Criticism of a kindly

nature may be indulged in, but any controversial conversation on the Fiscal Question is to be discouraged. Any person discovered talking through his nose, in order to avoid wearing out his mouth, will be deported without delay to Montreal, or some other suburb of the capital.

Matinée hats are not to be worn at the evening performances. (Duchesses and other American ladies please note.) (NAC 4)

Minto called the last performance, attended by Lord and Lady Laurier and some 300 guests, "Harry's greatest success" (NAC 2, April 13, 1904). This was the only performance besides the dress rehearsal attended by Lady Minto, who was carried in on a stretcher because of the leg she had broken while skating two weeks earlier. *Bluebeard* received high praise from *Saturday Night* magazine, and from the audience:

> On Monday evening the initial performance of the theatricals at Government House came off, when *Bluebeard* was presented for the first time on any stage, and everyone was unanimous in pronouncing it a complete success in every sense of the word, the music being pretty and catchy, the dialogue clever and witty, and ... the costumes were exceedingly handsome and gorgeous. *(Saturday Night,* April 23, 1904, p. 8)

A measure of Graham's skill and popularity was seen when the reviewer added: "To Captain Graham is due the unprecedented success of the performance, as besides being the author of the play, and also general supervisor of proceedings, he undertook the impersonation of three different characters, and was on the stage almost continuously throughout the evening, constituting the life of the play" (*Saturday Night,* April 23, 1904, p. 8).

Little else in the way of theatre was performed in the ballroom of Rideau Hall, although Minto referred to a "nigger minstrel performance" on New Year's day in 1903. Although, in the absence of Graham, it was only "got up a few days ago," Minto called it "quite excellent." The evening included the appearance of a "Mr. Sopes ... giving an excellent conjuring entertainment as a break to the minstrels" (NAC 2, Jan. 1, 1903).

One dramatic event of special significance at Rideau Hall under the Mintos was the outdoor performance of two of Shakespeare's plays, *As You Like It* and *The Comedy of Errors* by Ben Greet's British company, the Woodland Players. The forest scenes from *As You Like It* were performed in the afternoon, and *The Comedy of Errors* in the evening on Monday, June 8, 1903 to raise money for Lady Minto's cottage hospitals. The terrace on the upper lawn of the house served as a stage while chairs for an audience of a thousand people were set up on the croquet lawn below. It was described as "the first of the kind ever given by a professional company in America" (*Ottawa Free Press*, June 6, 1903, p. 10). Significantly Minto made no comment on the plays in his journal after noting that they took place. He was always supportive of his wife's projects but apparently had little interest in Shakespeare.

Another event at which he supported his wife was a children's fancy dress ball on December 29, 1903 when he commented, "Polly had worked immensely hard at it and it was a great success" (NAC 2, Dec. 29, 1903). Hundreds of children from the ages of ten to eighteen represented all the characters in both *Alice in Wonderland* and *Through the Looking-Glass* in what Minto called "our most successful function" (NAC 2, Jan. 1, 1903). Although not a formal drama, the dressing and marching of so many children had its dramatic moments. A lengthy description of the event was given in the *Citizen* under the headline, "A Unique Entertainment Promoted by Their Excellencies and Participated in by Many Youthful Ottawans—Dancing Was Superb." The colourful review is worth quoting at length:

> Wonderful indeed was the sight the lofty white and gold ballroom at Government house presented last night. Wonderland, with its fascinatingly funny characters and quaint

personages, had become a reality. First and foremost in the procession came Alice, the sweet and demure little heroine of Lewis Carroll's delightful book. She was dressed in a blue frock, her hands placed in the pockets of her little white apron, her long hair falling in a shower of gold about her shoulders, with blue stockings and little black ankle-strapped shoes upon her feet. The white rabbit came next and was followed by the dodo, who was capital as indeed were all the characters ... Never was an idea better conceived and carried out than this ball with its varied and intricate characters. The parents of the children who lined the walls showed much appreciation and enjoyment of the wonderful sight. Their Excellencies, the Governor General and Countess of Minto and house party entered shortly before the procession and took up their positions on the dais in front of the high Christmas tree which still stood in all its glory at the far end of the room." (*Citizen*, Dec. 30, 1903, p. 9)

Before giving a list of the parts played by all the children, the account described their procession and dances and gave credit to a Professor Macquarrie who trained them. After the performance a celebration reminiscent of the Dufferin theatricals was held:

Refreshments were served at a buffet in the small dining-room and supper was served at half-past ten in the Racquet court, where the tables were adorned with Chinese lilies, begonias and azaleas and silver candelabra shaded with red. The ball ended at 12 o'clock and every one departed feeling that they had witnessed a sight never to be forgotten. (*Citizen*, Dec. 30, 1903, p. 9)

So successful was the evening that tableaux from it were planned to be given at a later date at the Russell Theatre in aid of Lady Minto's Cottage Hospital fund (*Citizen*, Jan. 5, 1904, p. 9).

One other play was presented at Rideau Hall in May of that year as part of an at-home given in the ballroom one afternoon by Lady Minto for some 100 lady guests. Minto apparently did not attend, nor did he record it in his journal, but the *Citizen* noted the next day he was "laid up with a cold caught while out sailing on the river" (*Citizen*, May 28, 1904, p. 3). Perhaps the most interesting thing about the play was that it was performed in French, possibly the first ever at Rideau Hall, with three of the Minto children taking part. The local paper reported on the biblical drama and the performances of the Minto children:

> But the pleasantest part of all was a delightful little surprise which had been prepared for the amusement of the guests in the form of a short French drama entitled *Hagar* ... chairs had been arranged in front of the stage ... the curtain arose upon a scene in the desert ... (Lady Eileen playing Hagar) displayed her wonderful histrionic talent to great advantage. (Violet playing the angel) acted and looked the part to perfection ... (Hon. Esmond Elliot) performed his part in a child-like and unconscious manner which was as charming as it was natural (*Citizen*, May 28, 1904, p. 3).

This play was probably not directed by Graham. He left for England the next week with Eileen and Lady Minto, who would not return until the end of July.

In Ottawa the Minto family frequently attended plays, musicals, and concerts outside Rideau Hall, mostly at the elegant Russell Theatre, where they had their own box. Minto's taste in theatre was operettas, opera bouffe, and musical entertainments, and he recorded many of these in his journal. Some of his favourites included *The Climbers* (Mar. 11, 1902), *The Runaway Girl* (Mar. 14, 1902 and Sept. 2, 1903), *San Toy* (Sept. 22, 1902), *When Johnny Comes Marching Home* (Nov. 12, 1902), *The Daughter of Hamelskar* (?) (Dec. 22, 1902), *The Show Girl* (Dec. 28, 1903), *HMS Pinafore* (Apr. 27, 1903), *The Country Girl* (Dec. 28, 1903 and Feb. 24, 1904), *The Red Feather* (May 24, 1904), and the popular English comedian George Grossmith (Feb. 26, 1902). Several times he

Sir Henry Irving
(Bodleian Library, Oxford)

reported that other members of the household went to the theatre while he stayed home. More serious drama he attended when famous British actors were touring, and he often visited them backstage or invited them to Rideau Hall for lunch. Such was the case with Martin Harvey, who performed in *The Only Way*, which Minto described as "good, but not so wonderful a piece as I had been led to believe" (NAC 2, Jan. 26, 1903). *Dolly Varden* he called "the best thing I have seen here beautifully put on stage, and the leading lady Lulu Glaister quite excellent. Rather in the Nellie Farren style" (NAC 2, Sept. 28, 1903). When Lily Langtree appeared in *Mrs. Deering's Divorce*, which he found "very amusing," he "went behind and sat talking in her room for a bit ... she having very much aged ... I never knew her beyond a mere introduction" (NAC 2, Oct. 12, 1903). The meeting recalls Minto's theatre-going activities before coming to Canada and his acquaintance with people in the theatre world.

When Canadian-born Margaret Anglin, daughter of Timothy Anglin, a former Speaker of the House of Commons, played in *Cynthia* for two performances, Minto joined in the enthusiasm of other Ottawans and declared her performance as the leading lady "excellent" (NAC 2, Dec. 9, 1903). He was similarly impressed when he and his wife attended a French play starring Charlotte Wiehe, who was described as "the latest sensation in exotic actresses and although a Dane no Parisienne could be more Parisienne than the pretty and talented artist from Copenhagen, whose acting has been called by the great Henrik Ibsen 'psychology in action'" (*Citizen*, Jan. 2, 1904, p. 5).

Henry Irving and his company presented *Waterloo* and *The Bells* in Ottawa, and lunched at Rideau Hall. Some actors even skated there before the performance, about which Minto had reservations; he considered "the first excellent but in *The Bells* (Irving's) articulation was to me so indistinct, that it qualified very much his fine acting" (NAC 2, Jan. 30, 1904). Ten days later the Forbes-Robertsons were at the Russell with *The Light that Failed*, and were treated not only to lunch and a skating party but also with a band. Minto declared their play "quite excellent" (NAC 2, Feb. 9, 1904).

The viceregal household frequently attended concerts and entertainments, both amateur and professional, some by choice and some from a sense of obligation. As we might expect, the Governor General's response was mixed. But it was always honest, and he made no secret of the fact that he was no lover of classical music, even while recognizing its pre-eminence. He attended performances by world-famous singers and musicians, and sometimes met or entertained them whether he appreciated their work or not. One such person was British composer C.A.E. Harriss, whose Mass for Queen Victoria received its first Canadian performance at Notre Dame Basilica in Ottawa. Minto thought it "quite beautiful though I am no judge of high class music" (NAC 2, Jan. 29, 1902). Half the proceeds went to the church, and half to Lady Minto's cottage hospitals. When Emma Albani, another Canadian, sang at the Russell she stayed at Rideau Hall. Minto thought "her voice quite excellent" and her part-ner "Mrs. Jones's very nice but not big enough for this house" (NAC 2, Jan. 28, 1903). He was not so generous in his description of a lady who sang at a tea given by Lady Minto at Rideau Hall for a group which included Lady Laurier; the singer was "a creature (Mengis or some such name)—a fat lady of about 20, with a most beautiful soprano voice—cer-tainly beautiful, but personally I dislike this sort of freak" (NAC 2, Feb. 3, 1904). His honesty is revealed in his assess-ment of several musicians who came to Rideau Hall for lunch before performing at the Russell: "Mrs. Foster ... a magnifi-cent contralto—also a good violinist De Seve (?), and a most tiresome pianist Reneau" (NAC 2, Apr. 7, 1904). But he was unrestrained in his praise of Madame Nordica, the Chicago soprano, who "did the whole thing herself, any number of songs, quite delightful" (NAC 2, May 19, 1904).

Minto was most at home when he heard a good band, whether it was the Coldstream Guards, Phillip Sousa's com-pany, which often played at the Rideau Rink in Ottawa, or the Grenadier Guards, who gave a special concert for him shortly before his departure from Ottawa and were "quite excellent and played (many) of my favourite tunes" (NAC 2, Nov. 4, 1904). He was elated by a State Concert in his honour organized by his composer friend Harriss on his last night in Ottawa. He did not describe the event until he was on board the *Tunisian* sailing back to England, and he was still bubbling with enthusiasm:

> State Concert at the theatre (in Ottawa), the principal piece *Pan* composed by Harriss and the whole under his management—the idea of a state concert was his too—*Pan* I thought excellent—and the whole thing a huge success— the house crowded, gallery too ... a splendid sight such as has never taken place at Ottawa before ... the chorus sang *Auld Lang Syne* ... and the whole scene one can never forget. (NAC 2, Nov. 20, 1904)

He could also be devastatingly brief in his descriptions of concerts and entertainments he did not like, as in the case of the Normal School Entertainment he described as "quite awful" (NAC 2, May 30, 1902), or the St. Patrick's Day concert which was "deadly" (NAC 2, Mar. 17, 1903), or the singsong at the Russell given by the 43rd Regiment, probably a farewell gesture to himself, which he called "almost the most awful performance I ever attended" (NAC 2, May 18, 1904).

On their travels around Canada the Mintos attended plays and concerts that followed a similar pattern to those they saw in Ottawa. On at least two occasions he heard Calvé sing, in Montreal in *Carmen* (Oct. 18, 1899), and in Toronto at Massey Hall, where he was accompanied by the visiting Duke and Duchess of Cornwall and York, and where they were welcomed by the Mendelssohn Choir (Hubbard 106). On their tour of the North West in 1900 they attended two cultural functions in Winnipeg, one a Scottish concert on their outward journey, which Minto labelled "too deadly for words" (NAC 2, June 24, 1900), and a children's fancy dress ball on their return journey in which their own youngsters took part.

The local paper called it "A Brilliant Assembly of Youth and Beauty at Government House Last Night" (*Winnipeg Free Press*, Oct. 6, 1900, p. 1). In Prince Albert they all attended private theatricals in the town hall, although Minto made no comment on their quality (NAC 2, Sept. 26, 1900). On docking in New York on their return from the aborted coronation of Edward VII, the Mintos attended the matinee of a production called *Chinese Honeymoon*, which Minto thought "very amusing" (NAC 2, July 26, 1902). On his frequent Montreal trips he attended plays like *Sherlock Holmes* (Nov. 17, 1902), opera bouffes, including Sullivan's *The Emerald Isle* (Nov. 26, 1902), entertainments such as a Hallowe'en Concert by the Caledonian Society (Oct. 31, 1899), and classical concerts like the one given by Zella de Tuzan at Windsor Hall (Dec. 3, 1902). In Toronto he attended a concert at Massey Hall organized by Harriss as part of a music festival (Apr. 16, 1903) and another with Harriss and Britain's Sir Alexander Mackenzie conducting. In Ottawa five days later, Harriss conducted another concert where, Minto noted, there was "a crowded house, and a great success, but, as at Toronto, the music above me" (NAC 2, Apr. 21, 1903). Between these two concerts he took in another at St. Patrick's Hall in Ottawa, a benefit concert in aid of Lady Minto's cottage hospitals, for which performers were brought from New York and Montreal, and helped make it "a great success" (NAC 2, Apr. 18, 1903) in the new hall. On their extended tour of Ontario which began ten days later on October 28, they saw plays in Toronto with the famous actor Willard, whom Minto found "excellent" in *The Neildbman* (?) (May 5), but "very disappointing" in *David Garrick* four days later (May 9). In between they heard the Kneibel Violin Quartet from Boston at Toronto's Association Hall, which Minto found "very good indeed but not my style of music" (NAC 2, May 6, 1903). He certainly did know what he liked. He left no record of attending cultural events outside Toronto on this tour, which included London, Windsor, Detroit, Guelph, Berlin, Brantford, Hamilton, Brampton, Gravenhurst, Peterborough and Belleville. Lady Minto seemed not to have been a keen theatre or concertgoer when she travelled without Minto, but she did note attending a "Patriotic Concert" in New York a month after both of them had attended a similar concert in Montreal (Mary Minto, Feb.-Mar., 1900).

The Mintos' interest in music had its effects on their children, especially on Ruby, who took first-class honours in a music competition in Toronto in 1902. When she telegraphed the news to her father (Lady Minto was in England at the time), he was delighted and noted proudly in his journal, "such a triumph" (NAC 2, May 28, 1902).

Indeed, his interest in music was the occasion of trouble for him more than once. The first incident was early in 1899 when Samuel Aitken from the Associated Board of Musical Examiners of the Royal College of Music and the Royal Academy of Music in London came to enforce musical standards in Canada. His methods aroused the opposition of music teachers in Canada, and Minto unwisely supported Aitken, who was soon afterwards recalled to London. Miller summarized the events of the lively dispute, and concluded with a comment on Minto's role:

> A more cautious, perceptive, and experienced man or a less impatient one, might have avoided entanglement in this silly affair. A shrewder man might have attempted to seek or impose peace where he found misunderstanding and strife. But as subsequent events would demonstrate, Minto was at first none of these things. (Miller 64)

A year later a musical concert was the occasion of another imbroglio involving Minto. This time the culprit was General Hutton, who would become another embarrassment for Minto. As part of his larger analysis of the Hutton affair, Miller gave an account of this incident as well. In order to raise money to help the families of Canadian troops wounded or killed in the South African war, Minto agreed to attend a recital at the Russell Theatre in Ottawa sponsored by the British newspaper, the *Daily Mail*, and to host at a later date a dinner for the organizers, believing that the $5,000.00 raised would go to the Red Cross Relief Fund. But Hutton, without telling Minto, arranged for the money to go to the Soldiers' Wives League, of which his wife was president, and whose funds would not necessarily help Canadian soldiers at all. Minto, who only learned of the diversion during the recital, scolded Hutton at the intermission and cancelled the organizers' dinner. Untypically, Minto did not comment on the performance of the singer, Mr. Sharpe, but in his long entry for that day he called the whole affair "a mix-up ... Governor General thinks he is supporting Red Cross, but it is really for Mrs. Hutton's 'Working League' ... rather a jumble altogether" (NAC 2, Jan. 4, 1900). Four days later the following announcement of a National Patriotic Fund appeared in the *Ottawa Citizen* under the headline "Relief Fund for Wives and Children of Our Soldiers. His Excellency Patron": "His Excellency is anxious that the proposed patriotic fund should assume as far as possible a Canadian national character and that the population generally will not hesitate to contribute the smallest sums from 10 cents upwards" (*Citizen*, Jan. 8, 1900, p. 6). It did not say if any more concerts would be held for the victims of the Boer War.

As in other cultural matters, Minto took a passing interest in art. Presumably he visited some galleries in London and on his holidays on the continent. Buchan related that one year "they went to Spain, saw the pictures of the Prado" (Buchan 110). And we know that because of financial difficulties the Mintos had to sell one London house and some paintings (Stevens and Saywell xxi). They supported the Royal Canadian Art Association and attended some of their exhibitions, but they did not get actively involved with it. Nor did Minto have much to say in his journal about the exhibitions he saw, besides a reference to "some really nice ones" (Mar. 20, 1902), and a "very bad" one on another occasion (Apr. 8, 1902). When he was more personally involved with the owners of paintings or the subject matter he had more to say. When he and his wife went on one of their longer visits to Montreal in 1902, they visited two homes on one day which had collections of paintings, and Minto was impressed with the Corots and Reynoldses he saw (Nov. 30, 1902); three days later they visited his friends the Baumgartners and saw "some beautiful modern pictures ... by German artists" (NAC 2, Dec. 3, 1902). He got more involved with the paintings of Robert Harris, who painted a well-known portrait of Lady Minto. On that same visit to Montreal he went to Harris's studio with her but found the paintings "rather disappointing" (NAC 2, Dec. 6, 1902). When the Mintos went to the RCAA exhibition in Ottawa in 1903 to see the Harris portrait of Lady Minto, the Governor General made the most pointed comments he ever made on a painting: "very good but scarcely think he has improved on his first few sittings here ... hair is too dark—but still a good likeness" (NAC 2, Apr. 22, 1903). We may suspect his criticism comes more from affection for his wife than from a trained eye. Still, he had supported Harris being awarded the CMG in the Coronation Honours of 1902; he also supported the sculptor Louis-Philippe Hébert, who received the same honour at the Governor General's levee in 1904. It was Hébert's prominent statue of Queen Victoria that the Duke and Duchess unveiled on Parliament Hill in 1901, a ceremony the Mintos had performed the previous year for another statue of the Queen in Montreal on the grounds of Victoria College (Mary Minto, Nov. 1-2, 1900).

Minto had some uncomplimentary comments on church architecture in Canada when he spoke of the "tawdry style of Roman Catholic churches" and went on to generalize about "the barns we sometimes accept as places of worship, vide St. Bartholemew's (the Anglican church across from Rideau Hall)" (NAC 2, July 19, 1904). And he even had a thought about the barns where we hang our paintings when he suggested that Rideau Hall itself might become the National Gallery of Canada and that a new Governor General's residence be built (Hubbard 96). Neither suggestion was ever taken up, but Minto would be pleased to know that the splendid new National Gallery, which opened on May 21, 1988, is not far from his former residence on Sussex Drive.

Minto took a more active interest in the preservation of native Indian artefacts than he did in other forms of art. He had developed a respect for the Canadian Indian when he was Lansdowne's chief of staff during the Riel Rebellion of 1885, and he was especially concerned about their welfare when he travelled to the North West in 1900 and at other times when he was Governor General. He witnessed and never forgot Lansdowne's condescending treatment of an Indian prisoner, Chief Poundmaker, in 1885, and believed that the government made a mistake in hanging Riel. His concern for the Indians' welfare continued in his support for them in dealings with the federal government in Ottawa; Miller put the matter quite bluntly: "On behalf of his friend Standing Buffalo, Minto carried on a running battle with the Department of the Interior which seemed determined to destroy Indian culture" (Stevens and Saywell xxi). He fought continually, although not always successfully, for the Indians' right to dance their own dances, and on one occasion in Qu'Appelle, Saskatchewan in 1902, he overturned Commissioner Laird's ban and "informed the Indians in Laird's presence that he saw no harm in their dances and invited them to dance in the Commissioner's presence" (Miller 176). He held the same attitude towards traditional Indian dress, which he thought much more civilized than the highlander's kilt, no mean comparison coming from a Scot.

Minto's concern was epitomized in his efforts to preserve a collection of Indian artefacts purchased by the Bank of Montreal from the estate of Mrs. F.D. Freeman. When he heard the bank was going to sell them on the open market, he tried to get a Canadian museum to buy the collection. On February 4, 1903 his journal had a long entry on his subsequent efforts to get the British Museum to purchase the collection, and seven weeks later he reported triumphantly, "Mr. Anderson (Bank of Montreal) came by appointment for a few minutes in order that I might tell him I had arranged with the

BM to take the Freeman collection of Indian curiosities"
(NAC 2, Mar. 24, 1903). His initiative indirectly encouraged
the creation of a national museum for Indian and many other
Canadian artefacts which was officially opened in Ottawa in
1912 as the Victoria Memorial Museum. It is now the Museum of Nature, native artefacts now being displayed in the elegant new Canadian Museum of Civilization in Hull, Quebec.

Minto's love for Canada and its past also bore fruit in the
construction of a Canadian archives building begun in 1904,
the last year of his Governor Generalship. He had become
interested in documents from Canada's past during his yearly
residence in Quebec City. His tours of the city and its ruins
led him to inquire about their history, and he discovered to
his horror that the collection and preservation of Canadian
historical documents were in a state of chaos. As Buchan
described the situation:

> They were rotting uncatalogued and uncared for in cellars
> and basements: no one department was responsible for
> their custody (though there had been a Canadian Archivist
> since 1872), and no attempt was made to fill up the gaps
> in them, with the result that they were virtually useless for
> the purposes of the scholar. (Buchan 187)

In a letter in 1903 Minto had made specific recommendations to Laurier, the Prime Minister at the time:

> It appears to me that the appointment of a Deputy Keeper
> of the Records would be of the greatest value to the history
> of the Dominion ... For this appointment, both on account
> of his ability and literary taste, I should like to mention Mr.
> Doughty, the Parliamentary Librarian, with whom I have
> been in close touch in connection with the old plans of the
> defences of Quebec. (quoted in Buchan 187)

Laurier accepted Minto's recommendation for both a Dominion Archivist with wider powers, and for the construction of
a sturdy stone building on Sussex Drive, which remained the

home of the National Archives until it was replaced by the present building on Wellington St. in 1967. Minto's recommendation of Arthur Doughty was also accepted, and under Doughty the Archives made great strides for the next thirty-one years. The former Archives building now houses the National War Museum, and is situated next to the new National Gallery. Years later Lady Minto recalled the Archives as one of her husband's finest achievements: " ... Through his influence a Public Archives Department was inaugurated ... and has an imposing building now" (Mary, Countess 248).

Hand in hand with Minto's concern for an archives went his interest in Canadian history and especially the preservation of historic sites in Quebec City. In a long entry in his journal he complained about the "lack of interest in Quebec history and disregard for relics and remnants of the past" (NAC 2, Aug. 20, 1902). His concern showed itself most strongly when Laurier sent for his signature an order from the Privy Council in 1903 for the construction of a road across the Plains of Abraham. Minto refused to sign, and Laurier agreed with him, saying he had not looked carefully at the document. Legislation was then passed declaring the Plains a National Memorial, and Minto spoke of the importance of their preservation in one of his last speeches to the citizens of the historic city.

It should not be surprising that when Minto showed concern for education in Canada, it was with the teaching of history in Canadian schools, although he had been no lover of formal education for himself. However, "being dissatisfied with existing text-books, (he) induced the Government to undertake the preparation and issue of documents for Canadian history, of which the Board of Historical Publications and the brilliant work of Dr. A.S. Doughty were the ultimate fruit" (Buchan 188). Minto's ceremonial duties with regard to education were not undertaken with the same enthusiasm, as was evident in the laying of a foundation stone at Ottawa University, which he termed a "terrible ordeal" (NAC 2, May 24, 1904). The other guest of honour at the ceremony was

Cardinal Gibbons of Baltimore. Minto performed a similar duty in Calgary for "a new College which is hoped may grow into a University" (NAC 2, Sept. 9, 1904). He must have attended with greater alacrity the ceremonies at which he received honorary degrees from the University of Toronto, Queen's, McGill, Laval, and Bishop's universities.

Minto's term in Canada was twice extended, once by Chamberlain in 1903 for an extra year beyond the customary five-year appointment, and again in 1904 for two months when a general election was called and Laurier thought it unwise to have an administrator in Minto's place. The Minto family sailed for England from Quebec City on the *Tunisian* on November 18, 1904 after many tributes and fond farewells. During the voyage Minto confided one last time to his journal how much Canada and Canadians had meant to him:

> So our time in Canada is over at last, and it has been a great wrench parting from so many friends ... and leaving a country which I love and which has been very full of interest for me ... the six years have been far from ordinary years ... and now the task is over and the appreciation of the country one has worked for is more grateful (?). (NAC 2, Nov. 20, 1904)

At one point Minto considered living in Canada after his term of office. But the Foreign Office had other ideas, and after spending the next year mainly at his ancestral home in Roxburghshire, he succeeded the distinguished Curzon as viceroy of India. During his five years there he carried out several important reforms in conjunction with the Secretary of State, John Morley, and, said the *Dictionary of National Biography*, "no Indian viceroy ... was so universally liked and respected by (the Indian princes)" (Roberts 174).

In 1910 Minto returned to England and retired at his ancestral heritage to manage and enjoy the 16,000 acres he possessed. His final years were graced with many honours, particularly the year 1911, which saw him receive the freedom of the cities of both London and Edinburgh, a Doctor of Letters from his alma mater, Cambridge, which he visited for the occasion for the first time since his graduation in riding clothes, the rector-ship of Edinburgh University, and being one of four peers to hold the panoply at the coronation of George V. He was also made Convener of Roxburghshire, where he held most of his property and spent his final years. In the spring of 1913 he became ill and died at his beloved Hawick on March 1, 1914.

Lady Minto survived her husband by twenty-five years, most of which were spent as lady-in-waiting for Queen Mary. Their elder son and heir, Lariston, served as aide-de-camp in 1918 to the Duke of Devonshire, then Governor General of Canada, and married a Canadian, Marion Cook, at St. Patrick's Church in Montreal in 1921. The present (2001) and sixth Earl of Minto thus had a Canadian mother.

After his death Minto was applauded with many superlatives, notably those of Lord Kitchener and later Lord Buchan. Kitchener called him "the best, most gallant, and able administrator that England ever produced" (Buchan 340), and Buchan, recalling his principal passions, said: "Minto was preserved from the hardness and narrowness of the ordinary sportsman by his liberal education, the cultivated traditions of his family, and his perpetual interest in the arts of politics and war" (Buchan 345). Laurier was more measured and more just in his praise when he said that Minto "had much common sense, a stronger man than was thought. When he came to Canada first, he was absolutely untrained in constitutional practice, knew little but horses and soldiering, but he took his duties to heart, and became an effective governor, if sometimes very stiff" (Skelton 86). While Canadians might wish he had a greater interest in other arts besides politics and war, they were beneficiaries of his sporting background and his broad sympathy for a wide variety of cultural and human activities.

Works Cited

Buchan, John. *Lord Minto: A Memoir*. London: Thomas Nelson & Sons, 1924.

Gwyn, Sandra. *The Private Capital: Ambition and Love in the Age of Macdonald and Laurier*. Toronto: McClelland & Stewart, 1984.

Hubbard, R.H. *Rideau Hall: An Illustrated History of Government House, Ottawa, from Victorian Times to the Present Day*. Montreal and London: McGill-Queen's University Press, 1977.

"Mary, Countess of Minto." *Myself When Young by Famous Women of Today*. Ed. The Countess of Oxford and Asquith. London: F. Muller, 1938. Cited as Mary, Countess.

Miller, Carman. *The Canadian Career of the Fourth Earl of Minto: The Education of a Viceroy*. Waterloo: Wilfrid Laurier University Press, 1980.

Minto, Mary. *A Record of the Distances travelled to, from, or in Canada during The Earl of Minto's Tenure of Office as Governor General of Canada. Nov. 1898-Nov. 1904*. 2 vols. Manuscript in the Rhodes House Library, Oxford. Mss. Can. Cited as Mary Minto.

Montreal Star.

NAC 1 (National Archives of Canada, *Aberdeen Papers*, Martin Griffin to Lady Aberdeen, Jan. 24, 1899. MG27, IB5, vol. 2).

NAC 2 (National Archives of Canada, *Lord Minto's Journal*. MG27, IIB1, vol. 40).

NAC 3 (National Archives of Canada, *Minto Papers*, Graham, *Across Canada to the Klondyke*, p. 5. MG27, IIB1, Reel A-132). Also in Harry Graham, *Across Canada to the Klondyke* (Toronto: Methuen, 1984). Edited and with an introduction by Frances Bowles. pp. 11-12.

NAC 4 (National Archives of Canada, *Minto Papers*, Bluebeard Programme. MG28, I 139, vol. 8).

Ottawa Citizen.

Ottawa Free Press.

Roberts, Paul E. "Elliot, Gilbert John Murray Kynynmond, Fourth Earl of Minto." *Dictionary of National Biography 1912-1921*. London: Oxford, 1922.

Saturday Night.

Skelton, O.D. *Life and Letters of Sir Wilfrid Laurier*. Vol. II. Toronto: Oxford, 1921.

Stevens, Paul, and John T. Saywell. *Introduction. Lord Minto's Canadian Papers: A Selection of the Public and Private Papers of the Fourth Earl of Minto 1898-1904*. Vol. 1. Toronto: Champlain Society, 1981.

Winnipeg Free Press.

Lord Grey.
(NAC PA-042405)

Chapter 8

Grey Cups, Tea Cups and the British Empire: Earl Grey at Rideau Hall, 1904-1911

Minto was succeeded at Rideau Hall by his brother-in-law, Albert Henry George Grey (1851-1917), the fourth Earl Grey. Grey was a descendant of the former Prime Minister of England, the second Earl Grey, who had authored the Reform Bill of 1829. He had inherited the title from his uncle, the third Earl, Henry George Grey, who had been Secretary of State for Colonies, 1846-1852, but had no children. So on his death in 1894 the title went to his brother Charles's second son, who would become Governor General of Canada ten years later.

Lord Grey's family connections were intimately tied to royalty, a fact which contributed to the strong imperialist approach he took to almost everything. His father, General Charles Grey, had been private secretary to both Queen Victoria and to Albert, the Prince Consort. Grey's mother, Caroline Eliza Farquhar, had been an attendant of the queen; her title in *Burke's Peerage* is described as "Extra Bedchamber Woman to Her Majesty Queen Victoria" (1177). It is thus not surprising that the future Governor General was born at St. James's Palace in London, and counted among his close friends King Edward VII and Edward's successor George V, both of whom were on the throne during parts of Grey's tenure in Canada.

Grey's schooling took place at Harrow and at Trinity College, Cambridge, where he took a first in the law and history tripos in 1873. He must have worked hard to attain this, for his early schooling did not augur well for academic success. As his official biographer, Harold Begbie, said: "His schooldays were undistinguished ... he got into a set which rather despised devotion to grammar-books, and which regarded the clever fellows with some contempt" (27). But he also distinguished himself in athletics at Cambridge, so much so that one of his cohorts described him as "the beau-ideal of manly English youth ... I fancy that Bertie Grey was about the third best (racquet) player in his time at Trinity" (Begbie 32-3). This combined interest in athletics and intellectual pursuits characterized Grey's time as Governor General in Canada, and made him perhaps the most well-rounded and one of the most popular holders of the office up to that time.

It was not surprising, then, that in 1875 Grey travelled to India with Edward, Prince of Wales, to broaden his education. On this occasion, however, he suffered a sunstroke in Goa, as a result of which he lost most of his hair and returned immediately to England. Like his brother-in-law Minto, he enjoyed the busy social life of London, and there developed his appreciation of theatre and other arts, which he also shared with the people of Canada. Speaking of these years Begbie said:

> Without any profound knowledge of aesthetics ... he was eagerly responsive to loveliness. No man so impulsively and wholesomely ever gave himself to such frank and catholic adoration of beauty—beauty of every kind. He was a great admirer of Marie Hall's violin playing, of Sarah Bernhardt's acting, and of Pavlova's dancing. (38)

It was probably at this time that he got to know the actress Mrs. Patrick Campbell, and gave her the financial support which enabled her to continue her career, as noted by the Canadian journalist Hector Charlesworth in his *More Candid Chronicles*. Charlesworth also commented that Grey "was a keen lover of theatre and a first-rate judge of acting" (392).

However, duty called Grey far from the aesthetic pleasures of London when his elderly uncle, the third Earl, gave him the management of his estate of Howick in Northumberland in 1894, although he would not succeed his uncle as Earl for another ten years. He had already married Alice Holford, daughter of an art collector who was also a Member of

*Lady Grey, from **The King's Book of Quebec**, 1908.*
(NAC PA-057309)

Parliament for Gloucestershire, and would have five children by her, one of whom died in infancy, and another—Victoria, the eldest—would die in Ottawa during his term of office. Of the other three children, a son Charles Robert succeeded him as Earl, and daughters Sybil and Evelyn both outlived him.

Grey also got involved in politics; he ran unsuccessfully for Parliament in 1878, and then held the same seat in Northumberland County from 1880 to 1886. His career in the House of Commons ended in 1886 when, as a Liberal member, he voted against his leader Gladstone's Home Rule Bill for Ireland, and was defeated in the next election.

By this time Grey was committed to a life of public service, and it mattered not that he held no more elected offices. Three important men influenced him and led him to devote his energies to the cause of British Imperialism throughout the world. These men were Cecil Rhodes, the founder of the British South Africa Company and the diamond millionaire who gave his name to Rhodesia; Giuseppe Mazzini, whose life he studied assiduously and from whom he learned the ideal of serving one's fellow man; and Horace Plunkett, the Anglo-Irish statesman who taught him the importance of seeking peace and co-operation as the solution to the Irish question and indeed to all the world's problems. Whatever inspiration he derived from these men, it was all applied to furthering the cause of the British Empire, the dominant ideal of Grey's life. He spoke of it in virtually every public address he made, and preached it from one end of Canada to the other when he served as Governor General. Closely allied with his belief in the Empire was his belief in the power of Christianity, and he invariably linked the two, as he did when he confided to his biographer:

> Mazzini said that foremost and grandest amid the teachings of Christ were those two inseparable truths
> — There is but one God, and all men are the sons of God.
> If the nation acts on those truths there can be no limits to the glory and greatness of these little islands. We shall have,

Lord Grey in a motor car at the front of Rideau Hall, 1907.
(NAC C-006892)

in trade, profit-sharing and copartnership, making an end
of lock-outs, strikes, and unrest: round our crowded centres
of industry the garden suburb will supplant the slum: and
in our Church, instead of theological controversies and the
indifference of the laity, we shall have the enthusiasm of an
instructed and a happy democracy for beauty and truth.
The real grandeur of the Empire is yet to come. When it
comes it will be seen to be the grandeur of a people that has
obeyed the commands of Christ. (Begbie 102-3)

Grey's enthusiasm for the Empire could lead him to make
extravagant statements, as when he spoke of World War I in
a letter to Joseph Pope, Canada's first permanent head of the
Department of External Affairs: "You talk of this terrible war
and how shocking it is ... The war is the grandest thing that
ever happened. Reports from all parts of the Empire tell me
the same thing" (Pope 251). One wonders if he would have
said the same had his son died in the war, as Lord Minto's son
and Grey's nephew Esmond did in Flanders in 1917, as Lord
Lansdowne's son Charles did in the same war in 1914, and as
Lord Dufferin's eldest son and heir did in the Boer War in
1900. Grey's love of the Empire was more aptly expressed by
a friend Moreton Frewen, who said:

> Albert loved beauty with all his heart and mind. He loved
> a beautiful woman: he loved a beautiful horse. But there
> was never beautiful woman nor beautiful horse in all this
> wide world could compare in his eyes with the beauty of
> the British Empire. It was to him the magic beauty of the
> world ... He loved the Empire. It was for him the supreme
> achievement of British genius. It sufficed even his enthusi-
> astic nature. He was the greatest lover the Empire has ever
> had. (Begbie 114-6)

Grey was able to serve the Empire in various other ways before
he became Governor General of Canada, first as administrator of Rhodesia from 1896-1897, and then as a member of
the board of directors of the British South Africa Company in

1889. He also served as Lord-Lieutenant of Northumberland from 1899-1904, at which time he was appointed Governor General by Prime Minister Balfour. Like many another Governor General, Grey hesitated before accepting the appointment, probably for financial reasons. On this score he was reassured by his wife's aunt, Lady Wantage, who offered to supplement his salary if he accepted the position. He also hesitated because of his awareness of the sensitivity of the position of Governor General in Canada, and of his own tendency to be outspoken in the pursuit of his own ideals. As it turned out, he was for the most part able to forward the cause of both Canada and the Empire during his term of office, and to avoid the pitfalls of his enthusiastic nature. In fact, Canada became for Lord Grey the centrepiece of the Imperialist Federation he so strongly advocated, and he saw Ottawa not only as the capital of the Dominion he envisaged, but of the British Empire itself. He found a sympathetic but realistic supporter in Sir Wilfrid Laurier, who was Prime Minister of Canada throughout Grey's tenure, and who left office one week before Grey's term expired. Grey got along splendidly with Laurier, and indeed with the Canadian people as a whole. He loved the beauty and wide spaces of Canada, he loved ordinary people, and he loved travel, sport, music and drama. Like Laurier, he foresaw a great future for the country. Each had a vision of a glorious destiny for Canada—Grey of a Canada as the centre of an Imperial Federation, and Laurier of a twentieth century belonging to Canada. The fact that both visions proved to be wrong did not prevent them from admiring and co-operating with one another in most of their dealings. Grey also worked closely with the British ambassador in Washington, James Bryce, to promote Canada-U.S. relations. He presided over the entry of Alberta and Saskatchewan into Confederation in 1905, and, ever since his first visit to Newfoundland that same year, encouraged it to follow suit. Mary Hallett summed up well his and Laurier's mutual contributions to Canadian life when she said: "It was fortunate for Canada and Britain that in this difficult transition period in

Imperial relations a Governor General of Grey's energy and charm was associated with a Prime Minister of Laurier's strength and patience" ("Grey" 939).

As a sports enthusiast, Grey is best remembered as the donor of the Grey Cup, now awarded for excellence in professional football in Canada. It was originally donated as "a perpetual challenge cup for competition in rugby football, to be emblematic if possible, of the amateur championship of the Dominion" (*Citizen*, June 1, 1909, p. 8). No matter that, in the 1995 season, five of the thirteen teams in the league were American, and that the Grey Cup was won by the Baltimore Stallions that year. The following year all nine teams were Canadian again.

The first Grey Cup game, played at Toronto's Rosedale Field on December 4, 1909, was won by the University of Toronto, who defeated their local rivals from the Toronto Parkdale Canoe Club 26-6. The cup was purchased for $48.00 but in fact was not presented at that first game. Lord Grey had not yet obtained the cup, "apparently because his term as Governor General had been extended and the need for a memorial (to himself) had become a lot less urgent" (Proudfoot F1). It was only the following March after "an increasingly sharp exchange of correspondence among officials of the CRU (Canadian Rugby Union), the University ... and the vice-regal staff in Ottawa" that the Cup was finally delivered to the University (Proudfoot F1). The University of Toronto was the victor all three years it was awarded during Grey's residence in Canada, right until the Hamilton Alerts defeated the Toronto Argonauts in 1912. Although Grey did not do the ceremonial kickoff in any of the three games during his term in Canada, his successor, the sixth and present (2001) Earl did kick the ball prior to the Grey Cup game in Vancouver in 1986. The Cup has survived fire, theft, joyous imbibing, and battering at the hands of victorious players and coaches across Canada. It is still presented to the winning team, but since 1987 must be deposited in the Canadian Football Hall of Fame in Hamilton two months after the

Hockey at Rideau Hall, ca. 1905.
(Bodleian Library, Oxford)

game. So the Grey Cup did not leave Canada for long, even if it was won by an American team in 1995. In 1988 the Toronto Historical Board commemorated the first Grey Cup with a plaque erected in Rosedale Park.

Grey was not as enthusiastic about Canada's official winter sport, ice-hockey, as were his predecessors Stanley and Minto. Yet one of his first public acts in Ottawa was to face off the puck in a memorable hockey game between the Ottawa Silver Seven and the Dawson City Nuggets in 1905 (Hubbard 108; see *Addresses to H.E*, p. 37). Ottawa won the two games, and thus the Stanley Cup, in the final series 9-3 and 23-2 respectively, with the famous Ottawa player one-eyed Frank McGee scoring 14 goals, eight in succession, in the second game. This series was commemorated on March 23, 1997 with another team from Dawson City travelling a similar route by land and sea through Canada and the United States to play some alumni of the Ottawa Senators at Ottawa's splendid new Corel Centre. No Governor General faced off at this game, won by Ottawa 18-0, though politicians and doctors were there to help raise money for the Canadian Special Olympics and the Ottawa Heart Institute.

Grey did not attend games regularly, but Ottawa boasted three championship teams during his time, the Silver Seven in 1905 and the Senators in 1909 and 1911. There is no record of Grey bending over his wireless set late at night to get the scores of games the way Minto did. Still, Grey was in attendance at what has been called "the greatest game," played on March 17, St. Patrick's Day, 1906 at Dey's Skating Rink on Gladstone Avenue in Ottawa. Roy MacGregor, the talented sports writer for the *Ottawa Citizen*, described this game on October 8, 1992, the day that Ottawa regained its status as a National Hockey League city after a hiatus of 58 years. It was the second of a two-game-total final for the Stanley Cup between the Ottawa Silver Seven and the Montreal Wanderers. Montreal had won the first game in Montreal by a lopsided score of 9-1, so there seemed little chance the Silver Seven would win the cup. Miraculously, with the help of a natural hat trick by Harry Smith in the second half of what was then a two-period game, Ottawa came back to lead the game 9-1 and thus tie the series 10-10 with only minutes remaining. At this point, *The Sporting News* of the day wrote: "The madness was such that Governor General Earl Grey, quite an elderly man [he was 57 at the time] and not known to be athletic, was said to have leapt four feet in the air, and one fan who had not spoken to his wife in years rushed up and kissed her" (*Citizen*, Sept. 8, 1992, p. D1). However, both Grey's and the uxorious fan's celebration was premature. Montreal recovered to win the series 12-10, although Ottawa won "the greatest game" 9-3. The modern Ottawa Senators also won the match with Montreal on September 8, 1992, but it did not reach the Stanley Cup playoffs until five years later.

Grey's enthusiasm was directed more naturally towards skating and tobogganing parties, which continued at Rideau Hall during his time every Saturday afternoon in the winter, and often took the form of moonlight parties (Hubbard 110). His daughter, Lady Victoria Grenfell, left a beautiful description of such a party in a letter to Lady Wantage:

> Two huge bonfires burn and crackle close to the two rinks both of which are lit up by rows of Chinese lanterns on wires all round them. Then the toboggan slide is lit the whole way down with a line of Chinese lanterns on each side of it and the party is opened by a procession of couples on skates each holding a torch and skating a long serpentine march to the music of the band. The tatoo of torches with all the lanterns and coloured Bengal lights really made it look like Fairyland. It was a glorious night with a splendid full moon. (*Grey Papers*, Jan. 10, 1906; see Hallett, *Fourth Earl*, p. 76)

The Grey family also became involved in figure skating in Ottawa. Besides supporting skaters at the Minto Club, named after his brother-in-law, Grey donated a Grey Cup for skating.

Ice Castle at Rideau Hall, 1907.
Photo by John Woodruff (NAC C-008525)

With the view of assisting the Minto skating club to encourage and develop figure skating in Canada, and to evolve a national Canadian style which will combine the best features of the English, continental and American styles His Excellency the Governor General has offered a national challenge trophy to be competed for annually under the following conditions:

Every Canadian skating club, or branches thereof, may send one or more teams of four (two ladies and two gentlemen) to the place selected (Ottawa in the first instance). The competition to be:
1. Combined figure skating of four to a center.
2. Combined figure skating in pairs.
3. Individual skating. (*Citizen*, March 14, 1906, p. 8)

Grey attended many skating competitions, and often presented awards to the winners. In fact, his youngest daughter Evelyn became an excellent skater and won several competitions in Canada. In 1911, when she was 24 years old, she skated for the Minto Club in the national championships in Montreal and won the "ladies only" competition. The Minto Club won the aggregate award, for which it received the Earl Grey Trophy. We are told that Evelyn's

was a remarkable performance, when it is remembered that her career as a skater began only four or five years ago, and that she was then handicapped by lack of that early experience on the blades which falls to the lot of the ordinary Canadian. It therefore required natural aptitude, conscientious practise, and clever head work to enable her to rise to the top. (*Citizen*, Feb. 28, 1911, p. 8)

The winning team, "The Grey Trophy four," was rewarded with an exhibition in Boston, to which they were accompanied by the Governor General, Countess Grey, and daughter Sybil. Again, Evelyn received high praise for her performance as "one of the participants in an international skating carnival patronized by a notable gathering of Boston Society folk." The Minto Skating Club quartet was described as "a crack organization. Lady Evelyn Grey also appeared in pairs, and was warmly greeted for her share in the graceful and picturesque performance" (*Citizen*, March 17, 1911, p. 8). The standards and tradition set by the Mintos and Greys have continued to inspire and produce award winners at Ottawa's Minto Skating Club to this day.

Although the Greys were not known for fancy dress balls at Rideau Hall as were the Dufferins and the Aberdeens, they were involved in just such an event sponsored by the Minto Club in February of that same year. Over two hundred skaters took part, arranged in "courts", Countess Grey being the convenor of the principal court. The *Ottawa Citizen* gave a detailed description of the various groups, and then of the costumes worn by the Grey family: "His Excellency wore the costume of a general of the eighteenth century. Lady Sybil Grey was a court lady of Louis the XIV period. Lady Evelyn Grey wore an officer's costume of the eighteenth century" (*Citizen*, Feb. 21, 1911, p. 3). The groups remind us of the historical characters at the Aberdeens' Historical Fancy Dress Ball of 1896, although the ones at the skating carnival had a more international flavour, with Puritan costumes, Robin Hoods, and Spanish gypsies.

Grey was also a sportsman in the manner of the traditional English gentleman: he loved fishing, hunting, horse-riding and horse-racing. He was described by an authority on these sports to his biographer Begbie as "a nice horseman, a good shot without being a professor, and a master fisherman." The authority was particularly impressed by Grey the fisherman: "What Albert could do with timber and gut was almost magical. He'd kill three salmon to my one. He seemed to have a perfect instinct, an infallible instinct, and you never saw a man kill a salmon with less fuss. He was a beautiful fisherman" (Begbie 50). There is not much recorded in Canadian newspapers of the time about Grey's fishing prowess, but apparently he exercised it mostly during his residence in Quebec City in the summer months. There are accounts of fishing trips in Quebec in both his first and last summers in

Canada. The first is from *Le Soleil* (June 29, 1905, p. 8), which noted that, while Lady Grey was taking part in the official opening of the Lawn Tennis Court at the foot of the Citadel, His Excellency was on a fishing trip on the Cascapé-dia River in the Bonaventure region of Quebec. The second reference is a brief note in the *Citizen* (June 29, 1911, p. 1) that Sir Louis Davies will be acting Governor General while Lord Grey is on a salmon fishing trip in the Saguenay district of Quebec. The same edition of the *Citizen* noted (p. 11) that Grey was the captain of the cricket team at Rideau Hall, another sporting activity of his which received scant notice in the Canadian papers. By this time Canada was preparing to welcome Grey's successor, the Duke of Connaught, whose background and imminent arrival now received as much attention as the activities of the incumbent.

Grey's hunting expeditions received scarcely more atten-tion in the newspapers, and one suspects that he wanted it this way. On October 31, 1905 the *Citizen* (p. 5) noted that writs for a by-election would be issued on the Governor Gen-eral's return from a hunting trip in the Kippewa region of Quebec. A week later, on November 5 (p. 9), the same paper added that his brother-in-law, Major Holford, was with him on the trip as a guest of the Kippewa Fish and Game Club, and that he visited mines in nearby Cobalt, Ontario. It seems these were private holidays, and Grey did not have reporters following him around Northern Quebec and Ontario, as a Governor General would today. But his own sense of inquiry and duty compelled him to combine good work with person-al pleasure. More pointedly the *Winnipeg Tribune* praised Grey for mingling with the people on a visit to Manitoba in 1909 rather than going "chicken shooting" as his predecessors did. It said:

> Earl Grey is revolutionizing this system, and will spend two
> weeks in Winnipeg, so that the citizens will begin to look
> upon him as a new adjunct to the population. He will min-
> gle with the crowd, and will make a study of conditions

here. Furthermore, His Excellency has decided to visit
Winnipeg and the west every year or every other year,
and thus set a good example to all lieutenant governors.
(*Winnipeg Tribune*, Oct. 4, 1909, pp. 1, 4)

No doubt the paper had in mind Grey's Minto in-laws who visited Manitoba on several occasions and spent much time shooting game and being photographed with the birds they shot.

If Lord Grey did not wish his hunting and fishing trips
to be widely publicized in Canada, there was no way he could
or wanted to disguise his interest in horses and horse-racing.
At that time there was no race-track in the Ottawa area; the
Connaught track, in Aylmer, Quebec near Ottawa, did not
open until 1912, when Grey's successor, after whom the track
was named, arrived. Hence Grey had to indulge his passion
for horse-racing by travelling to Toronto and Montreal. He
and his family became regulars at the spring races at the
Woodbine track in Toronto, and often attended the horse
show there. He was also a favourite guest speaker of the
Ontario Jockey Club in Toronto. So well known was his
equestrian enthusiasm that one suspects this was the reason
he was not so warmly received by the press in Toronto. He
was, in fact, denounced from the pulpit while attending and
betting on the races in that city. In April 1905, he gave a
speech to the Toronto Club and opened the Horse Show. Perhaps in anticipation of the Horse Show, the *Globe* welcomed
him in a tepid manner:

> Already the Earl and Countess Grey have begun to establish
> themselves in the good graces of our somewhat democratic
> citizens. It will be all the pleasanter for them in years to
> come to reflect that whatever good will Canada bears them
> shall be due to their personal merits rather than the circum-
> stance of their exalted rank. (*Globe*, April 26, 1906, p. 8)

Some of the Greys' personal interests were covered in the next
day's newspaper with the headline "The Horse Is King Today"
(*Globe*, April 25, 1905, p. 1), noting that the Greys' presence

helped draw a large crowd to the show. There is not the same pride in the Governor General as that shown in the Ottawa papers, or even in the Quebec papers. In fact, when Grey returned to Toronto to attend the King's Plate and races on several other days at the Woodbine track less than a month later, the paper noted how he was denounced from the pulpit of the Toronto church he attended. Under the headline "Strikes a Blow at Gambling Evil" (*Globe*, May 22, 1905, p. 12), it noted a sermon by Canon Welch at St. James Cathedral, who declared that gambling involved evil, unclean money. It was well known that Grey had been gambling on the horses. The story was picked up by the *Ottawa Citizen* (May 23, 1905, p. 4), which headlined it "To Earl Grey: Toronto Preachers tell him of the great naughtiness of attending races at Woodbine." It followed up the story with an account of Grey's words to the Ontario Jockey Club on the same visit, noting that Grey "plainly showed that he had not taken seriously to heart the reflections of a couple of Toronto pulpits upon his association with the Club" (*Citizen*, May 27, 1905, p. 12). The unrepentant Grey thanked the Club for the exciting time he and Lady Grey had at the races.

His subsequent May visits to the Woodbine track almost every year he was in Canada did not arouse such indignation. In 1908 he arranged an unveiling of a statue of Queen Victoria in Hamilton on May 25 around his visit to the Toronto races where he presented the trophy for the Queen's Plate; he asked to have the unveiling on the morning of the 25th so that he could get to Woodbine on the afternoon of the same day. The *Citizen* was again privy to Grey's plans and to Hamilton's reactions to them when it announced "Hamilton's Statue: Earl Grey's Racquet Causes Aldermen Some Pain," and went on to describe how "Alderman Dickerson said it was too bad that such a small matter as the unveiling of a monument of the late Queen should interfere with His Excellency's attendance at the races" (*Citizen*, May 8, 1908, p. 1). On the same visit he attended services at both St. James Cathedral in Toronto and St. Alban's Cathedral in Hamilton, but apparently received no reprimand there. In his nostalgic farewell address to the Ontario Jockey Club in 1911, when he spent a full week in Toronto while the races were on, he cheered up his listeners by reminding them that his successor, the Duke of Connaught, Queen Victoria's son, would be a most eager guest at future gatherings (*Citizen*, May 24, 1911, p. 5). Earlier that month he and the British ambassador to the United States, James Bryce, were "cheered lustily" as they entered and were escorted to the centre of the ring at the second annual Horse Show in Ottawa. At this show he presented another Earl Grey Cup, "a solid silver cup, given for the best mare or gelding bred in Canada, suitable for cavalry or saddle purposes" (*Citizen*, May 4, 1911, p. 1). Then in a telling headline—"Montreal Show Next"—the *Citizen* announced that Grey and his suite would leave for the opening of the twelfth Montreal Horse Show on May 10. As his term was approaching its end, Grey obviously wanted to indulge in the things he enjoyed most in Canada.

While Lady Grey shared her husband's enthusiasm for many of the sports he encouraged in Canada, she also took the initiative and devoted her energies to causes which first ladies at Rideau Hall had supported in the past. Although not so flamboyant as Lady Aberdeen, she championed several of the causes of her predecessor, like the Victorian Order of Nurses, and the National Council of Women, of which she was elected president in 1905. She was assiduous in promoting the building and improvement of hospitals both in Ottawa and across Canada. On February 10, 1910 the Governor General officially opened the Lady Grey Hospital on a five and a half acre site in Ottawa. For many years, until 1961, it was a hospital for tuberculosis patients. Now an expanded complex for patients with mental disorders, it is called the Royal Ottawa Hospital, and contains a new Lady Grey Building completed at a cost of eight million dollars in 1987, when the original Lady Grey pavilion was demolished.

Her most distinctive contribution to life in the nation's capital was the establishment of the Lady Grey Garden

Awards, given annually to those who developed beautiful gardens in the city. The purpose of the competition was "to encourage the love of flowers in Ottawa and to improve the appearance of the gardens here" (*Citizen*, June 30, 1906, p. 9). Her plan was perhaps inspired by the Garden City scheme in England in which Lord Grey was deeply involved, reflecting his social consciousness and concern for the working classes. Mary Hallett summarized the nature of Garden Cities and Grey's involvement thus:

> Grey's interest in social reform led him to active participation in the scheme to establish Garden Cities in which he invested considerable sums of money. Garden cities were developed by private enterprise to relieve the city slum areas. They were planned areas in the suburbs where low rental houses with gardens were located on tree-lined streets. Each Garden City had ample land for public parks. Industries were encouraged to locate in the vicinity. (Hallett, *Fourth Earl* 13)

Lady Grey's plan was actually a new version of a garden competition begun by her sister-in-law, Lady Minto, and was announced in the *Citizen* on May 16, 1906. The new, more democratic nature of the awards was described in the paper:

> The new rules issued by the committee for the Lady Grey garden awards remove from it the element of competition, but make it possible for every householder to enter for a prize, no matter how small the garden may be, on equal terms with the wealthier citizens. Eighty points are allowed and every amateur gardener gaining from 80 to 100 per cent. of points will receive a silver medal and a certificate; those securing 60 to 80 per cent. will receive a bronze medal and certificate. This is a very liberal offer and should stimulate every owner of a garden to enter for a prize. While the relative sizes of the gardens will be considered by the committee, extra labour and originality shown on small plots may offset the better effect obtained in a large garden with less effort. This very generous offer of Lady Grey

should cause Ottawa to become a city of gardens. (*Citizen*, June 2, 1906, p. 6)

The names and addresses of all entrants, and the eventual winners were published in the *Citizen*; the winners were later received and awarded their prizes at Rideau Hall. The number of people who entered was rather small—about 25 each year—but the publicity given the awards no doubt added to the awareness of the joys of gardening in Ottawa, and helped develop the spirit that inspires large numbers of gardeners in the capital at the present day. It is no accident that the most popular phone-in show on gardening in the national capital area today is hosted by the chief gardener at Rideau Hall— Bill Lawrence.

Lady Grey's efforts were supplemented by those of her husband, who directed the planting of thousands of tulip and daffodil bulbs in the city imported from England in the fall of the year (*Citizen*, October 18, 1907, p. 1). The dearness of the awards to the heart of Lady Grey was shown by the fact that special note was made of the final report of the awards committee presented to her four days prior to the Greys' departure from Ottawa (*Citizen*, October 7, 1911, p. 7).

Another activity in which Lady Grey showed leadership was in the promotion of art in Canada, as one might expect from the daughter of an art collector. Advances were made in the acquisition of a portrait collection for Rideau Hall, as was noted in a contemporary publication:

> The present Governor-General is striving to make the interior of the Vice-Regal residence artistically handsome as well as serviceable, and to form therein the nucleus of a portrait gallery ... The conservatories are very fine and are the especial care of Her Excellency the Countess Grey. (from *Canada, Life and Resources*, quoted in Hubbard 257, note 75)

Hubbard noted that the portraits which Grey was acquiring were those of Edward VII and Queen Alexandra, Durham,

Elgin, Dufferin and Stanley, and that these portraits were still in the house in 1977 (Hubbard 111).

Grey also negotiated for paintings to be hung in the National Gallery, which became one of his favourite institutions in Canada. He it was who encouraged its separation from the Royal Canadian Academy of Art, and thus its development as a separate organization. At the same time he was a supporter of the Academy, and opened many of its annual exhibitions while he was in Canada. Thus, at the opening of the exhibition in 1907 Grey commended the Academy,

> "(f)or holding out a helping hand to struggling artists, and for educating the public minds in matters of art, having at the same time zealous regard for Canada's reputation as a nation of art in foreign exhibitions. Those are great objects and I hereby wish you the greatest success in attaining them." ... He congratulated the academy on the approaching removal of the National gallery pictures from their present quarters to the Victoria museum, and hoped that they would be rearranged in their new quarter so as to show the successive steps leading to the present conditions of Canadian art. (*Citizen*, July 7, 1909, p. 2)

In encouraging the appreciation of art beyond the capital Grey promised the Canadian National Exhibition in Toronto paintings from his own collection (*London Free Press*, June 4, 1906, p. 4). Then as he prepared Rideau Hall for the arrival of his successor the Duke of Connaught, he planned for the removal of the chapel, and the construction of a new facade for Rideau Hall. These plans were not carried out before the arrival of Connaught. And Grey's vision of a new Rideau Hall in Rockliffe Park above the Ottawa River, like many of his visions, was never realized (Hubbard 116).

Lord Grey was also a literary man; he did a fair amount of reading and some writing. His papers at the University of Durham contain several books and pamphlets, many of them on the subject of politics, including Canadian politics, and the cause of imperialism. Some are on literary topics, including a lecture by the Shakespearean scholar J.J. Jusserand, "What to Expect of Shakespeare," the British Academy first annual Shakespeare lecture (1911), with an inscription by the author to Earl and Countess Grey. His speeches in Canada and the United States have been published in various volumes, including *Addresses to His Excellency Earl Grey and His Speeches in Reply* (1908), and *Dinner Given by the Pilgrims of the United States to His Excellency Earl Grey, G.C.M.G., Governor General of Canada* (1906). He wrote prefaces to works he supported such as *The King's Book of Quebec* (1911). The only full-length book he wrote was *Hubert Hervey, Student and Imperialist: A Memoir* (1899), about a lieutenant in the Rhodesia Horse who died in 1896 while Grey was Administrator of Rhodesia. Grey graciously agreed to write the memoir at the request of the officer's sister. Like so many of his speeches and writings, the book was a paean to the British Empire, and written in the florid and patriotic style of a man for whom the Empire was the highest ideal. It bore the following quotation from the book's subject on the title page: "It is a grand thing to die for the expansion of the Empire" (Grey, *Hubert Hervey*).

Grey was visited in Canada by various writers, including Rudyard Kipling, Ryder Haggard, Ernest Thompson Seton, and Stephen Leacock, all of whom shared his enthusiasm for the Empire. Kipling received extensive coverage in the local papers, and was hailed in a *Citizen* headline as the "Vigorous Foster Parent of the New Spirit of Empire" (Oct. 19, 1907, p. 11). He addressed a Canadian Club luncheon in the railway committee room of the House of Commons, attended by 400 diners, including the Prime Minister, Sir Wilfrid Laurier, and another 200 who could not get seats for the luncheon but were admitted for the speeches. Although Grey did not attend the luncheon, Kipling's eloquent words on the glorious future of Canada and the Empire might have been spoken by the Governor General himself:

> I take you very seriously indeed—very seriously, and I think you perhaps do not realize how great Canada bulks in the

imagination of the other great communities within the empire. I am sure that you cannot realize how all that she does, how every act and word is watched, and keenly watched, throughout the empire. A false step, a hasty word, an ill considered weakness here, is felt, seen, and heard wherever our flag flies—is watched and discussed by the remotest races and religions that abide under that flag. Now there are certain things which a man cannot, must not do, merely because it is quite possible for him to do them—there are certain things which a man must do precisely because it appears impossible that he should do them. (Cheers.) That obligation lies a millionfold heavier on a nation—it is as a nation among nations that you stand today. It is as a great nation among nations that you will be judged. (Loud and long continued cheering.) (*Citizen*, Oct. 22, 1907, p. 9)

Grey persuaded Leacock to make a tour of the Empire lecturing on Imperial organization (Hubbard 112). After the British novelist Mrs. Humphrey Ward visited the Greys at Rideau Hall, she wrote a novel entitled *Lady Merton, Colonist* (1910) in which she included a character based on Grey, and another—the central character—based on Mackenzie King, a favourite for whom Grey saw a bright political future.

Grey's interest in music and drama is best shown in the Earl Grey Musical and Dramatic Competitions, held each year from 1907-1911. While he was not the concertgoer or playgoer that Lorne or Minto were, he did attend many performances in Canada, and was visited by several well-known performers. Both he and his wife's taste tended toward choral music and opera, as shown in their presence at *Carmen* at the Russell Theatre in Ottawa, one of three operas—the others being *La Bohème* and *Manon*—presented by the Grand Opera Company of Paris in February 1911. Everything about the performance was applauded, including the presence of the party from Rideau Hall:

There was good opportunity for the chorus and every opportunity was taken advantage of. The chorus is admirably balanced, there is a perfect blending of voices and the way they took the attacks and sustained the notes was a revelation. The production was costumed and staged in a most satisfactory manner and both vocally and in acting left nothing to be desired ....

The orchestra of thirty-six musicians and its brilliant leader were warmly applauded last night. Each act was followed by repeated curtain calls.

The audience was quite a brilliant one including Their Excellencies and a party from Government House. (*Citizen*, Jan. 6, 1911, p. 7)

On Monday, February 6 of the same year, when the Governor General left Ottawa for St. John, New Brunswick to attend a curling tournament, Lady Grey left for Toronto for five days to take in, among other things, a Mendelssohn Choir concert (*Citizen*, Mar. 3, 1911, p. 3). An article on the "Music Festival of Empire" noted that the movement had its origins in Canada in 1901, and had the support of Earl Grey, who, in a speech to the Canadian Club in Winnipeg, urged its members "to aim at having the best schools, the best churches, the best music, the best art, the best newspapers, and the best literature in the Dominion" (*Citizen*, Mar. 18, 1911, p. 11). He was a supporter of Canadian musicians, both professional and amateur, including the renowned Emma Albani, whose farewell concert he attended at the Russell Theatre on April 11, 1906, and the prima donna Pauline Donalda, who gave a benefit concert for research on tuberculosis at the Russell Theatre on March 21, 1910, one month after the opening of the Lady Grey Hospital for tuberculosis in Ottawa. The *Citizen* was ecstatic about the singing of Madame Albani and of all her fellow-Canadian performers:

The sentiment of patriotic pride which Canadians naturally take in one of their own who has achieved such marked distinction, and the fact that it was the farewell of the great diva, together with the genuine experience of the performance, were contributory elements in the remarkable welcome accorded Madame Albani and her company at the Russell theatre last night. Perhaps no more enthusiastic reception was ever given a great artist, the songstress being enthusiastically recalled again and again while a special carriage was necessary to carry home the floral bouquets practically showered upon her. What added to the satisfaction over the complete triumph of the cantatrice was the fact that sharing honours with her was an Ottawa girl, Miss Eva Gauthier, who simply captivated the audience. The members of the assisting company are all artists. (*Citizen*, Apr. 12, 1906, p. 2)

Among Grey's papers at the University of Durham is a pamphlet entitled *Cree Hymns with some most useful prayers* published in Winnipeg (Grey Papers no. 1109). Grey's enthusiasm for music, as for so many other things, was often related to a higher social good. Thus, in describing Grey's involvement in social issues in England, his biographer noted that Grey "was the first man who started that movement which eventually secured band music in public parks" (Begbie 169).

Grey was a more avid lover of plays than of music. Like Minto before him, he had frequented theatres in London, and was acquainted with several well-known performers. The Canadian critic, Hector Charlesworth, estimated that Grey was a keen lover of the theatre and a first-rate judge of acting, and that he "backed Mrs. Pat Campbell so she could become an actress" (Charlesworth, *More Candid* 392). In Ottawa the Greys supported both amateur and professional theatre. In fact, their first public appearance in Ottawa after the official welcoming ceremonies was at the Russell Theatre on December 13, 1904, the day of their arrival in the capital, to see *The Girl and the Bandit* (*Citizen*, Dec. 14, 1904, p. 2). It is worth noting that it was a play they saw first on their arrival in Ottawa, and not a hockey game, although Hubbard (p. 108) stated that "his first act was ... facing off the puck in a hockey match between Ottawa and Dawson City." The play was the first of many the Greys attended at the Russell Theatre during their tenure. On several occasions they were visited by the actors who came to Ottawa with their companies. Among the well-known performers they saw were Johnston Forbes-Robertson, Sir Charles Wyndham, May Moore, Edward Terry, H. Kyrle Bellew, Sarah Bernhardt, and E.A. Sothern. In her diary on February 23, 1905 Lady Grey showed her own astuteness as a critic when she noted of a performance of *Loved the Man* (sic) by Forbes-Robertson's company at the Russell that in spite of "a very crowded house," she "expected to be much touched, but did not care for it and felt no emotion whatever" (*Grey Papers*, Box C). On December 6 and 7, 1905, Sarah Bernhardt appeared in Ottawa for the first time in a two-night stand that included *Adrienne Lecouvreur* and *Camille*. The enthusiastic *Citizen* reviewer noted her playing before a less than full house at the Russell, and the appreciation of the Greys for her performance:

> Mme. Bernhardt, the Divine Sarah, the queen of tragedy, who holds undisputed sway over the world of drama, opened a two-night engagement at the Russell theater last evening. And the enthusiastic reception accorded her was magnificent though it must be considered a reproach on the theatre-going public that there were a few, though only a few, vacant seats. For certainly no more wonderful personage or more wonderful acting has been seen on a Canadian stage.
> ... Between acts Their Excellencies, the Governor-General and Countess Grey, sent Mme. Bernhardt a large bouquet of magnificent crimson carnations. (*Citizen*, Dec. 7, 1905, p. 9)

On a trip to New York City in 1910, Grey persuaded Forbes-Robertson to bring his company to Canada with their production of *The Passing of the Third Floor Back* in aid of the Ladies' Benevolent Society. Besides Ottawa, the company performed in Montreal, Kingston, Hamilton, London and Toronto (*Citizen*, Mar. 26, 1910, p. 10). Here again, Grey showed his readiness to use the persuasive powers of his office to enlist artists for a worthy cause. While Ottawa audiences may have become blasé about Grey's attendance at the Russell Theatre, the presence of the Governor General could inspire manifestations of great loyalty to king and empire among audiences elsewhere, as it did in Winnipeg on October 11, 1909. A review of G.M. Cohan's visiting New York production of *The Talk of New York* devoted the first four paragraphs to the distinguished audience, including a description of the effect of the vice-regal family on all present:

> Their excellencies were most cordially greeted by an audience which filled the handsome theatre to its capacity, the occupants of the galleries were particularly exuberant in their patriotic zeal, the higher priced sections being not quite so demonstrative, yet evidently sincere in their expression of esteem for the vice-regal ruler who has won the hearts of the people of this great northwest by his urbanity and manly methods, and almost democratic manners.
>
> The strains of the national anthem welcomed the vice-royal visitors on their arrival, and the forty or fifty performers on the stage, accompanied by the orchestra, right lustily sang *God Save the King* at the conclusion of the play, in which many among the audience joined, the scene being most inspiring at both times, the feeling of loyalty to the "old flag" being present in overwhelming force. (*Winnipeg Tribune*, Oct. 12, 1909, p.5)

However much Grey's presence encouraged Canadians to attend concerts and plays, and however much money he raised for worthy causes by sponsoring charitable events on the stage, Grey's most ambitious investment in music and drama was the Earl Grey Musical and Dramatic Competitions, which were held every year from 1907-1911. Not much has been written of these—there is no separate entry in *The Oxford Companion to Canadian Theatre*—yet they were the forerunner of the Dominion Drama Festival and its successor Theatre Canada, of the Stratford and Shaw Festivals, and of the many music festivals that enliven the Canadian landscape today.

Louis-Philippe Hébert's **Grey Trophy for Music and Drama**,
1906, Bronze.
Photo by Patrick Altman (Musée du Québec)

In the fall of 1906 Grey decided to hold the annual competition "with a view of encouraging the sister Arts, music and drama, throughout the Dominion of Canada" (Lee 65). The invitation also went out to Newfoundland, though it was not yet in the Canadian Confederation and only entered the first of the five competitions. A central committee, under the chairmanship of Sir John Hanbury-Williams, was set up in Ottawa to administer the competitions, and the Governor General called upon the Lieutenant-Governors of the nine provinces of Canada to assist with the project. Indeed, one of the factors that made him set up the competitions was the impression made on him by a Canadian choir at the ceremonies celebrating the entrance of Alberta into Confederation in 1905. A trophy was commissioned from the distinguished Montreal sculptor Louis-Philippe Hébert to celebrate both music and drama, and the identical trophy was presented to the winners in each category. The design of the trophy was described as follows:

> The figures represent Music and the Drama. Music is represented by a man with a lyre, not classic, but rather Watteau period. The Drama is represented by a woman towards whom Music turns his eyes for inspiration. As the woman holds up the horror-stricken mask of Tragedy, she herself is smiling, to suggest Comedy. As acting and music are always crossing the border into each other's territory, each figure has a foot on the stile which divides them. (*Citizen*, Jan. 31, 1907, p. 1)

Hébert was not happy with the directions Grey gave him for the trophy, especially the Watteau style he was to use, and while he did follow Grey's instructions, he refused to sign the sculpture.

However intimately the trophy depicted the man and the woman, they had a very uneasy relationship during their five-year marriage in the competitions. The organizers were never able to balance the relative contributions of music and drama, and invariably music was under-represented. Nor was there a clear demarcation of what constituted a proper musical entry. In the first competition, the D.P.F. Minstrels of Ottawa competed against the Quebec Symphony Orchestra, and it was left to the discretion of groups presenting operas or operettas themselves whether they should compete for the music or for the drama trophy. At one point shortly before the deadline for entries in the competition of 1909, there was only one music entry; by the time the festival took place there were three. In fact, the total number of music entries over the five years was 22, while the total for drama was 39. Nevertheless, the experience and opportunity received by the various groups encouraged several of them to compete more than once, and to undertake the personal and financial sacrifice involved in participating in the competitions. For a complete list of each year's competitors, winners and adjudicators in drama, see Appendix 1.

To match the prizes offered in drama, individual music prizes were added in the Toronto (1910) and Winnipeg (1911) competitions for male voice, female voice, piano, and violin. The adjudicators' remarks were invariably kinder to the musicians than they were to the actors, and one feels that this was not because the musical groups were of a higher calibre than the theatre companies. No musical group received the harsh criticism of some of the theatre groups. As in the case of drama, the adjudicators for three of the music competitions were from the United States, while only two competitions were judged by Canadians. The colonial mentality was still operative in the Earl Grey Competitions. For a list of competitors, winners, and adjudicators in music, see Appendix 2.

Both humorous and tragic events surrounded the first competitions. One sad story was related in the *Citizen* about the Quebec Symphony Orchestra, which went on to win the first music competition. Its arrival in Ottawa was not auspicious. Forty members of the orchestra came by the Russell Theatre at 11 p.m. to deposit their instruments and then find lodgings in the city. To their chagrin the theatre was locked. "'This is a pretty sight for the Quebec Symphony orchestra to be in,' cried the leader of the group … (but) there was 'nothing doing' for the Quebecers, so they laughed it all away as a good joke and shouldered the tubas and drums on tired-out shoulders and footed it to the hotels" (*Citizen*, Jan. 29, 1907, p. 8). They were the first musical group on the program the following night, and on the last night were rewarded for their endurance when they learned they had won the first Earl Grey trophy for music.

The organizers certainly took the rules seriously in the case of drama, and indeed changed them based on the experience of earlier festivals. From the outset individual plays, or two one-act plays, were limited to a stage time of one to one and a half hours, so that in many cases the companies were forced to do only parts of full-length plays. Actors had to be amateurs, although it was allowed that the "stage manager" (at that time another word for director) could be a professional—which gave considerable advantage to the companies which employed professionals. After the 1907 competition Lord Grey, on a visit from Johnston Forbes-Robertson, gave him his copies of the judge's comments and discussed the competition with him. Forbes-Robertson was so impressed with what he read and heard that he wrote:

> I have read the resumé and the verdicts on the amateur performances with the greatest interest, pleasure and profit. They are to me admirable words of wisdom, and do the judges the very greatest credit. I am strongly of the opinion that these wisely-written papers should be made further use of both here and in England in some form or another. (*Citizen*, May 25, 1907, p. 3)

As a result of consultation with Forbes-Robertson and members of the competition committee, under the chairmanship of Sir John Hanbury-Williams, new regulations were drawn up for 1908 and made available to all who wished copies of them. Amazingly, the ambiguity of the competition was maintained in that "Each company must state for which trophy it desires to compete, and comply with the rules accordingly" (*Citizen*, May 25, 1907, p. 3), as if the organizers were not clear about what constituted the categories of the competitions.

The competition was open to companies from any city or town in Canada and Newfoundland. Each province and Newfoundland could send two companies, one musical and one dramatic, but Ontario and Quebec could send four companies, two musical and two dramatic. The committee was grappling with problems of balanced representation that still confront festivals and organizations today. A competition was to be held at the provincial level if more than two (or four, for Ontario and Quebec) companies applied to enter the festival. For the 1909 competitions in Montreal the territorial representation was altered to give more flexibility and more discretion to the organizers. Thus, "The executive committee reserves the right to reduce the number of entries from any one city or province in case the total number of entries exceeds the number which can be conveniently accommodated during the week of the competition" (*Citizen*, Oct. 9, 1908, p. 9). The largest number of local entries for any competition was from Winnipeg, with five plays and five musical groups; the competition attracted no musicians from other parts of the country.

Originally, the choice of selections to be performed was at the discretion of the companies themselves; for the 1909 competition this rule was modified so that "The character of the entertainment (musical or dramatic) shall be subject to the approval of the executive committee" (*Citizen*, Oct. 9, 1908, p. 9). This regulation was later refined by the judge in 1910 so that "in future contests the artistic value of the play itself, apart from the acting and ensemble be a factor for consideration by the judges" (Lee 72). In 1910, special prizes of $100.00 and $50.00 were announced "for the most original two-act plays" and "for the most original musical composition of any kind" (*Citizen*, Jan. 4, 1910, p. 12), but there is no newspaper record that these prizes were ever awarded.

The individual qualities judges looked for in a production remained consistent from Langdon Mitchell's 1907 adjudication to Hector Charlesworth's in 1911, namely:

1. Originality of production, if written by an amateur.
2. Stage setting.
3. Excellence of the company in acting together as a unit.
4. The promptness of entrances, exits, and the picking up of cues.
5. Grace or ease of carriage and manner.
6. Diction.
7. Dress.
8. Make-up. (*Citizen*, May 25, 1907, p. 3)

The number of performers in each group was limited to 75. In 1909 the number was raised to 100 and the number of speaking parts in each play was to be six. Some of the problems in attracting musical groups to the competitions lay in the large groups which were encouraged to participate; often the problems of financing a journey to another city made it prohibitive for groups to come from afar, as when the competitions were in Winnipeg.

Yet come they did, especially for the competitions in drama. In 1907 the group that came farthest won the trophy for drama—the Winnipeg Dramatic Club—with a performance of a new Canadian play *The Release of Allan Danvers*, a piece written especially for the occasion by "Ernest James Wilson," a composite personality who turned out to be Ernest Beaufort of the *Winnipeg Tribune* (who became a drama adjudicator in 1910), Major James Devine, D.S.O., and Wilson Blue. Devine authored another play for the competition in 1911 entitled *The Mills of the Gods*, produced by the Philanderers' Amateur Dramatic Club of Winnipeg. The 1909 competition was won by the Thespian Club of Ottawa with two one-act plays, *Food and Folly* and *The Light of St. Agnes*. When the competitions moved to Montreal in 1909, the drama trophy was taken by the John Beverley Robinson Amateur Players of Toronto with George Bernard Shaw's *Candida*. And when the performances were in Toronto in 1910 and had the first Canadian adjudicators for drama—the trio of Hector Charlesworth, Ernest Beaufort, and B.K. Sandwell—it was Toronto's Dickens Fellowship of Players who won with a dramatization by Albert Smith of Dickens's *The Cricket on the Hearth.* The last competition, in Winnipeg, was won by another western group—the Edmonton Amateur Dramatic Club with *The Tyranny of Tears* by C. Haddon Chambers. The city of Winnipeg—chosen to host the competition of 1911 on the suggestion of Lord Grey himself—certainly made great efforts to win. They entered five plays—the earlier rule of one play per province outside Ontario and Quebec had obviously been dropped or ignored by this time. Winnipeg did win, however, in the musical category—not in the dramatic category as implied by Ross Stuart in *The History of Prairie Theatre*—with *The Chimes of Normandy.*

Individual prizes in drama began in 1908 with a donation by the famous Canadian actress Margaret Anglin of a bracelet for the best actress. That year it was won by the Ottawa Thespians' Mrs. W.W. Edgar; the following three years it was won respectively by Mlle. Jancy of Le Cercle Littéraire Saint-Henri of Montreal, by Pattie Maclaren of the London Dramatic Club, and by Ruby Michie of the London Dramatic Club. In 1910 and 1911 the well-known English actor J.E. Dodson was persuaded to match Miss Anglin's donation with a signet ring for the best actor, which in turn went to Basil G. Morgan of the Dickens Fellowship of Players of Toronto, and by Albert E. Nash of Edmonton. In the final year of the competition Grey donated another prize himself "for beauty and purity of diction," qualities dear to his heart. The prize—a silver cigarette case with an engraved inscription—was won by Harry L. Hayes of Ottawa, who played the title role in *David Garrick*, and was presented in a ceremony at Rideau Hall in September, shortly before Grey's departure from Canada.

There were tragic moments surrounding the competitions as well. On February 3, 1907, the day after the first competitions in Ottawa, Lord Grey's daughter and eldest child Victoria, for whose christening Queen Victoria had stood as a sponsor, died at the age of 29 while visiting Ottawa with her husband Lieutenant-Colonel Arthur Grenfell. She had contracted typhoid fever while they were visiting Mexico, and battled it in her last days at Rideau Hall, the week of the first Earl Grey Competitions. The *Citizen* noted Grey's absence because of "family illness" from some days of the competitions, but the exact reason for his absence was only revealed on February 4, when the competitions were over. That year also the Toronto-based Margaret Eaton School of Literature and Expression withdrew from the drama competition because of the death on January 31 of Timothy Eaton, founder of the department store chain that bore his name, and husband of the group's founder. The group was replaced on short notice by the Garrison Dramatic Company of Toronto. Only in 1911, in Winnipeg, did the Margaret Eaton School return to the competitions with the play it was scheduled to present in 1907—Goldsmith's *She Stoops to Conquer*.

The adjudicators were often blunt and harsh with the dramatic productions at the competitions—proof that they were not just a social occasion for the elite. Some of the memorable comments were made in 1908 when they criticized Miss Frances de Wolfe Fenwich's production of her own one-woman play *The Society for the Protection of Suffering Servants*:

> There were seven different characters set down for impersonation by Miss Frances de Wolfe Fenwick, and in not one single character of the seven did the lady, either in make-up, deportment or speech, present the art of impersonation. She was unnecessarily loud in voice and grotesque in action. The lady had only seven characters to present, on which she wasted force enough to have presented seven more, and still have voice to spare for another week's rehearsal before giving another performance. (Programme 89)

In 1910, the Toronto Associate Players' choice of a play by Arthur Law was censured:

> Arthur Law's farce *A Country Mouse* ... reeks with veiled suggestion and we considered it fortunate that the original last act of this play, which was condemned on its original production in London, was omitted. Harmless though the piece may be in its general effect on the average audience, it can easily be seen that any father might reasonably object to his daughter taking part in so cynical a production, the very humour of which turns on a lack of morality and of respect for the conventions of morality. (Programme 121)

In 1911, the Winnipeg Thespians' production of *Liberty Hall* was given as bad a review as any jaded reviewer could give a play: "This production was so bad as to be hardly worth the courtesy of a criticism ... It would perhaps be cruel to point out the ineptitude of most of the performers" (Programme 166).

Yet the critics could be generous too, and often recognized the hard work and dedication of the groups that travelled far to give their best. In the first year of the competitions, Mr. and Mrs. Stephen Leacock both performed in the McGill University Dramatic Club's production of Shaw's *Arms and the Man*. Mrs. Leacock received special praise:

> The lady who played the part of Raina seemed to be very nearly a mistress of the art of acting. Her repose was excellent; her movements exact, well-timed and full of significance; her diction was very nearly perfect. She was well-made up and she played thoroughly in character and with an excellent sense of comedy. It was undoubtedly a remarkable performance. (Programme 77)

Although other performers were pointed out as well, not a word was said of Mr. Leacock's acting by the adjudicators. But it appears that Leacock was no mean actor himself. In its review of the production, the *Citizen* praised his performance as Sergius Saranoff as one "that revealed considerable experience in stage work. His acting was most natural and never more so than in his final decision to marry Louka" (*Citizen*, Feb. 4, 1907, p. 2).

Dora Mavor, who received an honourable mention in 1911 for her performance as Kate Hardcastle in the Margaret Eaton School's *She Stoops to Conquer*, was praised in glowing terms, although the production as a whole was not well received:

> The only individual performance that came near being truly satisfactory was that of Miss Dora Mavor as Kate Hardcastle. She made an exquisite picture and her vivacity and charm lent many graces to the part. Her personality is hardly a commanding one, but her handling of the English tongue is the essence of refinement. (*Programme* 163)

She had been similarly praised for her work as Lady Phyllis de Beauchamp in the Catherine Merritt Company's 1910 production of Merritt's *A Little Leaven*, although the other actors, except for a Major Fletcher, were described as having a "general lack of talent" (*Programme* 127). This praise Dora Mavor received in spite of her contention in later years that she was "so disillusioned with the 'pointless socializing' among the amateur groups she vowed to work toward professional status" (Lee 77).

There was indeed socializing at the Earl Grey competitions. Whether it was pointless or not is a matter of one's personal taste. Most theatre groups enjoy socializing when they have travelled hundreds, or even thousands of miles, to enter a competition, or when they are hosting actors who have come to compete with them from far away. This was certainly true of the Dominion Drama Festival, just as it was true of the Earl Grey Competitions. Many would say it is part of the festive spirit that goes with any festival. Still, Canadians should be grateful if the Earl Grey Competitions, for whatever reason, persuaded Dora Mavor to choose a career on the stage.

From the outset Earl Grey set the tone for happy times for the visiting musicians and thespians. In the week of the first competitions in Ottawa, no events were scheduled for Wednesday so that the performers from St. John's, Halifax, Quebec City, Montreal, Ottawa, Toronto, Hamilton and Winnipeg could be vice-regally entertained. In an eloquent story headlined "Festivities at Rideau Hall," the *Citizen* described how the grounds were decked out for the tobogganing and skating party that evening, and how delighted all the participants were. Before giving a list of all the guests, it concluded:

> Pathways to this place, pathways to that; no one seemed to look for the path toward home. It might have lasted for a whole night, that big family gathering; but it came to an end as most good things do. Yet long before departure, the guests had an opportunity to meet Their Excellencies, and chat for a moment with the patron whom they have good cause to remember. Supper was laid in the curling rink. (*Citizen*, Jan. 31, 1907, p. 11)

The devotion of Grey to drama and music can be noted when we recall that, on this very night, his daughter lay ill in Rideau Hall with the typhoid that would kill her in four days. Festivities were held in the three other cities that hosted the event in later years, but never was a day of the week set aside for the festivities alone.

The Earl Grey Competitions were the first organized Canada-wide competitions in the arts, and for that reason alone were important. They gave Canadians an awareness that the arts could be celebrated more widely across the country when the time was ripe, as it was twenty years later when the Dominion Drama Festival was organized in a more efficient and representative way. And the DDF organizers were aware of their debt to the Earl Grey Competitions. The earliest document in the DDF papers in the National Archives of Canada is the 175-page programme of the Competitions from which I have freely quoted. If the organizers of later festivals

Audience at Tercentenary Celebrations, Quebec, 1908.
(NAC PA-024716)

learned something from the Earl Grey Competitions, it was that music and drama deserved their own separate competitions. The Duke of Connaught, who succeeded Grey, showed he had learned this when he supported a separate music festival until the outbreak of World War I. And the organizers of the DDF were clear that theirs should be a drama festival only. Other festivals can look back to the initiative taken by the amateurs who took part in the Earl Grey Competitions. As B.K. Sandwell said in his reminiscences of the Competitions, entitled "Early Festivals: Hard on Judges and Audience," one year before the Stratford Festival opened:

> In spite of the long hiatus which intervened between the Earl Grey Trophy competitions and the Dominion Drama Festivals, there is no doubt that it was Earl Grey who started the practice of a Canada-wide competition for amateur stage players, and the contribution that he made to the progress of the dramatic art in Canada should not be forgotten. (Sandwell 4)

Even with the success of the Earl Grey Competitions, Grey's greatest dramatic gesture as Governor General of Canada was his organization of the celebrations surrounding the tercentenary of the founding of Quebec in 1908, and in particular the gigantic pageant that was the keystone of those celebrations. He began talking of such a celebration in the fall of 1907, a mere year before the events themselves. But with his typical enthusiasm and energy, he established an organizing committee and set the wheels in motion for events that would last twelve days, from July 20-31, 1908.

The celebrations marked two quite distinct events that some might have seen as incompatible. One was the founding of Quebec City by Champlain in 1608; the other was the battle of the Plains of Abraham in which the English under General Wolfe defeated the French under General Montcalm in 1759. The battle of the Plains was to be commemorated because Grey wanted to complete a project begun by his predecessor Lord Minto—the establishment of the Plains as a national battlefield park. It took all Grey's powers of persuasion and tact to unite the two events in one celebration. He saw their coming together as an occasion to bring French and English in Canada closer together, and to show their unity as a model of different races living in harmony in one country. All this Grey set out to do in spite of the fact that the first Earl Grey was with Wolfe at Quebec, and that his father was an officer in the British army that crushed the Papineau rebellion in Quebec in 1837.

Grey also had a higher aim in mind, one that flowed from the dominating passion and ideal of his life—the manifestation of the glory of the British Empire. This was emphasized by Grey on many occasions during the tercentenary, but particularly at a state dinner on the sixth day of the celebrations. The dinner was attended by the Prince of Wales, later King George V, and many visiting dignitaries, Canadian, Imperial, and International. In his speech Grey said: "The influences which will radiate from this tercentenary week will tend to the unification of the Empire and to the strength and glory of the Crown" (*King's Book* 287). He even persuaded five of his vice-regal predecessors—Lorne, Lansdowne, Stanley, Aberdeen, and Minto—to support a fundraising campaign in England for the preservation of the battlefields.

He had an ambitious plan to erect on the Plains a statue of an Angel of Peace, which was to be six inches higher than the Statue of Liberty in New York (Hallet, *Fourth Earl* 155). He organized fundraising committees for this project too, but sufficient funds were not forthcoming, and the project was abandoned. Other plans for beautifying the battlefields did succeed—including the improvement of the grounds, the removal of two buildings that defaced the property, a seven-mile driveway around the Plains, and a museum. Supervising all the improvements was a Battlefields Commission set up and financed by the federal government.

Guests for the celebrations, besides the Prince of Wales (Grey had wanted King Edward VII to attend.), included the Vice-President of the United States, a special envoy from

Frank Lascelles in Indian dress at the Tercentenary of Quebec, 1908.
(NAC PA-024127)

France, and "such an assemblage of other distinguished individuals as the new world had never seen before" (*King's Book* 384).

The pageant was under the direction of Mr. Frank Lascelles, a renowned director of pageants, who came from England to direct the Canadian pageant when a pageant he was to direct for the city of London that year was postponed. He had already directed a successful pageant in Oxford, and had a reputation as the finest director of pageants in England. He also had great tact and understanding. Thus, the script he chose, by a French-Canadian Ernest Myrand, with music by Joseph Vézina, had virtually no English in it; only one comic scene with a British envoy was in English, and this was translated into French for the onlookers. There were some 4500 participants in the pageant, as well as 12,000 Canadian troops for the military display at the end. Spectators paid a fee to attend the pageant, but on the last afternoon 15,000 children who had been unable to see it before were given free admission.

The natural outdoor setting for the pageant was ideal for the events being depicted. *The King's Book of Quebec*, a 388-page, two-volume, lavishly illustrated book on the preparations and celebrations of those ten days, described it thus:

> Like an ancient Greek choosing a site for a theatre that was to be part of the scenery surrounding it, Mr. Lascelles chose the best among the good. His open stage for 5,000 performers and his auditorium for 15,000 spectators stand between the fields of the first and second Battles of the Plains, overlooking a magnificent and most historic reach of the St. Lawrence. Wooded ground, sloping down to the right, afforded cover to the multitude of actors, without hiding the view beyond. Through it runs the path up which Wolfe climbed to victory; a half-mile up stream is Sillery Point, where the French challenge rang out; and a half channel over is where Wolfe recited Gray's *Elegy* when making his last reconnaissance in a boat, the day before the battle. Close in under the cliffs is Champlain Street, along

which Montgomery led his Americans to death and defeat in 1775. And a few yards from where he fell is the wharf where the first Canadian Contingent embarked for South Africa in 1899. (*King's Book* 306-7)

The nine scenes represented in the pageant were as follows:

1. Jacques Cartier in Canada, 1535-36.
2. Jacques Cartier at Court, 1536.
3. Champlain at Court, 1608.
4. Champlain at Quebec, 1620.
5. Arrival of the Ursulines and Hospitaliers, 1639.
6. Dollard's Canadian Thermopylae at Long Sault, 1660.
7. Laval receives de Tracy, 1665.
8. Frontenac repulses Phips, 1690.
9. Review of the Historic Armies of 1759, 1760, 1775, 1812.

To emphasize the broad significance of the events and to concentrate on their unifying rather than on their divisive elements, Grey insisted that the military and naval displays be given as much prominence as the rest of the pageant itself. Thus the final scene, a Review of the Armies, included troops representing the French army in 1759 and 1760; the British fleet and army in 1759 and 1760; and the combined forces of English and French which fought the Americans in 1775 and 1812. In these displays, far from re-enacting the battle on the Plains of Abraham, the English- and French-Canadian troops marched side by side.

Then, as this formation became complete, all the participants in all the eight other scenes come thronging in on both flanks, inspiring strains of all the music and the pealing of all the bells. Just when these also are in position, they and all the armies burst out together into the swelling chorus—
O CANADA!
And then—last touch of all in this most deeply moving scene—the whole great audience springs to its feet and, literally "with heart and voice" joins the living exponents of

The Grey Cup, donated by Lord Grey for Canadian football.
(Canadian Football Hall of Fame & Museum Collections, Hamilton, Ontario)

Canadian history in the one Anthem of all who stand by
Crown and Empire—
     GOD SAVE THE KING! (*King's Book* 388)

These are the final words of the *King's Book of Quebec*, apart
from an appendix which consists of a letter from Grey to Sir
Georges Garneau, Mayor of Quebec, thanking him and
many others who made the celebrations a success, including
"Mr. Lascelles, by whose genius the glories of French achievement in Canada have been revealed to an admiring and grateful people" (*King's Book*, Appendix). The twelve days of celebration were given unstinting praise from all reports, as in the
Citizen's headline and day-by-day description of several days
of the celebrations on July 27 (p. 2): "The Tercentenary A
Great Success: Brilliant Events of the Past Week at the
Ancient Capital."

The success of the pageant and of all the celebrations was
due to the inspiration, enthusiasm, and sensitivity of Lord
Grey, who was determined to make Canadians aware of their
heritage—French, British, and Imperial. The pageant goes
down in the annals of many great pageants in the province of
Quebec. Whatever form the celebrations take to mark the
four-hundredth anniversary of the founding of Quebec, they
will have difficulty matching those of the tercentenary.

The tercentenary pageant was the most spectacular of the
vice-regal dramas presented to date—surpassing even those of
the Dufferins and the Aberdeens. Nor would any Governor
General in the twentieth century attempt to match Grey's
spectacle. Hector Charlesworth's 1925 comment on the tercentenary has been correct: "The result was a spectacle that
for variety and vividness will not be equalled in Canada in
this century" (Charlesworth, *Candid* 285).

*   *   *

This achievement is a fitting point at which to end the
detailed study of the cultural activities of Canada's Governors

General. There were many highlights in the contributions from Monck to Minto, from the theatre productions of the Dufferins through the encouragement of Canada's artists and scholars by Lorne and the cups for hockey by Stanley and for football by Grey to the magnificent balls given by the Aberdeens and the example of fancy skating provided by the Mintos. But Grey's pageant on the Plains of Abraham outdid them all, and it seemed that subsequent Governors General realized they could not match this spectacle or, indeed, the spectacles of his predecessors.

Works Cited

Addresses to His Excellency Earl Grey and his speeches in reply, having relation to the resources and progress of the Dominion (al. *Resources and Progress of the Dominion*). Ottawa: S.E. Dawson, 1908.

Begbie, Harold. *Albert, Fourth Earl Grey: A Last Word.* London: Hodder & Stoughton, 1917.

Burke's Genealogical and Heraldic History of the Peerage, Baronetage, and Knightage. 105th ed. Edited by Peter Townend. London: Burke's Peerage Limited, 1970.

Charlesworth, Hector. *Candid Chronicles: Leaves from the Note Book of a Canadian Journalist.* Toronto: Macmillan, 1925.

——. *More Candid Chronicles: Further Leaves from the Note Book of a Canadian Journalist.* Toronto: Macmillan, 1928.

The Globe (Toronto).

Grey, Earl. *Hubert Hervey, Student and Imperialist: A Memoir.* London: Edward Arnold, 1899.

Grey Papers. University of Durham.

Hallett, Mary. "Grey, Alfred Henry George, Fourth Earl." *The Canadian Encyclopedia*, 2nd ed. James H. Marsh, ed. Edmonton: Hurtig, 1988, p. 939.

——. *The Fourth Earl Grey as Governor General, 1904-1911.* Ph.D. thesis, University of London, 1970.

Hubbard, R.H. *Rideau Hall: An Illustrated History of Government House from Victorian Times to the Present Day.* Montreal & London: McGill-Queen's University Press, 1977.

The King's Book of Quebec. Ottawa: Mortimer Co. Ltd., 1911.

Lee, Betty. *Love and Whisky: The Story of the Dominion Drama Festival.* Toronto: McClelland & Stewart, 1973.

MacGregor, Roy. "Memories of when Ottawa held ... 'The Greatest Game.'" *Ottawa Citizen*, September 8, 1992, p. D1.

The Ottawa Citizen.

Pope, Maurice, ed. *Public Servant: The Memoirs of Sir Joseph Pope.* Toronto: Oxford University Press, 1960.

Programme of the Earl Grey Musical and Dramatic Trophy Competitions, September 1906-April 1911. National Archives of Canada, MG28, I 50, Reel M-1656.

Proudfoot, Jim. "Grey Cup game to draw a record $4 million gate." *Toronto Star*, November 21, 1989, p. 51.

Sandwell, B.K. "Early Festivals: Hard on Judges and Audience." *Saturday Night*, July 5, 1952, p. 4.

Le Soleil.

The Winnipeg Tribune.

Appendix I

Earl Grey Drama Competitions, 1907-1911

Note: Author's name is given where it is available.

1907

Place: Russell Theatre, Ottawa
Dates: Monday, January 28-Saturday, February 2
Adjudicators: Langdon Mitchell, New York, and Kate Douglas Wiggin Riggs (Authoress of *Rebecca of Sunnybrook Farm*, etc.)
Best Play Production: *The Release of Allan Danvers* by Ernest James Wilson (i.e., Ernest Beaufort, Major James Devine, and Wilson Blue), produced by the Winnipeg Dramatic Club

Other Entrants:

1) St. Mary's Dramatic Class (alias, St. Mary's Total Abstinence Society), Halifax: *Captain Swift*
2) Toronto Garrison Dramatic Company: *His Excellency the Governor*
3) Garrick Club, Hamilton: a) *The Deacon* by H.A. Jones, b) *Kitty Cline* by Frankfort Moore
4) Ottawa Dramatic Club: *Gringoire* by Théodore de Banville
5) McGill University Dramatic Club, Montreal: *Arms and the Man* by G.B. Shaw

1908

Place: Russell Theatre, Ottawa
Dates: Monday, February 24-Saturday, February 29
Adjudicator: F.F. Mackay, New York
Best Play Production: a) *Food and Folly* by W.W. Edgar and H. McDonald Walters; and b) *The Light of St. Agnes* by

Mrs. Minnie Maddern Fiske, produced by the Thespians
Club of Ottawa
Margaret Anglin bracelet prize: Mrs. W.W. Edgar, Thespians Club of Ottawa

Other Entrants:

1) Ottawa Garrison Dramatic Club: *Joseph Entangled* by
   H.A. Jones
2) Ottawa Players Club: *Marble Hearts, or The Artist's
   Dream,* by Charles Selby
3) Frances de Wolfe Fenwick Club (Montreal): *The Society
   for the Protection of Suffering Servants* by Frances de
   Wolfe Fenwick
4) Aubrey Amateur Stock Company (Montreal): *The Chorus Lady* by J. Forbes
5) Montreal Amateur Dramatic Club: *A Game of Bluff*
   by Grace L. Furniss
6) The New Garrick Club of Montreal: *Naval Engagements*
   by Charles Dauce
7) Garrison Dramatic Company (Toronto): *Brother Officers*
   by Leo Trevor
8) Dickens Fellowship of Players (Toronto): *The Cricket on
   the Hearth* by Albert Smith

1909

Place: His Majesty's Theatre, Montreal
Dates: Monday, April 19-Saturday, April 24
Adjudicator: John Corbin, New York
Best Play Production: *Candida* by G.B. Shaw, produced by
the John Beverley Robinson Amateur Players (al. The Amateur Players Club of Toronto)
Margaret Anglin bracelet prize: Mlle. Jancy, Le Cercle
Littéraire Saint-Henri (Montreal)

Other Entrants:

1) Ottawa Players Club: *David Garrick*
2) Walters Dramatic Company (Ottawa):

a) *Eyes of the Heart* by Minnie Maddern Fiske; and
b) *Op-O-Me-Thumb* by Frederick Fenn and Richard Pryce
3) Conservatoire La Salle (Montreal): *Les Précieuses Ridicules* by Molière
4) Montreal Dramatic Club: *The Bells* by Leopold Lewis
5) Le Cercle Littéraire Saint-Henri (Montreal): *La Princesse de Bagdad* by Alexandre Dumas, fils
6) McGill University Dramatic Club (Montreal): *A Russian Honeymoon*
7) Dickens Fellowship of Players (Toronto): *Little Nell*
8) Garrison Dramatic Club (Toronto): *Caste* by T.W. Robertson

1910

Place: Royal Alexandra Theatre, Toronto
Dates: Monday, April 4-Saturday, April 9
Adjudicators: Hector Charlesworth (Toronto), B.K. Sandwell (Montreal), and Ernest Beaufort (Winnipeg)
Best Play Production: *The Cricket on the Hearth* by Albert Smith produced by the Dickens Fellowship of Players (Toronto)
Margaret Anglin bracelet prize: Pattie Maclaren, London Dramatic Club
J.E. Dodson signet ring prize: Basil G. Morgan, Margaret Eaton School of Literature and Expression (Toronto)

Other Entrants:

1) The Toronto Associate Players: *A Country Mouse* by Arthur Law
2) The Associate Players of the Margaret Eaton School of Literature and Expression (Toronto): *The Land of Heart's Desire* and *Kathleen ni Houlihan* by W.B. Yeats
3) Miss Catherine Merritt's Company (Toronto): *A Little Leaven* by Catherine N. Merritt
4) The Montreal Thespians: *The Bells* by Leopold Lewis
5) The London Dramatic Club: *Jack Straw* by Somerset Maugham

1911

Place: Walker Theatre, Winnipeg
Dates: Monday, April 24-Saturday April 29
Adjudicator: Hector Charlesworth, Toronto
Best Play Production: *The Tyranny of Tears* by C. Haddon Cham-bers, produced by The Edmonton Amateur Dramatic Club
Margaret Anglin bracelet prize: Ruby Michie, London Dramatic Club
J.E. Dodson signet ring prize: Albert E. Nash, Edmonton Amateur Dramatic Club
Earl Grey prize for Beauty and Purity of Diction: Harry L. Hayes, Ottawa Players Club (The prize consisted of a silver cigarette case with an engraved inscription.)

Other Entrants:

1) The Strollers' Dramatic Club (Winnipeg): *The Chimney Corner* by H.T. Craven
2) The Bohemian Company of Players (Winnipeg): *A Pair of Spectacles* by Sidney Grundy
3) The Winnipeg Thespians: *Liberty Hall* by R.C. Carton
4) The Philanderers Amateur Dramatic Club (Winnipeg): *The Mills of the Gods* by Major James Devine, D.S.O.
5) St. Alban's Amateur Dramatic Club (Winnipeg): *The Chimney Corner* by A.T. Craven
6) Ottawa Players Club: *David Garrick*
7) The London Dramatic Club: *Lady Huntsworth's Experiment* by R.C. Carton
8) The Associate Players of the Margaret Eaton School of Literature and Expression (Toronto): *She Stoops to Conquer* by Oliver Goldsmith

Appendix II

Earl Grey Music Competitions, 1907-1911

1907

Place: Russell Theatre, Ottawa
Dates: Monday, January 28-Saturday, February 2
Adjudicator: G. Walter Chadwick, Boston
Winner: Quebec Symphony Orchestra

Other Entrants:

1) D.F.P. Minstrels, Ottawa
2) St. Johns's Boys' Brigade Band, Newfoundland
3) St. Lambert Choral Society, Montreal

1908

Place: Russell Theatre, Ottawa
Dates: Monday, February 24-Saturday, February 29
Adjudicator: Horatio W. Parker, Yale University, New Haven, Conn.
Winner: Canadian Conservatory of Music Orchestra, Ottawa (al. Ottawa Symphony Orchestra)

Other Entrants:

1) Ottawa Choral Society
2) Orpheus Glee Club, Ottawa
3) Quebec Symphony Orchestra

1909

Place: His Majesty's Theatre, Montreal
Dates: Monday, April 19-Saturday, April 24
Adjudicator: Dr. A.S. Vogt, Toronto
Winner: Canadian Conservatory of Music Orchestra, Ottawa

Other Entrants:

1) Association Chorale Saint-Louis de France, Montreal
2) First Baptist Choral Society, Montreal

1910

Place: Royal Alexandra Theatre, Toronto
Dates: Monday, April 4-Saturday, April 9
Adjudicator: Howard Brockway, Auburn, New York
Winner: Ottawa Symphony Orchestra (formerly Canadian Conservatory of Music Orchestra)

Other Entrants:

1) Choir of Bloor St. Presbyterian Church, Toronto
2) Choir of St. Paul's Methodist Church, Toronto
3) The Peterborough Operatic Company (production: *The Geisha*)
4) The Conservatory Madrigal Club, Peterborough
5) The Maurice Pouré Orchestra, London

1911

Place: Walker Theatre, Winnipeg
Dates: Monday, April 24-Saturday, April 29
Adjudicator: Donald Heins, Ottawa
Winner: The Winnipeg Amateur Operatic Society (production: *The Chimes of Normandy*)

Other Entrants:

1) Grace Church Choir, Winnipeg
2) Broadway Symphony Orchestra, Winnipeg
3) Zionist Church Choir, Winnipeg
4) Dr. Ralph Horner's Choir, Winnipeg

Prizes were also given for piano, violin, female voice, and male voice in 1910 and 1911.

Afterword on their Successors, Connaught to LeBlanc, 1911-1999

The involvement of Governors General in the cultural life of Canadians did not end with Lord Grey and the re-enactment of the battle of the Plains of Abraham. This was however the most spectacular of many spectacles and other cultural activities sponsored by Governors General both before and after that most dramatic of events. Since then there has rarely been the same direct involvement of a viceroy in the cultural affairs of the country. There have been notable exceptions to this, as, for example, in the role played by Lord Bessborough in the establishment of the Dominion Drama Festival, and of Vincent Massey in the deliberations of the Massey Commission and the establishment of the Canada Council.

I have concluded this afterword with the activities of Romeo LeBlanc. Since the incumbent—Her Excellency Adrienne Clalrkson—is in the mid-term of her office at Rideau Hall, I have not included her in this book. Should the book be re-issued when her term is over, I would certainly add a section on her cultural activities, which, to this point, have been impressive.

Indeed, another volume might be written examining the activities of Governors General who succeeded Lord Grey, to illustrate their high level of taste in cultural matters. No doubt their example was followed by their friends and by other Canadians. A brief survey of some of their activities will illustrate to what extent that example was evident.

Duke of Connaught

The Duke of Connaught (1850-1942), the third son of Queen Victoria, returned to Canada as Governor General in 1911 and held the post until 1916, halfway through the Great War. While his own training was largely military, he had a serious interest in operatic music and sometimes attended touring performances of operas, specifically, *La Boheme, Tosca, Madame Butterfly,* and *Faust.* He went to hear and hosted at Rideau Hall singers such as Reinhold von Warlich, Pauline Donalda, and Nellie Melba. He also attended touring performances starring the English manager-directors Sir John Martin Harvey and Sir Johnston Forbes-Robertson. He and his wife Princess Louise Margaret visited the art collections in Montreal of Sir George Drummond and Sir William Van Horne, and went to see Paul Kane's paintings at the Royal Ontario Museum in Toronto. Their daughter Princess Patricia was a serious artist who painted both at Rideau Hall and across Canada on viceregal tours around the country. For a brief time the Governor General continued to sponsor the Musical and Dramatic Competitions begun by his predecessor Lord Grey, but allowing them to die was a sign that encouraging culture for all Canadians was not one of his priorities.

Duke of Devonshire

Connaught was succeeded by the Duke of Devonshire (1868-1938), who was married to Evelyn, daughter of the former Governor General Lord Lansdowne. Devonshire's term (1916-1921) included the final war years and the years of a growing sense of Canadian identity that followed. But his cultural activity in Canada was sporadic, due partly to the pressures of the war in Europe and its aftermath. One interest he acquired in Canada was a love of hockey, and he even faced off the puck in a game between Ottawa and Hamilton in 1920.

Baron Byng of Vimy

Baron Byng of Vimy (1862-1935) also brought memories of the war to Canada, having commanded Canadian troops at Vimy Ridge in 1917. During his tenure at Rideau Hall (1921-1926) he built on those memories by involving himself in sports dear to Canadians such as figure skating. He even hired a professional skater to teach him and his household the basics of figure skating. He attended musical performances by such singers as Dame Nellie Melba and Dame Clara Butt, and was actively involved in at least one musical revue at Rideau Hall. *Oriental Ottawa*, said to have been written by Byng himself, parodied the Ottawa scene and used local streets for the names of the characters. Although his reintroduction of private theatricals at Rideau Hall was limited, he encouraged at least one other satire *On the Platform*, which used the formal and nonsensical dialogue forced upon dignitaries like himself at public functions on tours across Canada. This skit was occasioned by a tour of western Canada in 1924.

R.H. Hubbard claims that Lady Byng's major achievement in Canada was the creation of the enchanting rock garden on the grounds of Rideau Hall (Hubbard 154). But she is more widely known today for the Lady Byng Trophy, a cup she donated to the National Hockey League in 1925 for a player who combined sportsmanlike conduct with excellence in hockey. After Frank Boucher of the New York Rangers won the trophy seven out of eight seasons, he was given the cup; another was made, which survives in the league to this day and is awarded annually.

Lord Willingdon

Lord Willingdon (1866-1941) also donated cups for excellence while he was Governor General (1926-1931). In 1927 he donated to the Royal Canadian Golf Association the Willingdon Cup for amateur team competitions in interprovincial golf, a competition which is still alive. In 1928 he inaugurated the Willingdon Arts Competition for music, literature, painting and sculpture. Unlike the Earl Grey Competitions, this one did not include drama as a category. One important innovation at Rideau Hall in Willingdon's time was film evenings in the ballroom to entertain invited guests.

As we have seen, in the days of more active Governors General like Dufferin, the ballroom was given over to the performance of private theatricals, with the Governor General and his wife on stage.

Lord Bessborough

Besides bringing with him an abiding interest in horse-racing and fishing, Lord Bessborough (1880-1956) shared with Canadians a love for amateur theatre in his short term (1931-1935) in Ottawa. He and his French wife, Roberte de Neuflize, had acted regularly in the theatre they built in their Sussex home in England. On a tour of western Canada in his first year in office, they visited the little theatres in several towns and cities. For Canadians this interest in theatre culminated in the first Dominion Drama Festival in 1933, with groups from across Canada competing in Ottawa for the Bessborough Trophy for the best production of a play in English or French. In his efforts to establish the DDF, Bessborough was assisted by Vincent Massey and by Colonel Henry C. Osborne of the Ottawa Drama League (renamed the Ottawa Little Theatre in 1952), who met at Rideau Hall with some sixty other theatre enthusiasts in October 1932 to plan this bilingual country-wide drama contest that was to last until 1970. In that year it was renamed Theatre Canada and lasted another two years as a showcase rather than a competitive event. The national office of Theatre Canada closed in 1978.

The Earl of Bessborough was not the only member of his family to take an interest in theatre. His son Frederick, Lord Duncannon, played the lead in two of Shakespeare's plays at the Ottawa Little Theatre during Bessborough's tenure in Canada. In 1932 he played Hamlet in a production sponsored by his father, and the following year played Romeo in a production of Shakespeare's *Romeo and Juliet* directed by Bessborough's actor-producer friend Rupert Harvey. Betty Lee reports that "Duncannon received and refused an offer to appear in a Hollywood film version of the play" (Lee 108). At

Bessborough's urging Harvey had been adjudicator of the first finals of the Dominion Drama Festival in Ottawa in 1933.

Bessborough was also the first Patron of the Canadian Writers' Foundation, which was established in 1931 as the Canadian Authors' Foundation to grant financial assistance to Canada's finest writers in times of financial need. Initiated by Dr. Pelham Edgar, Professor of English at Victoria College, University of Toronto, its first President was Sir Robert Falconer. Edgar, who also took a leading role in the formation of the Canadian Authors' Association in 1921, served as its second President from 1943 to 1948. Its first beneficiary was the renowned storyteller Sir Charles G.D. Roberts, who received from 1933 to 1943 an annual grant of $2500.00. Many other distinguished writers up to the present have been assisted by the Foundation, and virtually every Governor General from Bessborough to Clarkson has been its Patron.

Lord Tweedsmuir

John Buchan Lord Tweedsmuir's (1875-1940) greatest legacy to Canadian culture is the setting up of the Governor General's Literary Awards in 1937, three years before his untimely death in office (1935-1940), the first viceroy to die while still Governor General. He was a prolific writer himself and wrote several of his books while in Ottawa and on his many tours around the country, including his autobiography *Memory Hold-the-Door* (1940). The first Literary Awards were for books published in 1936, the winners being chosen by the Canadian Authors' Association. In 1959 the administration of the Awards was taken over by the Canada Council. They remain the most prestigious awards for literature in Canada, among many other literary awards which have been established since then.

Susan, Lady Tweedsmuir, was interested in fostering literature as well, but of another sort. She initiated a Prairie Library Scheme under which 40,000 books were collected and sent to small communities in western Canada. She also encouraged women's institutes to write local histories, to the best of which she gave a prize each year.

The Earl of Athlone

Royalty again resided at Rideau Hall when the Earl of Athlone (1874-1957) was appointed Governor General by his nephew King George VI for a term (1940-1946) which covered most of World War II. His wife Princess Alice was a daughter of Prince Leopold, the son of Queen Victoria. His training was largely military, and he had in fact declined the post of Governor General of Canada in 1914, offered to him by his brother-in-law King George V; instead he chose to serve in the army during the Great War. When he accepted the position in 1940 he had already served as Governor General of South Africa from 1923-1930.

Due to the constraints of wartime Canada, Athlone's cultural initiatives were limited since his support of the war effort in Canada was primary. Culture and the war were combined in his regular attendance at benefit performances in Ottawa and elsewhere, and in his entertaining performers at Rideau Hall. Among those he heard and entertained were Sir Aubrey Smith, Sir Cedric Hardwicke, Yehudi Menuhin, the Hart House String Quartet, and the Ballet Russe de Monte Carlo. So frequent were these benefit performances that Hubbard says, " … a full account of such beneficial side-effects of the war would constitute a chapter in the cultural development of Canada" (Hubbard 205). Athlone also had the distinction in 1943 of speaking at the first convocation of Carleton College (now University) in Ottawa.

Lord Alexander of Tunis

A younger and more energetic Governor General was Lord Alexander of Tunis (1891-1969), who came to Rideau Hall for six years (1946-1952) after gaining the respect and admiration of the many Canadians who served under him when he was Field Marshall Harold Alexander in the Mediterranean area during World War II. He was the last of the British-born Governors General of Canada. His two passions were sport and art. He learned to ski so well that he became a skiing enthusiast in Canada; he did the ceremonial kickoff at his first football game, and faced off the puck at his first hockey game; he organized a snow-shoe race at Rideau Hall, and started off a dog-team race in Ottawa; he fished on Lake Erie, and square-danced with Princess Elizabeth and Prince Philip when they stayed at Rideau Hall in 1951. He even arranged for the Ottawa-born 1948 Olympic figure-skating champion Barbara Ann Scott to give skating lessons to his children.

Early in life Alexander wanted to be a professional painter. The war made demands on him that prevented his fulfilling this dream, but he never lost his love of painting nor an opportunity to engage in it. He took art lessons, and was a frequent visitor at the National Gallery. He opened and attended many art exhibitions in Ottawa and elsewhere in Canada, and sent a painting of his own to the 1947 Montreal Spring Exhibition . He had a special admiration for the Canadian painters Tom Thomson and Arthur Lismer, and befriended both amateur and professional painters. Indeed one famous picture shows him at his easel painting a view of Parliament Hill.

Vincent Massey

Vincent Massey (1887-1967), born into a prominent Ontario manufacturing and philanthropic family, was the first Canadian to be named Governor General. In his years in office (1952-1959), as well as before and after those years, he was a driving force for culture. He was both a collector and a connoisseur of art. Batterwood, his estate near Port Hope, Ontario, became a home for his collection of Canadian art. He was a trustee of the National Gallery of Canada for many years from 1925 on. When he was Canadian High Commissioner in London (1935-1946) he was chairman of the trustees of the National Gallery, Trafalgar Square, and on his return from London he gave many English paintings to its Canadian counterpart. In his time as Governor General he opened many art exhibitions, and established the Massey Medals for Architecture.

His greatest cultural achievement came when he was appointed chairman in 1949 of the Royal Commission on National Development in the Arts, Letters, and Sciences, popularly known as the Massey Commission. The resulting report which bears his name was published in 1951, and led to the establishment of the National Library of Canada in 1953 and of the Canada Council in 1957. He also gave strong support to the founding of the Stratford Festival, which opened its doors in 1953. In this connection it must be remembered that he came from a family with strong ties to the theatre, including his brother the famous actor Raymond Massey. Another result of his tireless efforts for the arts in Canada was the building of the National Arts Centre in Ottawa. Although it was not opened until 1969, two years after his death, the seeds for it were sown by a private committee he formed in 1959 to establish a national festival of the arts.

Other projects dear to Massey came about after he had left office. One was the Order of Canada, a system of honours to recognize Canadians of distinction, which distributed its first medals in 1967. His final years were devoted to the planning of Massey College in Toronto, which opened its doors to students in 1963. A striking self-enclosed residential building designed by the distinguished Canadian architect R.J. Thom, shut off from the hubbub of the surrounding Toronto streets, the college is intended to give Canadian scholars from many disciplines a collegial experience such as Massey had when he was a student at Balliol College, Oxford.

Georges Vanier

Other distinguished Canadians followed Massey as Governors General, but none left their mark on Canadian culture as he did. Georges Vanier (1888-1967), a diplomat and soldier, had served as ambassador to France from 1944-1953 before his long term (1959-1967) as Governor General. A deeply religious man, he had a chapel installed in a former bedroom at Rideau Hall so he could attend daily Mass, and fathered two sons who became role models for many Canadians—Georges, a Trappist monk in Oka, Quebec, and Jean, founder of L'Arche, a worldwide community for the handicapped. One of his lasting endeavours is the Vanier Institute of the Family, which grew out of a conference at Rideau Hall in 1964.

He was also a keen sports enthusiast. The Vanier Cup, emblematic of the championship of Canadian college football, was first awarded in 1965; in 1982 the game itself became known as the Vanier Cup. But his special love was hockey and, in particular, the Montreal Canadiens. He died the morning of March 5, 1967 after watching les Canadiens on television the previous night and then reading from St. Paul's epistle to the Galatians.

Roland Michener

The next Governor General, Roland Michener (1900-1991), had a distinguished political and diplomatic career before serving as the Queen's representative in Canada (1967-1974). He had been a Cabinet Minister in the Ontario legislature, a speaker of the House of Commons, and High Commissioner to India (1964-1967). As Governor General he became the first Chancellor of the Order of Canada, "conferred in recognition of exemplary merit and achievement in all major fields of endeavour" (Marsh 1584); it was instituted during his tenure on July 1, 1967, the one hundredth anniversary of Confederation.

One of his cultural legacies is the Michener Awards for public service in journalism, established in 1969 to commemorate his daughter Wendy, a film critic, who died that year of a brain embolism. One event in the Micheners' time was reminiscent of the heyday of the private theatricals of the

Dufferins: a play in the ballroom at Christmas time performed by the Micheners' grandchildren with the Governor General as Santa Claus and Mrs. Michener as Queen Victoria. Michener himself became an exemplar of good physical conditioning with his regular jogging and energetic tennis playing, practices that continued long after he left Rideau Hall, and enabled him to enjoy a healthy and useful life almost to the age of ninety-one. In his later years he often appeared in television commercials as a symbol of physical fitness. The Blood Indians of Alberta made him their honorary chief, and in deference to his jogging named him Running Antelope.

Mrs. Michener was exemplary in her own right, being an accomplished musician and writer. She both studied and taught at the Toronto Conservatory of Music. The multilingual Norah Michener wrote her Ph.D. thesis in philosophy at the Pontifical Institute of Medieval Studies of the University of Toronto on the French philosopher Jacques Maritain, under whom she had studied there. Her thesis was "Maritain on the Nature of Man in a Christian Democracy", which was published as a book in 1955. She also wrote a food column for *Canadian Homes and Gardens* and a cookbook under the pseudonym Janet Peters.

Jules Léger

Jules Léger (1913-1980) assumed the post of Governor General (1974-1979) after serving as ambassador to Mexico, Rome, Paris and Brussels and as undersecretary of state for Prime Ministers Pearson and Trudeau. Earlier he had worked on the editorial staff of the Ottawa newspaper *Le Droit* and on the faculty of the University of Ottawa. He was a brother of Montreal's Paul-Émile Cardinal Léger. His activities were curtailed by a stroke he suffered in June of his first year as Governor General, six months after he took office, which damaged his speech and paralysed his left arm. Though he was able to resume his viceregal duties by December of that year, he did not have the vigour to initiate cultural schemes as many of his predecessors had done. He was greatly aided in his work by his wife Gabrielle Carmel both during his convalescence and for the rest of his term. They maintained friendships with several Quebec artists including Jean-Paul Lemieux, Alfred Pellan, and Jean Dallaire. And they held a series of chamber concerts at Rideau Hall which began in late 1975 with a program by the Orford String Quartet. In 1978 he established the Jules Léger Chamber Music Prize—an annual award of $5,000.00 to a Canadian composer. The first winner was R. Murray Schafer for his String Quartet No. 2, performed in the ballroom by the same Orford String Quartet. The Jules and Gabrielle Léger Fellowships, administered by the Canada Council, were established in 1979 in their honour to promote research and writing on the historical and contemporary contribution of the Crown and its representatives to Canada. He died the year after he left Rideau Hall.

Edward Schreyer

Edward Schreyer (b. 1935), of German and Austrian origin, was the first Canadian of non-English or non-French descent to hold office at Rideau Hall (1979-1984), and the youngest Governor General of modern times. He came to the position having served as a New Democratic Party member in Manitoba and in Ottawa for many years, including four years as premier of Manitoba. He and his energetic wife Lily made Rideau Hall more accessible to ordinary Canadians though he was often criticized for being ill at ease as a host. They travelled a great deal during their tenure both in Canada and abroad, visiting some 600 communities in Canada on 200 trips they made across the country. He even made Fort Garry, Manitoba an official residence of the Governor General for a brief time, adding it to the two long-standing residences of Rideau Hall and the Citadel in Quebec. They hosted a number of performances at Rideau Hall by Canadian artists, including les Grands Ballets Canadiens and the National

Ballet of Canada. On one occasion they made Rideau Hall available to the CBC for a concert that was simulcast on television and radio in January 1984 and included les Grands Ballets, the Orford String Quartet and soprano Rose-Mary Landry. Mrs. Schreyer was especially active in sponsoring exhibitions at Rideau Hall. One was an exhibit by Canadian artists and craftspeople; another was a fashion showcase in 1983 to promote Canadian designers; and a third in 1984 was entitled The Perfect Setting, a crafts competition to design stem-wear and place settings for the small dining room at Rideau Hall, which later toured the country.

One of the highlights of the Schreyers' time at Rideau Hall was a dramatic performance in 1979 to celebrate the fiftieth anniversary of the Persons Case when women in Canada were recognized as persons by the British Privy Council and thus became eligible for appointment to the Senate. The landmark decision was marked by a musical *Heaven Will Protect the Working Girl*, performed by members of the Pears Cabaret of Toronto for 150 guests at Rideau Hall. A special stage was built for the occasion, the original stage in the ballroom having been dismantled in 1904. The Governor General's Persons Award, for work on behalf of women's rights, was inaugurated that evening and distributed to seven prominent Canadian women. A memorable contribution to Canadians from the Schreyers was the installation of the Terry Fox fountain in the driveway of the Governor General's residence.

On leaving office, Schreyer, who was then forty-eight years old, announced that he would donate his pension of about $60,000 per year until he reached the age of sixty-five to the newly formed Biological Research Support Foundation to examine problems faced by farmers and foresters. Schreyer's next assignment was ambassador to Australia, where he served from 1984-1988. His humanitarian instincts got him involved in other projects after he left Rideau Hall. Along with former U.S. President Jimmy Carter he has worked for Habitat for Humanity, an organization to help needy families around the world build their own homes. He was also associated with the Unification Church of Rev. Sun Myung Moon in its Summit for World Peace, although this involvement drew some criticism from Canadians.

Jeanne Sauvé

Jeanne Sauvé (1922-1993) became the first woman Governor General of Canada (1984-1990), a first among many firsts for this remarkable lady. In 1972 she had become the first woman French-Canadian cabinet minister when she was appointed Minister of State for Science and Technology in the Trudeau government. Subsequently she was appointed Minister of the Environment (1974) and Minister of Communications (1975). She was also the first woman speaker in the House of Commons (1980-1984). Her political career thus eclipsed that of her husband Maurice, who was Minister of Forestry and Rural Development (1964-1968) in the cabinet of Lester Pearson. Before entering politics Jeanne Sauvé had a brilliant career as a journalist in print, radio, and television.

Unfortunately poor health prevented her from making more of an impact than she did on Canadian life and culture when she became Governor General. Her inauguration was delayed four months because of an undisclosed illness, and she was often frail during her tenure and sometimes had to cancel engagements for health reasons. Nevertheless she was able to travel some 570,000 kilometres in Canada and abroad as Governor General.

Her appointment was greeted by many as a sign that a more formal and elegant style would return to Rideau Hall after the populist days of Schreyer. They were right, and she impressed many with her charm, grace, and social ease. But she did a number of things that alienated her from ordinary Canadians and gave her a reputation of being elitist and aloof. Most notable was the closing of the gates of Rideau Hall to people who had been accustomed to roaming and playing on the grounds of the eighty-eight acre property for many years.

The official reason for the closure was security, but many Ottawans who had used the property regularly were unforgiving, even after organized daily tours were permitted as a compromise.

Her interest in art, music, and theatre manifested itself on various occasions as was appropriate to someone who had been secretary-general of la Fédération des auteurs et artistes du Canada in the 1970s. One occasion was the launching at the Citadel in Quebec in 1986 of a photographic album *Canada* by Mia and Klaus, for which she wrote the preface. Another was her and her busband's patronage of the National Theatre School whose Board of Governors meeting she attended in Otttawa in 1988; no doubt her interest in theatre derived from her school days when she was often chosen for leading roles in plays. A popular innovation in 1987 was a yearly concert performance open to the public on the cricket pitch on the grounds of Rideau Hall to celebrate Canada Day, sometimes with Boris Brott conducting his Festival Orchestra.

Sauvé's greatest contribution to Canadian life was a genuine love and concern for children and young people. A mother of one son, Jean-Francois, she was always warm in her relations with children, and often spoke with optimism of the contributions youth could make to the nation. She hosted with delight at Rideau Hall the Christmas dinner for the Boys and Girls Club of Ottawa, which had become an annual event since the first year of Vincent Massey's time. In her first year sponsoring the dinner, she added the participation of a group of French-speaking youngsters from Le Patro d'Ottawa cultural centre. Mindful of her days as president of the Jeunesse Étudiante Catholique she once told a prayer luncheon in Montreal: "I can say, without being an unrealistic optimist, that the young people whom we are tempted to call indifferent, will one day teach us to live under the sign of God" (*Citizen*, June 8, 1985, p. F2). She promoted both youth and music in Canada in 1986 when she travelled to Banff for the opening of the Seventh Festival of Youth Orchestras. Evidence of this optimism and confidence in youth was the establishment in 1990 in her name, shortly before she left Rideau Hall, of a $10-million youth foundation to bring together young leaders from around the world. She even worked for this organization after she left Rideau Hall. In recognition of her accomplishments, the Department of Communications, of which she had once been Minister, created an award in her memory for women in the communications industry.

Her death came in 1993, just three years after she left Rideau Hall for private life in Montreal. Her husband had predeceased her by nine months.

Ramon Hnatyshyn

Sauvé's successor, Ramon Hnatyshyn (b. 1934), the son of Senator John Hnatyshyn, came to Rideau Hall after many years in the Conservative caucus under both Joe Clark and Brian Mulroney. Before that he had taught and practised law in Saskatoon, where he was born and raised. In the Conservative government he had served as Minister of Energy, Mines and Resources (1979-1980), Minister of State for Science and Technology (1979), and Minister of Justice and Attorney General of Canada (1986-1988). Shortly after he was defeated in the general election of 1988 he was appointed Governor General (1990-1995) and sworn in on January 29, 1990.

Known for his warmth and affability, he endeared himself to many Canadians in his new office. One of the first ways in which he did this was by reopening the grounds of Rideau Hall to visitors on June 2, 1990, after first inviting 400 families in the neighbourhood of the vice-regal mansion to a coffee party, and hearing their views on the matter. He invited the general public to other events on the grounds, in particular, a series of Sunday afternoon Summer Concerts at Rideau Hall each year. Music, in fact, was one of his favourite recreations and he fostered its enjoyment at Rideau Hall on several occasions. His early aptitude for the clarinet, which he played in a band while attending university, manifested itself at the annual garden party at Rideau Hall in 1993 when he played the clarinet with the Governor General's Foot Guards Band to the delight of the 10,000 who attended the party. The 1992 garden party featured folk groups from across Canada and was recorded by the CBC for broadcast on Canada Day. In 1991 he hosted a live-to-air CBC broadcast entitled *Christmas at Rideau*, which was released a year later by CBC Records as *Adeste Fideles*. As part of Celebration 92, to mark both the 125th anniversary of Canadian confederation and the 75th of Finnish independence, Hnatyshyn and his wife hosted a special concert at Rideau Hall which included a commissioned piano concerto by Canadian composer Srul Irving Glick, played by the Finlandia Sinfonietta and later broadcast on the CBC and in Finland.

Hnatyshyn reestablished the tradition, begun by the Dufferins in the 1870s, of public skating on an outdoor rink at Rideau Hall. While skating was permitted to the general public on the weekends, the rink was reserved for schools, social clubs and organizations during the week. This welcome practice was continued by his successor Romeo LeBlanc. Hnatyshyn's familiarity with other sports was not always so evident. When he and Prime Minister Brian Mulroney welcomed the 1992 World Champion Toronto Blue Jays to Rideau Hall, he referred to the "World Series Cup", confusing baseball's World Series and hockey's "Stanley Cup". On the same occasion he referred to the "Golden Glove", an award for boxers, rather than to baseball's "Gold Glove". If the spectators were mildly amused by these gaffes, they more seriously asked why Canadian teams with more Canadian athletes, like the champions of the Canadian Football League or the National Hockey League, had never been feted at Rideau Hall.

The Governor General's Performing Arts Awards, Canada's highest honours in the performing arts, are presented annually at a gala evening at the National Arts Centre and broadcast across Canada by the CBC. They owe their beginning to Hnatyshyn, who inaugurated them in 1992. They honour individuals for a lifetime of outstanding contribution to Canadian culture in many of its expressions. In their first year the awards were given to six performing artists who each received $10,000. Two related awards were presented: the Ramon John Hnatyshyn Award for Voluntarism in the Performing Arts (to Norman Jewison) and the National Arts Centre Award for outstanding achievement by an individual or group in the previous performance season (to Gilles Maheu and Carbone 14).

Hnatyshyn was not so noted for his support of Canadian authors, but he did support the cause for literacy. In 1990 he hosted a reception for well-known Canadian authors who contributed personal perspectives on literacy to a book entitled *More Than Words Can Say*, edited by Knowlton Nash of the CBC. That same evening the authors gave a reading from the book at the National Library. At the end of Hnatyshyn's term of office, his wife Gerda emerged as an author, along with Paulette Lachapelle-Bélisle, of *Rideau Hall: Canada's Living Heritage*, an elegant volume with some 200 colour photographs by Gene Hattori. Published by The Friends of Rideau Hall, a group organized by Mrs. Hnatyshyn to raise funds to renovate and redecorate the viceregal residence, the book is both a history of the country's best known home, and a guide through its 177 rooms and their decor. Published just before the Hnatyshyns left Rideau Hall, the book brought a heated response from former members of the National Capital Commission, which is responsible for maintaining official residences, who claimed the renovations lacked historical integrity, and that they were prevented by Mrs. Hnatyshyn's group from completing work they had begun on the residence. The book remains a lofty record of Rideau Hall updating much of R.H. Hubbard's *Rideau Hall: An Illustrated History*.

Romeo LeBlanc

The next Governor General, installed on February 8, 1996, was Romeo LeBlanc (b. 1927). Born in the village of Memramcook (L'Anse-aux-Cormier), New Brunswick, he was the first Acadian and the first person from Atlantic Canada to hold the post (1995-1999). Before entering politics he was a teacher, a correspondent for Radio-Canada, and Press Secretary to Prime Ministers Pearson and Trudeau. He spent twelve years as a Liberal member of the House of Commons, during ten of which he was a minister of four different departments, most notably Minister of Fisheries. In 1984 he was appointed to the Senate, of which he was speaker in 1993-1994.

Any assessment of LeBlanc's contributions to the cultural life of Canada will be based on his desire to be a populist Governor General, as he made clear in his installation address: "If I am to be known for anything, I would like it to be for encouraging Canadians, for knowing a little bit about their daily, extraordinary courage. And for wanting that courage to be recognized ... I hope we can call upon their experience to build a national program that will honour the many, many thousands of our fellow citizens whose quiet daily bravery assures the care of so many among us" (*Globe and Mail*, Feb. 9, 1995, p. A19).

In many ways he and his wife, Diana Fowler LeBlanc, carried out this populist agenda, as at his first New Year's levee which he held on January 7, 1996 in Ottawa, a week later than usual, so that many families could attend. At the levee he broke with tradition by having no receiving line and mixing freely with the public. In his desire to meet more ordinary Canadians in other parts of Canada, he held his other three levees in Quebec City, Winnipeg, and St. John's, Newfoundland. Similarly, beginning July 1, 1996, LeBlanc opened three more rooms in Rideau Hall for daily guided tours by the public, as well as two of the six greenhouses and parts of the gardens. He carried on Hnatyshyn's Sunday Summer Concerts series, and in 1996 added Saturday concerts as well. He invited two new groups of children from the National Capital Region to the annual Christmas party—le Relais de Jeunes Gatinois and Les Enfants de l'Ile de Hull. And he continued Hnatyshyn's practice of opening the rink at Rideau Hall to the public on weekends. He also gave a higher profile to Canadian scientists and engineers by presenting in 1995 the Izaak Walton Killam memorial prizes, the country's most distinguished annual awards in health sciences, natural sciences, and engineering.

LeBlanc instituted new awards for ordinary Canadians, in particular, the Governor General's Caring Canadian Award "to recognize the everyday caring and dedication of ordinary people who have made extraordinary contributions to their families, communities or country" (Governors General website). Four hundred and two of these awards were handed out during his tenure.

The Aboriginal Peoples were close to the hearts of both the Governor General and his wife. He proclaimed National Aboriginal Day in Canada in June 1996, and on the second annual celebration of that day on June 21, 1997 he unveiled on the grounds of Rideau Hall a sculpture known as an inuksuk by Inuit artist Kananginak Pootoogook. Mrs. LeBlanc, after receiving her own degree in social work, established the Diana Fowler LeBlanc Aboriginal Social Work Scholarship, available to First Nations people, Inuit and Metis in every province and territory of Canada to pursue a social work degree. The long-range plan for the scholarship was to raise money to enable ten students every year to study social work.

While LeBlanc was not a noted patron of the arts, he did give his support on several occasions to the promotion of the arts in Canada. Thus, he and his wife were patrons of the revived but short-lived Festival Canada at the National Arts Centre in the summer of 1997. He announced in 1999 the establishment of the Governor General's Awards in Visual and Media Arts to complement the other vice-regal awards for literature and the performing arts, although he was no longer Governor General when the awards were first distributed in 2000.

LeBlanc encouraged greater knowledge of Canadian history on the part of youth by announcing and unveiling the design for a millennium medal for high school students in

Canadian history in the 1999-2000 school year. Students taking Canadian history or Canadian studies in 3000 high schools across Canada were eligible for the award. Each school selected the student with the highest marks in either of these disciplines for the award.

Diana Fowler LeBlanc also left her own mark on Rideau Hall. Having begun studies in social work at McGill University before she came to Rideau Hall, she completed those studies and graduated with a bachelor's degree in 1996, thus becoming the only member of a vice-regal couple to pursue a university degree while they resided at Rideau Hall. She was further rewarded for her many good works by receiving an honorary doctorate from the University of Ottawa in 1998.

While chatelaine at Rideau Hall Mrs. LeBlanc was honorary patron of the Canadian Palliative Care Association, and visited palliative care centres across Canada. In an imaginative gesture she combined both art and social work by hosting a public exhibit of the paintings of the late Robert Pope, artist and cancer patient, whose paintings are of sickness and healing as experienced by the patient. She also helped the Children's Hospital of Eastern Ontario by sponsoring in 1999 in the tent room at Rideau Hall an exhibit of thirty-five teddy bears from across Canada. A teddy bear enthusiast herself, and honorary president of the Ottawa Limestone Teddies den, she hosted on the grounds of Rideau Hall the annual Teddy Bears picnic in support of the Children's Hospital in both 1998 and 1999, another example of the LeBlancs' readiness to reach out to help and embrace ordinary Canadians in their ordinary activities.

Romeo LeBlanc did not complete his five-year term as Governor General. Citing health reasons, he left the post after four years and eight months, three months before the dawn of the new millennium. One newspaper summed up those years thus: "His legacy as Governor General is not dramatic, but it does reflect Mr. LeBlanc's concerns for the lives of ordinary Canadians" (*National Post*, Sept. 9, 1999, p. A6). With no aspirations to greatness, LeBlanc once described himself as a "country bumpkin". This could never be said of his successor, the sophisticated Adrienne Clarkson, of whom he said with typical simplicity and self-effacement: "I think she probably will bring [to Rideau Hall] a flavour of the large cities, which I couldn't bring because I'm not from a large city" (*Ottawa Citizen*, Sept.10, 1999, p. A3). When Clarkson was installed as Governor General on October 7, 1999 she would indeed bring to the office a different approach to culture, but she would have a hard time matching LeBlanc's interest in and concern for the lives of ordinary Canadians.

Works Cited

The Globe and Mail.

Governors General website, Romeo LeBlanc <www.gg.ca>.

Hubbard, R.H. *Rideau Hall: An Illustrated History of Government House, Ottawa, from Victorian Times to the Present Day*. Montreal and Kingston: McGill-Queen's University Press, 1977. I am indebted to this book for many of the facts in the Afterword up to 1977.

Lee, Betty. *Love and Whisky: The Story of the Dominion Drama Festival*. Toronto: McClelland & Stewart, 1973.

Marsh, James H., ed. *The Canadian Encyclopedia*. 2nd ed. Edmonton: Hurtig, 1988.

The National Post.

The Ottawa Citizen

Conclusion

The main focus of this book has been the cultural activities of Canada's Governors General, in the rich variety that the term culture implies. While the first nine holders of that office since Confederation have received detailed coverage, I have tried to show in the *Afterword* to what extent their successors have followed in their footsteps. I have used the letters, diaries and journals of the Governors General or their spouses and children to tell their stories since their own words seemed to me interesting and immediate for giving insights into the contributions they have made, or have not made, to Canadian life. I have also given a portrayal of their characters and family background, as well as their lives and contributions before and after their residence at Rideau Hall, through incidents that remind us how human and how dedicated they were to the responsibilities they undertook when they agreed to become the Queen's or the King's representative in this country.

What has emerged from this survey is that the most memorable of the Governors General as far as Canadian culture is concerned are those who were willing and able to take initiative in areas where Canadians needed cultural leadership at the time. Thus, the Dufferins saw a lack of theatrical vigour in their midst, and entertained and enthralled their guests with private theatricals from the beginning of their tenure in Canada. Lord Lorne, as husband of Queen Victoria's daughter, was able to add the prestige of the royal family to art and learning in Canada by establishing, in the face of opposition, two important organizations, the Royal Canadian Academy of Art, and the Royal Society of Canada. Lord Stanley gave prestige to hockey by donating a cup in his name to a sport he never played but which later became Canada's official winter sport, and remains the most popular sport in the country. Originally donated to advance the cause of amateur hockey in Canada, today it stands for the pinnacle of professional hockey in the world. Though only six Canadian teams out of thirty now compete for the cup, the National Hockey League playoffs have become an annual rite of spring in Canada, helping Canadians to survive when spring itself seems to have forgotten them. Slightly less prestigious is the Grey Cup for Canadian football, which recently emerged from several years of expansion into the United States to become the coveted prize of an all-Canadian league again. The Aberdeens seized on the idea of spectacular historical balls in Ottawa, Montreal, and Toronto to make Canadians proud of their native, British, and Canadian heritages. Besides a football cup Lord Grey conceived the idea of almost two weeks of colourful events climaxed by a recreation of the Battle of Quebec to mark the three-hundredth anniversary of Champlain's founding of that city, as a means of making Canadians proud of their heritage in an empire that stretched around the world.

No contemporary or succeeding Governor General has matched the spectacle and imagination of the initiatives of Dufferin, Lorne, Aberdeen and Grey. While many other holders of the office made notable contributions to Canadian culture—Lansdowne in art, Minto in skating, Bessborough in drama, Tweedsmuir in literature, and Massey in arts funding—none matched the mark left by these giants of the nineteenth and early-twentieth centuries. With rare exceptions, these men and their spouses took initiatives undreamed of by other holders of the office. And they took the initiatives not only in their own residence of Rideau Hall, and in the city which they called home for the five or six or seven years they lived in Canada, but in several parts of Canada.

More and more since the time of Grey (1904-1911) the activities that Governors General inspired were taken over by the Canadian government, so that the Queen's representative is now more a ceremonial leader in culture than an actual one. Part of the reason for the lack of cultural leadership from the top is no doubt Canada's maturing as a nation during and after the First World War. With maturity came a touchiness about being shown the way by British-born viceroys, or by their Canadian-born successors. Arts organizations now receive much of their funding from the Canada Council, the result of the groundbreaking Massey Commission Report of 1951. Even work and renovations on Rideau Hall itself are in the hands of the National Capital Commission, so that when someone like Gerda Hnatyshyn undertook to oversee renovations there she was severely criticized by former members of the NCC who had worked on the residence and who felt it was their job to decide what should be done to it.

Could a present or future Governor General ever become a leader in Canadian culture as Dufferin, or Lorne, or Aberdeen, or Grey were? Yes, if they had the imagination and determination to lead in the face of opposition as these men and in some cases their spouses did. Since their political power is so limited, they may be tempted to think that they are limited in the cultural initiatives they can take as well. They should be bold enough to increase their involvement in culture, just as the Canadian Senate has recently increased its activity in the political affairs of Canada.

There are initiatives they can take, even at Rideau Hall itself. Since the gates to the lovely grounds were opened again by Governor General Ramon Hnatyshyn, he and his successors Romeo LeBlanc and Adrienne Clarkson have made ordinary Canadians feel welcome there again, especially through public invitations in the local newspapers to attend summer concerts and to skate on the outdoor rink in the winter. Many Canadians have accepted their invitations as they have accepted the offer of tours of the grounds and of the house itself. The elitism of the cultural activities at Rideau Hall of earlier days has gone, but so has the glitter of the events of those days. Perhaps it is time for the incumbents to stretch their imaginations to see how they could make ordinary Canadians aware of their culture by inviting them to attend more, and a greater variety of events at Rideau Hall. Perhaps they could put a permanent stage in the ballroom again, as the Dufferins did, and sponsor Canadian artists to perform and be televised on that stage for ordinary Canadians. Perhaps a new performance space could be constructed on the grounds of Rideau Hall—it is many years since any significant changes besides renovations were made to the buildings on the property—where plays, concerts, art exhibitions, conferences, public lectures, dancing, and singing could take place. Perhaps we might witness once again at Rideau Hall gala events like those described in this book, but now for all Canadians and for many weeks of the year. The same events could be brought to other parts of Canada by radio and television, as has been done from time to time in recent years.

For anyone offered the office of Governor General of Canada in the past, personal finances were often a consideration. Some declined to accept because the salary was not high enough; others accepted hoping they would be able to bring some of their earnings home with them. Some spent their own money to promote the cultural activities they believed were important for Canada and Canadians. Indeed Dufferin, the most memorable of all the residents of Rideau Hall, was warned not to be so extravagant in what he spent on balls, theatricals and dinners for his many guests. Current and future holders of the office might enhance their involvement in Canadian culture by being more "Dufferinish", or more "Sheridanish", as Dufferin was advised not to be.

In recent times, an example has been set by Ed Schreyer, who donated his $60,000 per year pension to the Biological Research Support Foundation after he left Rideau Hall. I would suggest that future holders of the office make a similar contribution to Canadian culture at the time they accept the office. For some it might mean donating their government or other pension to a cultural activity or foundation of their choice; those with sufficient wealth might donate their Governor General's salary to promoting Canadian culture in a way that seems important to them, just as the early holders of the office promoted culture in ways that were significant to them. Organizations like the Hnatyshyns' Friends of Rideau Hall might be established not only to renovate and publish a book on the building, but also to enhance the cultural activity that takes place there. We would indeed have a variety of causes supported by the Governors General, so that their enterprises might grow as haphazardly as has Rideau Hall itself. But the result might well be a special fondness for the office and for the unique events that it promotes, just as Canadians have developed a fondness for the uniqueness of the building known as Rideau Hall that some Governors General looked down upon.

At a time when many Canadians doubt the relevance of the role of Governors General, a greater emphasis on their cultural leadership, now that their political activity is so limited, would give them a higher profile and make them a larger symbol of Canadian unity. Not only would it help assure the continuance of the post of Governor General. It would also help assure the continuance of Canada itself.

Index

C